Get Unstuck!

Get Unstuck!

The ultimate guide to stop procrastinating and overthinking and finally move forward with your life and work.

Murielle Marie Ungricht

To my parents, Guy and Elizabeth. May you have found peace.
To Silvia, my dearest friend, without whom I would be lost in this world.
To my clients, for your trust and willingness. There would be no book without you.

To anyone who feels stuck. This is for you.

Table of contents

Preface

You can get stuck for many reasons, but one of the most common is being overwhelmed. You get a burst of inspiration and become carried away about how fantastic this new idea could be. As time passes, the vision of what you want to create or the new life you want to be living gets more elaborate. All the while, you're not taking action because this all happens in your mind. Then, just when you're about to go for it, you find yourself overthinking and overanalyzing what started out as a great idea. Eventually, you end up anxious, stressed, frustrated, or even burnt out – overwhelmed – before you even start. So, you do nothing.

Perhaps being overwhelmed is not your issue; you're simply caught up in the routines of everyday life, going through the motions. You feel like Bill Murray in the movie Groundhog Day, reliving the same day over and over again.

Maybe it's not routine or being overwhelmed that keeps you from doing what you love, but this habit of yes-but-ing that you've mastered. For each dream or goal you have, the excuses are right around the corner. You yes-but yourself out of everything. Again, this ends in doing nothing.

When every day looks the same, when all we do is procrastinate, when we endlessly overanalyze every decision we could make, we start to feel an itch. We know something's off, but we can't quite put our finger on it.

I spent countless sleepless nights imagining the life I truly wanted to live, where I was happy and successful, unafraid of making bold decisions or mistakes, and where each day would be exciting and new. But every morning, even though I could almost touch my dream, I would return to doing the same thing. I knew what I had; that was the comfort I chose over my freedom.

Secretly, I didn't believe what I wanted was possible. Perhaps you've felt, or feel, this way too.

If you're stuck, overwhelmed, afraid, or don't know what to do, don't worry; you're not alone. I've felt that way for a long time, and hundreds of clients have felt this way, too. That's precisely why I wrote this book. After almost a decade of doing this work, I knew it was time to share everything I learned about helping people get unstuck.

When I became a coach, I'd come to a point where I knew my life desperately needed to change. On the outside, I looked like an accomplished businessperson with an excellent track record, but on the inside, things were different. I didn't love myself or the things I was doing. I was exhausted and constantly on edge. As soon as I reached a milestone, I focused on the next thing and the next thing – to what end? The worst part was that I ended up judging myself. Even when I accomplished something big, it was never good enough. I could have done a better job.

My life changed in 2010. During the summer, both my parents died – pivotal moments for me. Until then, I'd only ever done one thing: followed other people's dreams, things I thought I wanted but didn't choose for myself. I was not living the life I wanted to live – I was stuck. I fell into the trap of relentless productivity, trying to make everyone around me happy, doing what I thought was expected of me, and building a career and life that weren't my own.

When my parents passed away, I lost all sense of purpose. I suddenly didn't know who I was anymore or what I wanted. The biggest question in my life became, "Why did I put off doing the things I wanted to do for so long?" I asked myself, "How did I end up here? Why am I stuck in this life that I don't want to live?"

I had a lot of "stuff" to work through... my childhood, the messages I had internalized from caregivers and society, and challenging experiences that had left me feeling vulnerable and hurt.

This led me to understand that when we're stuck, we're suffering. Not knowing how to escape a situation you don't want to be in is painful. Overthinking and worrying about the right decision is stressful and causes anxiety. Procrastinating and breaking promises to ourselves leaves us questioning if we're even capable of achieving our dreams. Those are not great feelings. Instead of helping us get unstuck, they keep us where we are for longer.

If you're anything like I used to be, you have all these dreams and goals but don't know where to start or how to get there. You're not as confident as everyone thinks you are.

Perhaps you've been trying to be what the world expects you to be, and by doing that, you've ignored your dreams for so long that you don't even know what they are anymore. Or you're afraid you might have too many passions or ideas, and choosing one path and forgoing the others gives you cold sweats. What if you make the wrong choice? What if you don't like it? After all, you've started so many things before.

But deep down, you know it's now or never. You've dreamed about your life long enough. Now is the time to live it!

Now is the time to finally get unstuck. Are you ready? Let's go!

Antwerp, September 3rd, 2023,
Murielle Marie Ungricht

The MOVE Method and How It Came to Life

"Those who do not move, do not notice their chains."
– Rosa Luxemburg

The MOVE method is a four-step process I created to help you get unstuck. It's based on thousands of coaching hours helping creatives and entrepreneurs figure out what they really want and support them in moving forward. In a private coaching series, I work one-on-one with clients and guide them through the process in a structured and intuitive way. I've chosen to follow the same structure in this book, adding background information, thinking prompts, philosophical theories, neuroscience discoveries, and coaching questions, as you move through the book.

The four steps of the method – Mindset, Options, Vision, and Execution – were always part of my work, but they've become more precise and were finetuned over the years. They combine what I learned by getting myself unstuck, what clients have shared with me that worked for them, and the many hours of work and experiments clients were willing to take on when working with me.

To gain the most from the method, I invite you to move through it step by step and follow along. Some parts might be familiar to you if you're familiar with the self-development process. I invite you not to skim over those parts but to use them as a reminder of your knowledge. Each step builds upon the previous one; they're stepping stones to a greater understanding of yourself, how getting unstuck works, and what you can do to get yourself moving again. Let's take a quick look at each step.

- **Mindset.** This step is about understanding what being stuck really means and how we get stuck. We're looking for clarity and awareness. We want to figure out what got you stuck and what keeps you there. What we think we can or cannot do – our mindset – is fundamental to getting unstuck. The exercises and thinking prompts will help you to gain more clarity about why you are where you are and help you to start figuring out how to get moving again.

- **Options.** Our minds can keep us trapped and stuck, which means that if we change our minds, we change our situation. This is the foundation of freedom: having options. Like most valuable things in life, freedom is not something other people will give you; it's something you must take for yourself. You do it by taking responsibility for your thoughts, emotions, and actions. A starting point to do that is looking at all the things you could be doing and all the opportunities available to you.

- **Vision.** It's great to figure out how your mind works and realize there's no limit to what you could be doing, having, or being. However, if you don't have a clear idea of which direction to go, it can still be challenging (not to say impossible) to see what is possible for you, make a choice, and take a step. That's why you need a vision for your life and your work. What is it that lights you up in the morning? What do you really want? What is truly important to you? In Step Three, we try to make sense of all these questions from a perspective of expansion and limitless possibilities.

- **Execution.** The final step of this book, work, and method is about taking action. Once you have a clear vision, you need to start implementing it in a way that feels good and is sustainable over time. This is where you put a plan together and take your first steps toward getting unstuck. I won't lie; this step requires courage, especially if you've been stuck for a while. Taking action will feel weird and icky.

But do not worry, I'll send you on your way with a few final tools to help you stay unstuck so you don't get lost or stranded right before reaching the finish line – or, should I say, the beginning of the rest of your wonderful life!

In the pages of this book, you'll find a collection of client stories and experiences that I've selected to illustrate the themes and insights explored within. It's important to note that I've made every effort to protect the privacy and confidentiality of the people whose experiences I'm sharing in this book. To this end, all client stories have been anonymized and pseudonymized. Additionally, in some instances, I've merged stories or grouped them to convey overarching themes and messages better. I've chosen this approach to respect the anonymity of my clients while still presenting a comprehensive and meaningful narrative that emphasizes the essential lessons of *getting unstuck* from these shared experiences.

STEP ONE:
MINDSET

“All that we are is the result of what we have thought.”
– Buddha

In this step, you’ll learn:

- How to change your mindset by understanding how you think.
- The difference between a mindset that expands your reality and one that limits it.
- What it means to be stuck and how people get (and stay) stuck.
- The connection between being stuck and being afraid of change.
- The first step to getting unstuck and how change happens.
- That number one truth about life: everything always changes.
- How to embrace the messiness of change.

Chapter One: What Is Mindset?

"Nothing is impossible. The word itself says "I'm possible!"
– Audrey Hepburn

Wild and free. That's how I felt when I was eight years old, running with my arms open in the corn fields behind my grandfather's farm. One Saturday afternoon, I ran as far as the field was deep. When I turned around to see how far I'd gotten, the farm had become a tiny black dot on the horizon of a gigantic blue and white canvas. It was a fantastic summer day. The sun warmed my skin red while the wind dried my sweaty cheeks. The air smelled of dust, pine trees and grass. In the fields around me, cows were grazing and lying down lavishly. I crawled under an electric fence wire to join in and lay down in the warm green grass next to them.

Everything was possible that day. My entire life was ahead of me.

I had many dreams, and all of them felt achievable. There was no doubt or insecurity. Whatever I wanted to become, I was sure that I could, and I would. I wasn't sure yet of what I'd pick, but I would definitely become an astronaut, a lawyer, or an inventor. I liked the idea of making things that didn't exist, of discovering the vastness of the Universe, of helping those who couldn't defend themselves.

Those same ideals guide me in everything I do today.

Integrity, doing good, helping others, creating things, and never backing down from an adventure is how I live my life. But a little over a decade after that warm summer day, by the time I left university, I wasn't convinced I could reach my dreams anymore. Those ideals had made room for the demands of society. Years of domestication and conditioning had taken the wildness out of me. Instead of running in cornfields, dreaming of spaceships and lying down with cows, I was trying to be what I thought everyone expected of me. As a child, I'd let my creativity and inspiration guide my days; now, all I had were "have-tos." In those formative years, how I saw the world had dramatically changed. When I was eight, there was no limit to what I believed was possible. At twenty-two, I only knew the constraints of rules and limitations that had become part of my worldview. I no longer believed I could be or do anything I wanted. I thought I needed to follow the rules if I wanted to succeed.

I know I'm not alone in this. Almost everyone I talk to has known that place of freedom at some point in their life only to have lost it along the way. Perhaps you have, too. But the good news is, you can find your way back to it. Like I did. It all starts with your mindset.

When I was getting my thoughts sorted for this chapter and figuring out the most important ideas and concepts to share with you, so many things came up. Like how we go through life with inherited belief systems, which often hold us back from doing what we want or being who we desire to be. Or how the way we think about ourselves can make us feel good about ourselves or keep us small. I also kept reflecting on how what we do is the result of what we think and how important it is to think the right thoughts.

Clearly, there was a lot I wanted to cover, but I realized it all came down to one thing: your mind can be your worst enemy or your best friend. It can be the driving force that pushes you to go after your dreams or the most horrible nay-sayer that keeps you stuck forever.

We don't always think about our minds this way – working for or against us depending on our thoughts. Understanding the true power of your mind is a fundamental aspect of understanding mindset. Most people are controlled by their minds, but we can learn to flip things around and take control of our thoughts.

Our mindset influences not only the way we think but also the way we feel and therefore the way we act. In a way, everything comes down to your mindset:

- How you perceive the world.
- Your level of self-confidence and self-esteem.
- How much you love yourself.
- Whether or not you think like a do-er, a winner, or a yes-I-can-do-this kind of person.
- Your ability to recognize opportunities for happiness, success and love in your life and the life of others.
- If you stay stuck or not.

Your mindset guides all these thoughts, feelings and characteristics. *Knowing this is a priceless piece of knowledge!* It means that *you* are in control. No matter your situation, you can change your life simply by changing how you think about it.

We'll dive into how this can help you get unstuck in a minute, but first I want you to start thinking in a way that positively impacts all aspects of your life and work.

What kind of mindset do you have?

Your mindset is a combination of how you think and your beliefs about yourself and the world. Mindset makes you see the world around you in a particular way; it's what influences your actions and shapes your world.

An example of this is the "glass half full or half empty" idea. The glass holds the same amount of water but depending on your mindset, you see it as half full or half... empty. I'm sure you've experienced this, depending how positive you feel, you'll see a glass that still holds plenty and sometimes, well, there's not much in it. The same is true about the decisions that we make. They're never neutral, we always make them while thinking and feeling things. That's why it's a good idea not to make important decisions when you've just received big news (good or bad), had an orgasm, or bumped your toe against the bed. As Bishop T.D. Jakes famously said, "Never make permanent decisions on temporary emotions."

This brings me to another one of the characteristics of mindset: it can change. Depending on what's going on in your life, what you learn, what happens to you, etc. your views shift. When that happens, the world around you changes. Suddenly, you might see an opportunity you didn't see before, you think you can do something that until now seemed impossible, or someone you've known for a long time can suddenly appear different to you. All of this is related – at least partly – to your mindset.

In recent years, I've made it a point to push myself outside my comfort zone creatively. This led me to enroll in a screen-printing workshop, attend improv classes, do speaking engagements, be accepted to a writing academy, make reels for Instagram (what a comfort zone trigger that was), take impromptu trips, and even write a monologue that I brought on a stage last year. I thought up a million reasons why I should cancel doing it, but since I try not to break promises with myself (I'll come back to this), I had to go through with it. So glad I did. It was so much fun!

What's interesting about all those experiences – and life in general – is that the way you feel and think about something before you do it (have it, experience it) and after is often different. I call it the *elasticity of your comfort zone*. What looks unknown, dangerous or stressful before you do it often becomes "normal" once you've done it. The same is true of people, places, experiences, jobs, businesses – almost anything. We make assumptions about things based on little to no information, but once we get to know someone, experience something, go somewhere new, or start a new job, our opinion of it almost always changes. Things have a way of becoming familiar.

Maybe you've experienced something similar. It could be a person, a place or something you've done for the first time or a million times. One day you wake up with new thoughts, giving you a new lens through which you see the world. It often happens to me after I've done something I'm afraid to do. Like when I spoke at TEDx a few years back. The day after giving that talk, I woke up and I felt different. I had done something scary that was now part of my experiences. It made me more courageous, trusting that if I could do that, I could do other big and scary things. I always find those moments magical, and I try to use them to remind myself that what the world looks like to me depends on how I look at the world.

Your mindset dictates what you believe. What you believe creates what you see. Based on what you see, you'll take action, think specific thoughts, and behave in a certain way. Your mindset is like a philosophy of life. It's what defines how you see the world and how you interact with it. As a result, being able to have control over our mindset and cultivating a positive mindset that drives action and leads us to more happiness and fulfillment, is something we all should strive for. Luckily, we can!

Fixed or growth mindset?

We can't talk about mindset without mentioning Dr. Carol Dweck, who did extensive research on the subject and wrote down her findings in her best-selling book, *Mindset*. According to Dr. Dweck, you either have a fixed or a growth mindset. What's important to know when you feel stuck is that you can have a fixed mindset without realizing it.

Even with everything I've done so far, and with all the positive experiences I have from jumping into the unknown and landing on my feet, every time I try something new my first thought is that I won't be able to do it. I must fight against this tendency – this fixed mindset – to tell myself that I can't do something each and every day.

With a fixed mindset, your ideas and beliefs about yourself and the world are static, meaning you live your life believing that your qualities, intelligence, and capabilities are what they are and that there is little room for improvement. As a result, you see the world in an unmovable way, where things are the way they are and change is limited.

People with a fixed mindset often have inflexible beliefs about themselves that are expressed as excuses for why they cannot do, be, or have certain things. As a result, they might say and believe things like:

- I'm not smart enough to …
- I always procrastinate and never do anything.
- I'm not creative enough to …
- I'll never be good with money, so I shouldn't start my own business.
- I have no discipline or willpower.
- I'm too old to…

People who believe things like this don't believe in a world of possibilities. They have rigid beliefs about themselves and almost unalterable beliefs about the world. These beliefs might include the following:

- You need to be smart to start a business or go to college.
- You need a degree to be an expert at something.
- You're born an artist; you cannot become one.
- Only young people can change careers.
- Only a certain kind of person has enough discipline to be successful.
- Only math geniuses are good with money.

People with a growth mindset believe that what they don't know can be learned and that they're not the sum of a predetermined set of characteristics but rather that their skills, talents and intelligence can be nurtured and grown.

People with a growth mindset might say and believe things like:

- I can figure out what I don't know.
- I can learn to take action instead of procrastinating; that's why I'm reading this book!
- Creativity is a practice.
- The more I practice, the better I get with money.
- I can learn discipline and be consistent.
- You're never too old to…

People who say things like this to themselves have specific – growth mindset – beliefs about the world. These beliefs might include the following:

- Everyone's got a shot at college; you get smarter by going in the first place!
- The more I use my creativity, the more creative I become.
- I'm allowed to be myself and do things in a way that works for me, even if I procrastinate sometimes.
- It's not because I feel stuck now that I'll be stuck forever.
- You don't need a degree to be an expert at something; you can always learn.
- It's never too late to be what you want, change careers or start a business.
- Everyone has to learn to be better with money, so clearly, I can learn too.

A difference in mindset can significantly impact how you see the world. It's the same as the "half full and half empty" glass we discussed.

The more positive and growth-oriented your mindset is, the happier and more successful you will be and the easier it will be to get yourself unstuck. To help you get there, let's start with an exercise.

Prompt: What type of mindset do you have?

Take a minute to think about this question. You can always choose to put pen to paper and write your answers down or think about them and answer them mentally as you read. Whatever works for you is fine. Download a free workbook companion from my website at www.muriellemarie.com/get-unstuck-the-book.

How successful do you feel in what you undertake or want to accomplish?

To answer this question, look at how your life is organized. Your mindset is a determining factor, not only of the things you want to do but also of the things you're doing; it's essential to look at your life as a whole.

The most crucial point is this: your mindset influences your behavior. Your mindset is the driving force behind what you do, so it can restrict your actions, expand them, and make you take risks or not. Understanding this is huge!

Let's dig a little further. Look at the questions below, and answer them truthfully (nobody's watching, so don't worry, this is just for you!).

- How is your mindset impacting your life?
- Do you think you have a fixed or a growth mindset?

I know these are tough questions. Let's look at an example. Imagine you want to start something new: a creative project you think about a lot, a business you want to create, a change in your life that you know in your heart you must make, or any other idea that you can't seem to do anything about. Maybe...

- you think you don't know how to start,
- you know you must do something about it, but you're waiting for the right time,
- you have no time to do it at all, so you keep postponing it,
- you're afraid of what will happen if you take a step,
- you started, but you fear you won't succeed,
- you... (fill in the blank).

Whatever it is you're thinking, your mindset is what sets the tone. As a result, your mindset also drives your behavior and actions. That's precisely why it's so important to work on it.

If you've been feeling stuck, I guarantee you that your mindset plays a part in how you feel. Our mindset is one of the most important reasons we're not getting what we want out of life and achieving our goals. The truth is, there's nobody stopping us but our own thoughts. I know, it can be a hard pill to swallow, but it's true.

Chapter Two: What Does It Mean to Be Stuck?

"It always seems impossible until it is done."
– Nelson Mandela

When I was twenty-two, fresh out of College, I started as a freelance consultant for a media agency. My role was to help their clients, most of whom were Colleges and Universities, transition from print to the web. It wasn't easy. Most of them were so set in their ways and stuck that they couldn't see the benefit of being available on the internet. One client in particular, the marketing director of a famous College I won't name, commented, "People will always need to come to class to study; no computer will ever change that." That was back in the year 2000. Today, that College is one of the world's largest distributors of online courses.

Even though it's a big part, there's more to being stuck than mindset. To understand how we get unstuck, we must first look at how we get stuck, what being stuck really means and the complexity of getting started or moving forward – especially when you've been in that dreaded place for a while. What keeps us where we don't want to be is often a mix of practical considerations (overthinking and anxiety), emotional or mental blocks (inherited dreams or limiting beliefs, assumptions, and opinions) like in the case of that marketing director, and psychological factors (pain from the past or even trauma).

Nobody gets stuck on purpose

A lot of people feel resistance to this first step of the process. Perhaps you don't want to think about it and just want to flip through to Steps Three and Four, the practical steps, so that you can get moving right now. I want to ask you not to do that. In all the years I've been helping clients, I've learned that if you don't give yourself the time to examine what lies beneath the surface, if you don't recognize the complex web of thoughts, beliefs, emotions, inherited dreams, imagined problems, dangers and assumptions that are keeping you where you are, you won't be able to move forward sustainably or stay unstuck in the long run.

Understanding what is keeping you from taking action is the first step and a necessary building block. Give yourself the gift of time to work through the many layers that make you, you: an incredible human being with many qualities and a unique worldview.

Everyone can get stuck (even Vera Wang)

I love reading biographies of famous and successful people. You can learn a lot from the journey other people have taken to get where they are. One striking thing in all those stories is how everyone struggles and gets stuck sometimes. I've never heard of a life story that was just great, without obstacles, a straight line towards happiness and success. The road is always – always – paved with obstacles, insecurities, moments of doubt or even agony or good intentions.

Think of the people you admire, the ones whose life you'd like to live someday, or who are doing something you wish you dared to do. You might know some of them personally, or they could be unreachable superstars. Are they made of invincible material that never lets them doubt themselves or their decisions? Or are they made of flesh and blood like you? Do you believe they're never afraid or wondering what they're doing? Do you think they never experience setbacks or hardship? It's hard to imagine others being afraid and doubting their every step, especially with social media only showing us the best side of life, but everyone has hard times. Everyone gets stuck. It doesn't matter how famous, beautiful, or successful you are; life happens to all of us.

- Vera Wang, the revered fashion designer, was a competitive figure skater, journalist, and fashion editor before she ever sewed a garment together. It wasn't until she was 40 that she started thinking about becoming a fashion designer, and it wasn't until after she failed to make the 1968 figure skating Olympics.

- Van Gogh, the famous French sunflower painter, only sold one (one!) painting during his life. Even though he produced over 900 paintings, only "Red Vineyard at Arles" was sold while he was alive. Luckily for us, not selling his art never stopped him from painting!

- Michael Jordan, the athlete and basketball player who led the Chicago Bulls to championship victory six times, was dropped from the basketball team in high school. Jordan speaks openly about failure; he says he owes his success to all the missed shots he took during relentless practices, "I have failed over and over and over again in my life, and that is why I succeed."

- Walt Disney was fired from his first job at the Kansas City Star on account of him not having enough, guess what, imagination and creativity! A few years later, his first company went bankrupt. His career took a few more years of hard work and determination to finally take off.

These are only a few of the many life stories of people who got stuck and eventually figured a way out of it. Because there's always a way – that's the good news! Like the famous Amelia Earhart quote that's printed on my business cards says, "The most difficult thing is the decision to act, the rest is merely tenacity."

How about you? If you've picked up this book, I guess you might feel stuck too. Before we move on, I'd love for you to quickly assess where you are right now. When you want things to change, it's always good to know where you're starting from. Without that, how will you know you're making progress?

Prompt: How stuck do you feel right now?

To know where we're going, it's essential to know where we're starting from. As a coach, one of the first questions I ask clients is where they are on the journey to achieving what they want. Nobody starts from nowhere. Whatever we're trying to accomplish, we usually have some tools already in our toolbox.

As you embark on this journey, it's essential to first get clear on what it is you're stuck on. We'll use this information as we progress through the book, so take a few minutes to reflect on what you want from this experience.

Take a few deep breaths, ground yourself for a minute and then answer the following question, preferably on paper. Remember, you can download a free workbook companion for this book from my website at www.muriellemarie.com/get-unstuck-the-book) to help you keep track of your progress.

What are you stuck on right now? Be as specific as you can.

- Is it a person, a place, a job, or a lifestyle that keeps you stuck?
- Does it have to do with money, the place you live, or the people in your life?
- How does being stuck affect you? How does it make you feel?
- Have you tried making progress on a dream or goal for a while without success? What feels challenging about it?
- What area feels blocked when you think about your life or your work?
- If you weren't stuck, what would you be doing right now?

- If you weren't stuck, who would you be with? Where would you be?
- What would be different about your life or work if you could get unstuck right this minute?

Feel free to add all the details you need to get a clear picture of where you are right now. The clearer that picture, the better we'll know how to work from where you are to where you want to be.

It's important to remember that getting stuck is a part of life. But so is getting unstuck. You don't need a magic wand to get you out of the swamp you think you're slowly sinking into; what you need is a bit of resolve and the tools, ideas and mindset shift that I share in this book. That's it.

There's no magic trick or red pill to take, but there is a road to travel. Perhaps you'll have to walk it as often as I have because I get stuck too, and more often than I'd like to admit. For instance, it took me six years from when I said I would put pen to paper to write my first book. It took me the better part of four years to create my first online course and launch a podcast, and it took me another two years before I felt capable enough to write the book you're currently reading.

Everyone can get unstuck

I'm not going to lie. Getting unstuck takes bravery. Sometimes you need to muster courage you don't think you have or take a step without knowing where your foot will land. But the wonderful thing is that it becomes easier over time. Many things that used to block me have no power over me anymore. Like wondering what other people think of me or trying to please everyone. We'll discuss this further, but for now, I want you to know that the way you're feeling today is not the way you'll feel for the rest of your life.

Not even if you're stuck in an unhealthy or frustrating situation, like many of my clients when they come to me for help:

- In a job they hate, that drains the life out of them.
- Feeling like their abilities are underutilized and undervalued.
- In relationships that don't work for them anymore.
- Feeling misunderstood by family, friends or coworkers.
- On the verge of personal or professional burnout.
- Running on empty, building a business that isn't right for them.
- Following other people's dreams and ignoring their own.

The anatomy of being stuck looks very different from person to person, but at its core, it's always the same. Look at the examples below; what do they have in common?

- Making plans but never following through.
- Making promises to yourself or others and constantly breaking them.
- Staying in negative patterns that are bad for your health or wellbeing without ever taking action to change your situation.
- Waiting for your situation, relationship, or job to change so you can finally move on and do something else.

In each of these situations, we stay exactly where we are. To get unstuck, we need to change our situation. This means that we must change our behavior, make other choices and do things differently. To get to *that* point, we must first change how we think. But that's precisely what we're incapable of doing. We make promises to ourselves that we repeatedly break. We tell ourselves we'll try again tomorrow, the next day, and the next without ever making lasting changes.

If we do this long enough, we end up feeling lost and never get out of our rut. Or worse, we start to distrust our ability to change or take control of our lives. How would you feel if a friend kept telling you they'll help you clean out your garage only to cancel at the last minute every time? If that person stood you up a few times, would you still trust them to come and help you out? The same is true for the trust we have in ourselves. Break enough promises to yourself, and you'll unconsciously start to distrust what you tell yourself. It may look insignificant, but it has significant consequences: without self-trust, you don't believe you can do what you say you will. Stay in that mental place long enough and you'll stop trying altogether.

To move forward, you must listen to the promises you make to yourself and decide whether you will do what you say you'll do. If you're honest with yourself, you'll admit that you always know. The minute the thought pops up into your mind, you know whether you're going to act on what you tell yourself. The problem is that even when we know we won't do something, we still promise ourselves that we will.

How we get – and stay – stuck

Let's look at Thomas's case. This 48-year-old interesting, intelligent and funny project manager for an international organization specializing in digital transformation had given his best to the company for more than seven years. When I met him for the first time he was on the verge of burnout. He'd given his all to the company for four years, after which he'd been pushed aside by a narcissistic boss who was fifteen years his junior. Since then, he'd kept his head low and focused on his daily tasks. But the passion that had once allowed him to motivate teams and keep clients happy was gone. He woke up feeling bored, snoozed his alarm clock at least ten times before forcing himself out of bed, and dreaded the commute to the office, during which his anxiety and stress would systematically go up. He knew something needed to change; he knew he wasn't valued enough to stick around much longer, but he was recently divorced and had two teenagers at home. When I asked him what he really wanted to do, he told me he wanted to pick up his bike and cycle away. "It's time for me to focus on myself," he told me, "I've never done anything that was just for me. All my life, I've spent working and taking care of everyone else except myself."

Thomas's case isn't unique. I hear stories like this every day – where both sides of the scale are weighed down. With Thomas, he gets a comfortable paycheck every month but has become invisible at work, taking away his agency and job satisfaction. The problem is that Thomas knows and feels he has a potential to fulfill, a life to live, and passions to explore. His bike is calling him; he knows adventure lies ahead as soon as he sits on the saddle and starts to peddle. But he doesn't do anything; he keeps things the way they are, and he settles.

Perhaps you've settled too? Whether it's with a job, someone in our lives, or simply how things are, we all do it at some point.

What it feels like to be stuck

Being stuck is a feeling, not a fact.

This is something that I tell all my clients because when I was stuck, it helped me understand what was really going on. If you're feeling glued down right now, look around you. Is there someone else besides you keeping you there? Perhaps you're intuitively thinking, "Yes." If so, I want you to think again. Are you really, and I mean *really*, stuck where you are? Or do you just feel that way?

Especially when work, money or family are concerned, I hear clients tell me they have "no other choice but to keep doing what they're doing." But is that really true?

What being stuck often feels like:

- You're exhausted, stressed out, and always on the verge of a mental breakdown.
- Your passion for life seems to be gone.
- You feel like you've outgrown your life, your work or both.
- You're feeling frustrated, trapped, angry, helpless, hopeless and out of control.
- You're mad at yourself or others and resentful of anyone who seems to have it all figured out or doing what you'd like to be doing.
- You're hard on yourself and believe you're just not good enough.

Sound familiar? If so, I want you to know that you're not alone.

If I take what clients tell me at face value, I must believe that something terrible will happen to them if they change anything about their lives. After doing this work for almost a decade, I know it's not true. I've never met someone who had something terrible happen to them *because* they pursued their dreams. On the contrary, change, in most cases, and especially when you're the one directing it, is a good thing! It's scary, but it's the only way to grow, move forward and be truly satisfied and happy.

How fear keeps us stuck

Feeling stuck will show its ugly head in many ways, and all of them will make you believe you're better off where you are than where you want to be. But that's fear trying to protect you from making choices it thinks you might regret later. Here are a few ways fear shows up:

- You only see one way forward, and it's not what you want.
- You know things aren't working, but you don't understand why.
- You don't know what you really want.

- You know what you want but not how or where to start.
- You're waiting to feel ready to do something without having doubts.
- You have many ideas or passions, but the thought of choosing makes you cringe.
- You start new projects only to abandon them soon after you begin, in the middle or right before you're done.
- You feel empty, undervalued and on the verge of burnout or bore-out.
- You know you're meant for big things but are afraid to go for them.
- You're following other people's dreams, leaving your dreams unfulfilled.
- You allow fear (of failure, rejection, change, and so on) to keep you from doing what you want.
- You're waiting for someone else to do it for you.

Lucy came to me when she had just turned 28. A bright, enthusiastic professional who was making her way up the corporate ladder in digital marketing. Fresh out of college, she'd been offered a junior position, and now, six years later, she was still sitting at the same desk in the same chair, doing the same work for the same salary. "I'm so bored," Lucy told me during her first coaching session. "Whatever I try, I don't like what I'm doing anymore. Nobody seems to notice what I'm capable of, and they keep giving me smaller projects and difficult clients because they know I'll do it." Lucy couldn't imagine doing the same job for another year or even a few months. She was done but not ready to admit it to herself. "I want a career I can be proud of. I want to do something meaningful," she replied when I asked her about her professional goals. "I know I can make a difference; I just don't know how."

Again, this is something that can happen to anyone. We feel an itch, we know something's wrong, but we can't put our finger on what exactly or – and this is most often the case – we're afraid to admit it to ourselves.

I love when clients come to me at a crossroads like Lucy's. It's the perfect place to ask important questions because the answers are ready to be heard. I asked Lucy what she would do if she knew everything would work out for her. "If I could do anything?" After a long silence, Lucy said, "I think I would work with kids. I've been thinking about opening a kindergarten that would double as a children's bookstore. I've always loved being around kids, and reading to them or introducing them to books that changed my life as a child has been a lifelong dream." I looked at Lucy while she was talking. I could see her eyes come alive and sparkle. While she was dreaming aloud, a smile appeared on her face, and a glow of happiness that looked like it had been hiding for a long time within her. "It sounds like this might be important to you, Lucy." Lucy looked at me in disbelief. I could see how what I'd just said was making its way into her subconscious mind, where validation for what she knew to be true was waiting in all the memories of when she'd thought about her dream. As she dug deeper into her mind, her smile turned into a grin. "It will never work," she said nervously while picking at her blue woolen cardigan. "I've tried to make something of this dream before, but whenever I feel like I'm getting somewhere, eventually, I get stuck. I just don't think I have what it takes."

Can you relate to how Lucy is feeling? If you do, again, I want you to know that this is a natural feeling that many of my clients (and I) have felt at some point in our lives. Being stuck has a way of making us feel miserable. It can feel even worse when you've tried to do something about that feeling and nothing changed.

Getting stuck is one thing, but getting stuck repeatedly adds another layer of mental difficulty to an already complex problem. When that happens, you not only have all your ready-made excuses and reasons "why it will never work," you also have "proof" of what you're saying because you tried before, and it didn't work. Or so it seems.

Chapter Three: The Link Between Being Stuck and Being Afraid of Change.

"If I am an advocate for anything, it is to move.
As far as you can, as much as you can.
Across the ocean, or simply across the river."
– Anthony Bourdain

When Lucy was younger, her parents opened a small shop on the main street in their hometown. It was a beautiful place; they called it Little Italy. It had everything from olive oil to the best Italian pasta and everything else you could think of when imagining a warm afternoon in Rome or Venice. In the beginning, things looked bright. Everyone in town was excited about this exotic shop that felt like a holiday. But even though sales were good, and people kept coming, Lucy's parents lost track of their finances. After a few years, and to everyone's surprise, the shop went bankrupt. Her parents were devastated. To this day, it's hard for them to talk about it. They still can't explain what happened. But one thing is certain, if Lucy told them she was going to open a shop, they wouldn't be able to sleep at night. "We're not businesspeople," is what they would say. "Don't do it, Lucy; it will only break your heart." Of course, they don't know Lucy already tried it, at least a little bit. With her friend Martha, she went to a few book fairs last year, and they set up a corner called 'The Kindergarten Library.' They expected everyone with kids to be ecstatic about their idea and to let them read to their kids while watching them so they could go around the fair in peace, but Lucy and Martha only had three children to watch in the four days they were there. Martha concluded it was a stupid idea, and although Lucy didn't think she was right, she agreed with her. It didn't work. "What if I invest all my savings in this dream, and nobody shows up?" Lucy asked me. "I would be left with nothing, and my parents would be disappointed in me. I could never live with myself after that."

What Lucy is talking about is a deeply ingrained fear of change, fueled by many reasons why it's a bad idea, even to consider altering her circumstances or anything about her life. Even though this is one of the fundamental reasons why we get and stay stuck, the capacity we have to imagine all of the terrible things that might happen if we change anything about our current situation, is an evolutionary advantage that kept us alive and allowed us to evolve for the whole of human history.

Throughout my college years, I wore the same socks every time I had an exam. It wasn't a pretty sight if you're wondering what they looked like when I graduated. I still have them. A pair of Burlington's my mom bought me for my birthday right before I started university. I know I'm not the only one who adds a dash of superstition to important events in their life. There are stories of baseball players wearing the same worn-out shoes for important games or state officials signing every treaty with their lucky pen. Maybe you have a thing too. Those things are a way for our brains and nervous systems to try and control a situation we have no control over. There's no problem with it, as long as it doesn't stop you from doing what you want. Even though there is no correlation between my knowledge of a particular subject and the socks I'm wearing, I guarantee that my grades on the exams I took wearing random socks weren't as good as the ones I got wearing my lucky socks. That's how powerful our mind is. It's essential to let go of the need for control in situations we can't control, especially when we're stuck. The most common way that the need for control will show up is through the fear of change.

Why does our brain resist change?

Our brain has evolved into seeing and remembering danger. Many centuries ago, when humanity was emerging and we were roaming the planes of the savannah, a quick fight or flight response to a moving branch or a wild animal spotted in the distance could mean the difference between life and death. Following Darwin's theories on the natural evolution of species, only our ancestors with the fastest "fear" reflexes made it. This is the gift they passed down to their children and eventually to us. But here's the problem. What was once an indispensable tool and advantage for survival has yet to adapt to the world we live in today. Our brains and nervous systems are still on the lookout and ready to respond to life-threatening dangers, except there aren't many remaining.

As we have evolved as a species, we have traded most physical dangers for stress and the pressure to perform. Especially in the Western world, where we're groomed to be productive and "make" something of our time and ourselves. We're taught to care about brain-numbing jobs because we need the "security" they provide, and we're expected to be kind and understanding with others, including those who mistreat us. But none of this is as detrimental as this false belief that society engrains in us: *to care about what other people think of us.*

Have you ever stopped yourself from doing something you wanted to do because you heard that voice in your head say something like:

- "What will people think?"
- "I could never do that."
- "What if someone sees me?"
- "What if someone finds out?"
- "Everyone will make fun of me."

You can take the person out of the savannah, but you can't take the fight or flight response out of the person. As we evolved as humans, our reptilian brain (the oldest part of our brain, which responds so well to danger) gained some friends: the limbic system, our emotional brain, and the neocortex (or rational brain). These evolutionary additions make us agile, sensitive, and intelligent beings all at the same time. The problem is communication doesn't always flow well between them. The reptilian brain by nature remains on the lookout for danger, and its reactions, whether to danger or other situations, is of the "act first, think later" kind.

On the other hand, the neocortex is the part of our brain that helps us understand the world, see structures and systems, and organize our thoughts and feelings. When the reptilian brain senses danger, the neocortex wants to "understand" the threat or where it comes from. In that "translation," a lot is lost. Maybe our heart rate goes up and we start to sweat a little because we just thought about a big dream we have, and we get a little too excited about it, our reptilian brain and nervous system will immediately react. This response can (and often will) be misinterpreted by our neocortex. Instead of being equally excited about the prospect of achieving this big dream, our thinking brain wonders why we are sweating and breathing faster and concludes it must be because there's danger lurking in that dream.

This process often goes unnoticed because it happens so quickly and on an unconscious level (as does 95% of all our brain activity).[1] This neocortex and reptilian communication misfiring starts from the moment we are born, mainly because what the reptilian brain wants and how it reacts to the world around us is not how our parents want us to be. As we are being culturized, educated, and brought up, we are taught to "control" our impulses. Often, shame and guilt are used to get us to do that. Parents and caretakers use their love and attention as currency to get us to behave in a way they (and society) approve of. This leaves a trace. Don't get me wrong, we need to gain control of our reflexes and can't go around doing whatever our reptilian brain wants us to do. The problem is that our neocortex goes into overdrive. Pressured by a world that is too demanding and stressful, it wants to take control of everything in our lives and needs to give meaning to every impulse or emotion we experience. That's how we get to a place where even excitement about a dream causes anxiety and negative thinking.

Trained into anxiety, stress, and feeling stuck (like a puppy)

When my Labrador was a puppy, my now ex-husband and I purchased a trailer by the water to have a calm and relaxing place to go to when we needed to escape the city's busyness. It was an old camper we found by chance one day when we were walking in a place known for its forests and rivers. We knew it was meant for us as soon as we saw it. We also realized it needed to be stripped down and completely renovated. A week after that initial visit, we received the keys to our little crumbling castle. We called on some friends, and together we spent a weekend taking every rotten wall and floor out of the trailer. We installed wood flooring, upgraded the gas heater, removed two walls to make the living space and kitchen areas one big room, installed a new shower, and turned our bedroom into a luxury hotel room with a brand-new mattress and new bed paneling. In 48 hours, we had transformed it into our dream home, albeit a very tiny one.

As we were sitting down for a well-deserved cold drink and a slice of pizza, I wondered where my puppy was. By then, he'd been with us for a few months and never left my side. Every day since he'd become part of the family, he was right there behind me every time I stood up. When I cooked dinner, he was patiently waiting by my side until I was done (and had a little something for him to eat as well). When we started the renovation of the trailer, I remember him being excited and walking up and down the place, watching what everyone was doing. Because he was still a puppy, he was playful and looking for attention. But a renovation project is not the best place to make new friends, even when you're the cutest little dog in the world. Without realizing it, we'd pushed him away every time he came up to one of us for a hug or to play. When he was walking around the trailer looking at what was happening, we were telling him to get out or not to touch the wet paintbrushes or pots of glue. When I think about it now, my heart still hurts. For the better part of two days, we told this little fluff of love to bugger off just for being curious and loving.

When we finally sat down that Sunday night, proud of our work and eager to start enjoying our new little piece of heaven, my puppy was nowhere to be found. Finally, after calling him at least a hundred times, we found the little one hidden under a table, all the way at the back of the front porch to our trailer. It took a lot of convincing and patience to finally get him out from under that table. The poor thing looked so scared. Even when I kneeled to look at him and pet him, he wouldn't come out. I could see how every time someone said his name, he would cringe, his ears would flatten, and he would look at me to assess the danger and know if it was safe.

Just 48 hours earlier, when I would say his name, my loving puppy would come to me happy and ready to play. Now, when he heard his name, he thought he was in trouble. I learned that day how quickly he could be trained to believe something was wrong.

The same is true for us humans. We, too, will believe things about ourselves if we're just told them often enough. Even though they're not true, if we say demeaning or negative things to and about ourselves or have someone repeatedly say them to us, we will internalize what we are told. What we believe influences our actions. So we will start behaving in a way that confirms what we think about ourselves or what we are capable of. The more negatively we think, the more our actions can undermine us, thus reinforcing the excuses we tell ourselves why we can't or shouldn't do something. Then, we worry and ask ourselves what's wrong with us, what we did to deserve what is happening to us and feel sorry for ourselves. The problem is that we rarely look for solutions in this state of mind because we're so caught up in worrying, overthinking, or other negative thought patterns. That's why it's so difficult to change.

After realizing what had happened to my puppy, I focused on gaining his trust back and easing his anxiety. I could see how two days of being told off stressed him out so much that it drastically impacted his behavior. Luckily, it didn't break our bond. My dog still trusted me. After a few days, he returned to being his old self and followed me wherever I went. But it was a valuable lesson. What if I hadn't been there to restore his perception of how I (and, by extension, all humans) felt about him? How would that have influenced his life? Would he have grown into a depressed dog thinking something was wrong with him? Would he ever have trusted humans again? How would his perception of the world as a scary place have influenced his behavior? How would that behavior have reinforced how people treated him? And so on.

Of course, humans aren't dogs; I'm certainly not claiming they are. But how we learn to believe things about ourselves that aren't true can follow a similar path. If you, or other people, spend enough time trying to convince you that you're a certain way or that you can't do something, it will be hard not to fall into the trap. If after that, as our brains love to do, you start to look for confirmation of what you believe to be true about yourself, I guarantee that you'll find it. Finally, if you then use that "proof" to confirm what you think, well, tada! ... you've entered a getting stuck loop.

Are your beliefs keeping you stuck?

Even though nothing of what you think about yourself might be true, your beliefs influence your actions. Your actions reinforce your assumptions in an endless cycle of inability or unwillingness to change. When this happens, being stuck becomes your life, and changing your situation looks almost impossible.

When we take a closer look at what's going on, we notice that being stuck often happens because of one, or more, of the following reasons:

- **Fear and worry: you know what you have but don't see what you *could* have.**

  The fear of change and all the worries about what could happen or go wrong that accompany that fear can keep you from taking action. The old saying "You know what you've got, but not what you might get" keeps you stuck. Instead of taking a chance, you'd rather live risk-free, with a false sense of security, as Thomas did; remember him? "What if I fail?", "What if this isn't really what I want?", "What if something goes wrong?" are common questions clients ask at this stage or when they start thinking about change. The problem with the fear of change is that it keeps you stuck and unhappy by endlessly making you think about disaster scenarios when instead you should do something about your situation.

- **Internalized beliefs: we *all* have them.**

  They're passed down to us from our caregivers, society, family, friends, and loved ones. We construct them as we move through the world and experience life. Our behavior is mainly the result of the beliefs we internalize. Whatever we believe, we do. Whatever we do, we become. It's not that these beliefs are all bad; most help us make sense of the world. The problem is that we also internalize many beliefs that aren't true. "Being successful is not for me" is a great example. "You need an MBA to become an entrepreneur" or "I don't have the right degree to become a journalist." Research has shown that about 95% of what we think is unconscious[2]. Are we free when we act on autopilot this way? Further in this book we'll explore this critical question and how uncovering our internalized beliefs can help us get unstuck.

- **Negative thinking: some people see the good in everything, others call themselves realists, and then there are the *negative* thinkers.**

  My grandmother used to be like that. She was a brilliant and capable woman who spent her life waiting for horrible things to happen to her and her family (which almost never did). The problem with negative thinking is that it keeps you where you are. It reinforces your internalized beliefs and makes you constantly worry about adverse outcomes. You cannot believe in yourself and think of yourself as a helpless loser simultaneously. Luckily, as we'll explore, you get to choose what you believe.

- **Lack of clarity: ambiguity never disappears just by *thinking* about all your options.**

  Creatives and entrepreneurs, the generalist[3] kind especially, are prone to overflow with ideas, projects, and passions. They only need to start something new to have a flood of ideas appear unannounced, especially when they're in creative flow or focused on a task. I know, believe me, because I often go through this, and so do most of my clients. Having so many ideas can be overwhelming and make you feel as if you don't know what you should be doing. Who can pick between a million-dollar business idea and a life that includes healthy smoothies for breakfast and yoga on the beach every day? We can see ourselves doing both, and we want to. The thing with clarity is that it only appears when you pick something. Only then will you know if you like an idea or not. The good news is that if you don't, you get to change your mind and pick something else. Or, better yet, you get to keep the parts you like of different ideas and *combine them* into a life and work you love. How cool is that? More about this in Step Four of my MOVE method and the last part of this book.

- **Not knowing where or how to get started: picking the *first* thing you should do can be hard.**

  Once my clients have chosen what to start with, and yes that's a BIG (often scary) step forward, they encounter the next hurdle: needing to know where or how to take the next step. How do you build a million-dollar business? How do you relocate to a place where you can practice yoga on the beach every day? It can be overwhelming to think about it. But just thinking about something never makes it come true. In the end, you must go out and do it. The problem lies in wanting to have all the answers in advance. Building the resolve, courage, and resilience to take action with limited knowledge about what comes next is how you get ahead. We'll work on helping you do just that throughout this book.

- **Lack of self-confidence: believing in yourself is an *inside* job.**

  Negative thinking, fear, worry, lack of clarity, and internalized beliefs all add up to how good or bad you feel about yourself. Then there's the dreaded inner critic, our egos, perfectionism, and people-pleasing, the people in our lives who don't understand us and put unwanted pressure on us to "just do something" or who disapprove of our dreams, the family members with good intentions who want to warn us of all the dangers in the world... you get the picture. Spend enough time with these internal and external influences, and you'll lose all sense of agency. You'll start to believe you're incapable of anything, or worse, that you don't deserve better than your current circumstances. To get unstuck, you need to start believing in yourself (again), whatever you or anyone else says you can or cannot do. We'll work on that throughout this book as well.

- **Lack of creativity: building your *problem-solving* muscle to help you get unstuck.**
  It's hard to imagine that creatives and entrepreneurs could lack creativity. Still, when it comes to getting unstuck, we tend to be great at pretending we don't have one creative idea to help us get out of the muddy swamp that keeps us from moving forward. The thing with being stuck is that it paralyzes you. You focus so much on your situation that you forget you have the agency and the power to get out of it. It's not your fault; it's just how it works (otherwise, you wouldn't feel stuck, would you, or read this book?). Remembering that you have a choice and can come up with solutions and try them out is a significant first step – more about it in Steps Three and Four of my MOVE method later in this book.

- **Inner conflict: can only be resolved by making a *choice*.**
  When faced with life choices or career decisions, we often believe that what we're comparing looks the same. We think we're weighing off similar things against each other, like the difference between colors or types of pasta, so it feels hard, or perhaps even impossible, to make a choice. This inner conflict is painful. It can only be resolved by making a choice. The faster you do it, the quicker you'll be relieved from the pressure of not knowing what to pick. In a state of inner conflict, we tend to develop tunnel-vision and become egocentric. This is a normal reaction of our psyche, which is trying to figure out what is best for us to do when faced with seemingly very comparable choices. The choices we face are often not similar; we just make them out to be. We only look at a very narrow part of the options in front of us. Given two career options, for example, we only look at the difference in salary, the job description, and the company we might end up working for. In that equation, we don't consider how our coworkers will make us feel, how the coffee will taste, the freedom this new job might offer over our existing one, or any other life-altering effects of choosing one over the other. Once

we've made a decision, things change dramatically. Our brain does what it does best: it goes looking for confirmation that we made the right choice, so all of a sudden, the jobs that seemed so similar couldn't be further apart. The same is true of procrastination. Imagine you have an essay due in two weeks. You know you should work on it, but don't do it. Again, there's an inner dialogue (conscious or unconscious) with opposing views on what you should do next. This is nothing new and part of human nature. As far back as Plato, the Greek philosopher, people thought we had different centers in the mind, each with another cognitive relationship to the world that motivates us differently. The question is, what internal message should you listen to? More about that in this first step and Step Two of this book.

- **Self-deception: our minds *never* imagine the future the way it unfolds.**
We all think about the future. When we do, we imagine our lives, how we will feel, where we'll be, and potentially with whom. The problem is our minds don't imagine events the way they unfold, and the further into the future we look, the less we feel the impact it might have on us. That's why smokers are not turned off by the idea of lung cancer, even though the science is undeniable. It's so far off in the future and there are so many possible ways to die, that our minds don't give the impact of smoking on our life the importance it deserves. Something else our minds are good at is overestimating our ability to react to events the way we imagine that we will. Experiencing events feels very different from thinking about them. This has profound effects on us and how we change. We think we know the future, but we have no clue who we'll become as we move forward through life, have experiences, do things, and chase our dreams. Because of this self-deception, we make choices that often limit us. We underestimate how different we will be in the future, so we keep on wanting the same kind of things, thinking the bold

choices or options available wouldn't work for us when in fact, it's every choice we make that slowly changes who we are.

- **A love for excuses: listening to them always *sucks* in the long run.**
  I do things consistently every day. It helps me live the life I want and build the career and business I aim for. Every day before I get started on some of the tasks and habits that I've built over the years, I still hear the voice in my head telling me that I don't have to do it if I don't want to and that, in fact, I could just spend this time watching Netflix, doing some online shopping or doing nothing at all. If there's one thing we can say about that voice in our head and excuses in general, it's that they're tenacious. I've been doing this work for over a decade, and still the voice is there, ready to serve me up an excuse. Although the ideas it comes up with often sound more fun than mine, I've learned that listening to my inner voice might give me pleasure in the moment but always sucks in the long run. And that's what excuses do: they keep us from achieving our goals and keep us stuck.

- **Childhood wounds, attachment styles, and trauma: we must acknowledge their *impact*.**
  Last, but certainly not least, I've come to believe that our childhood wounds, attachment styles, and the trauma we might have experienced as children, or even later in life, play a massive role in how stuck we are and, most importantly, in how difficult it is to get unstuck. As someone who has suffered trauma, I know what it takes to heal and move past it. It's probably the hardest thing I've ever had to do in my life and something I will always have to work on. As a society, we don't acknowledge this enough. We love to put the work and pressure on the individual as if we can always fix ourselves alone. This isn't true. When trauma or attachment wounds are involved (which is something almost everyone struggles with to some degree),

we cannot do this work alone, and we cannot do it lightly. The first step is always to recognize and accept what is. Only when we uncover the automatic triggers and responses we have and the unconscious stuff that is keeping us stuck, can we start healing and move forward. We'll look at this in Step Four further in this book.

To get unstuck, look at your life with a beginner's mind

If you're familiar with coaching or the self-help aisle at your favorite bookstore, you might have heard about what I share in this book. You may have enrolled in a program once to improve your self-esteem or make all your fears and worries disappear. Perhaps you've been doing mindset work for a while or have tried all the meditation apps – to no avail. Or you're a skeptic who never tried any of those things and doesn't believe in woo-woo. Whatever your situation, I invite you to keep an open mind – what Buddhist and mindfulness teachers call a "beginner's mind."

Please look at the information in this book as new, just like a child who discovers the world for the first time and tries to make sense of it. Having a beginner's mind has helped me in so many ways. Before I practiced looking at things this way, I often got stuck in my thoughts. Opening myself up to the possibilities of things not being what I believed them to be, allowed me to slowly transform how I perceive the world and myself. Having a beginner's mind was instrumental in helping me get unstuck. It's an essential building block. Without it, I wouldn't have been able to change and finally move forward.

Getting stuck is a process that can take years. It's not something that happens overnight or that you can catch or fall into. Untangling what keeps you from doing the things you want will take time, too. And that's okay. Remember that resistance will show up. You will feel like the world is against you sometimes or that the people around you have it easier than you (even though we never really know people's lives or how they genuinely feel). In those moments, I want you to keep your heart and mind open to the possibility that this might also be part of the process.

I promise you there is a way out and I will help you find it. So read along; we're getting into the juicy stuff.

Chapter Four: The Myth of Change.

"The greatest discovery of all time is that a person can change his future by merely changing his attitude."
– Oprah Winfrey

Change is a tricky thing. Even though most of us know that change is often for the better, we fight it with everything we've got. That's because we usually only see the good in change after it happens, so we resist it, even when we know it would benefit us. Again, we know what we've got but not what we'll get.

We often think of change as something that happens to us rather than something we control. To some extent, this is true, even when we're the ones igniting change. But even a seasoned *changer* like me still feels resistance towards it. Because it's not just that we know what we've got, and not what we'll get. We also know who we are, but not who we'll become by changing. Although often unconscious, this is a big part of why people resist change. I know I must fit into the big new shoes of my big new dreams. It's not that I can't, but will I like the person that I need to be to do it?

As a professional coach, I know a business or career can only grow as much as the person or entrepreneur behind it. When I teach clients the mindset and practical techniques I've developed to help people move forward, I'm often met with delightful and enthusiastic disbelief. "I didn't know I could do things this way," or "Wow, this stuff really works," or, my favorite, "Do you mean I can apply this to whatever I want in my life?"

Change isn't a precious metal found on the surface of faraway planets; it's something you can have as much of as you want or need in your life – right now. There's one caveat though: change isn't easy. The formula for change may be, but as we've mentioned, when you apply it, you'll meet resistance, mental blocks, or other people claiming to want the best for you by keeping you where you are. For many, even with the formula firmly in their hands, taking the necessary steps to change remains difficult, if not impossible. So they get, and often stay, stuck.

Change often needs a breaking point

A few years ago, my ex-husband left out of the blue, claiming he was "confused and needed time to think." In reality, he wasn't confused at all. He was leaving me. He started a relationship with someone else and didn't have the guts to tell me. So he let me figure it out. It was a painful moment. In the months following our separation, I only wanted things to go back to how they were, even though our relationship had been rough for a long time.

Reading through old journals of the years leading up to our separation, I'm reminded of how miserable I felt, how much we fought, and how little love and warmth was left between us. A few times, I even wrote in my journal that I wanted to leave him, questioning how and when I should do it. But I never did. The idea of change felt too big and challenging. Divorce sounded scary and splitting our lives (and our assets) felt almost impossible. In light of all these unknowns, I convinced myself that my life "wasn't so bad."

That marriage ending turned out to be one of the best things that ever happened to me. It wasn't easy. Getting those assets split without tearing each other's eyes out was an exercise in maturity and forgiveness. After everything was said and done, it took me a while to find my bearings again and feel the natural joy I have for life come back, but once it did, I felt so grateful. I've never been happier or more successful. Now that I've gone through it, I know that given a choice, I wouldn't hesitate to do it all again. In the last years we spent together, nothing about us was fun anymore. Eventually, I'm sure I would have left my ex, but I was stuck, so it would have taken me a long time to do it.

Everyone has a different breaking point

To effectively change, most people need to arrive at a breaking point. As long as their circumstances aren't painful enough, they'd rather stay where they are. During that time, which can be years or decades for some, the fear of change is more significant than the pain of staying where they are – even if that means waking up every day wondering what they're supposed to do with their lives or why they can't seem to be content with what they have. This may sound familiar to you, dear reader. If it does, I want to tell you that you're not alone. I'd been in *stuckland* for years before I figured out how to move past my fears and blocks.

Staying stuck is often finding every possible reason in the book (not this one!) why there's absolutely no good reason for us to change: the kids, the house, the cushy job, the parents, the dog, the bad economy, the ... (fill in the blank with your favorite excuse). But there comes a time when even the best reason doesn't work anymore. Many people who finally got unstuck have in common that pivotal moment when, one way or another, they said: "Enough!" This is a different moment for everyone, but again, it's usually a breaking point.

Take my friend and former client Sara for instance, who was passed over for a promotion for the third time when she got pregnant with her second child while she'd been doing most of the work in an office of five sales reps, even during her first pregnancy and all the way through her maternity leave. Out of frustration and anger, she decided, "No more!" She took a cardboard box, filled it with the picture frame of her toddler and husband, grabbed Lucy, the succulent who lived on her desk, and left to never look back. Fast forward a few years and Sara is now the HR director of one of the biggest construction companies in the country. She leads various teams that amount to over a hundred people and has helped the company make a 180-degree turn back into profitability after a few difficult years of losing market share and business. Thanks to Sara, a lot of employees kept their jobs. Suppose she'd never reached her breaking point. In that case, Sara might still be working in a company that undervalued and underpaid her and the families of the employees she helped keep their jobs might be under a lot of stress and financial difficulties.

Or take my good friend Kristina, who got promoted to consultant in a multinational company specializing in cargo freight after having been given the lousiest admin tasks in the office for over two years. The promotion came with double the amount of work and two mandatory weeks of travel out of the month. When Kristina finally made the promotion, she was promised a long overdue raise, but that never came. Two months after taking on her new role, and the long hours and time away from home that came with it, the company hired a man five years younger than her and with only half her years of experience. When she got notice that his salary was almost double what she was making, she finally decided to quit. It dawned on her that she was worth so much more than what the people in that company were giving her credit for. It was time for her to step up and start advocating for herself; it was time for her to take control of the changes she wanted to make in her life and career instead of waiting for someone else to do it for her.

Kristina, just like Sara, took a leap of faith. Even though the first weeks without a job or a clear plan were stressful and scary, she firmly landed on her feet after a few months. Unlike Sara, Kristina decided to go after her lifelong dream of opening a bakery. The cupcakes, birthday cakes, and other delicious goodies she loved to make but only had time for on the weekend, became her focus. Kristina decided to start small and offer baking services for children's birthdays and company events. Soon enough, her kitchen became too small for the orders she was getting through the website she had put together herself. While looking for a small commercial kitchen downtown, she found the perfect brick-and-mortar shop to house her creations. As I write this, Kristina is working out the final details of her grand opening next week.

Kristina and Sara are great examples of how we can stay in careers for too long, often because of the money we're making or the illusion of security it provides. It's not hard to imagine why many need a breaking point to finally decide to leave. The same is valid for relationships.

It doesn't hurt hard enough yet

In 2014, when I was going through my growth journey, I picked up Amanda Palmer's book *The Art of Asking*. The music industry was amid a revolution, with initiatives popping up everywhere for artists to publish and sell their work online. In her book, Amanda Palmer, a multi-talented artist and singer/musician, makes a case for asking for help from your fans. If you're an artist, there are many reasons why you'll like her book. What stuck with me the most is an anecdote in the book, a short passage in which she talks about her emotional difficulties as a young adult and her bouts of self-destructiveness. To illustrate her point, she shares a story of a dog and a farmer. That story was an aha moment that unlocked so much wisdom for me and later, for many of my clients. It's so powerful that I wanted to share it with you. The story goes like this[4]:

A farmer is sitting on his porch in a chair, hanging out.
A friend walks up to the porch to say hello, and hears an awful yelping, squealing sound coming from inside the house.
"What's that terrifyin' sound?" asks the friend.
"It's my dog," said the farmer.
"He's sittin' on a nail."
"Why doesn't he just sit up and get off it?" asks the friend.
The farmer deliberates on this and replies: "Doesn't hurt enough yet."

When I read this story, it was as if my heart stopped. One nail was my marriage, another one was the demanding and selfish friends I had in my life, and yet another was the clients that paid me peanuts and called me on

Sunday nights to discuss their projects. Still more were all the "have tos" I had accumulated over the years trying to be liked by everyone, all the pressure I gave myself to keep on doing things I hated, and to do it all perfectly.

We're all sitting on nails. If you're lucky, it might just be one, but in most cases, there's more – when you finally feel them, when the pain outweighs the risk of changing, that's your breaking point.

I've had clients come to me after being fired by a toxic boss, going through severe burn-out, surviving a car accident, experiencing panic attacks for the first time or even losing a child. Some people have a high threshold for pain, others are unaware of what is going on before it's too late or the truth hits them in the face. Whatever the case – whatever *your* case – there comes a point everyone wants to change. With this book, I want to give you the nudge you need to get up now before the nail hurts too much.

The bad news is: nobody's coming to save you or make change happen for you. That's the big fat lie, what I call *the myth of change*. The good news is: you *do* have the ability to change your life. You have the power to change. There's always something you can do, a step, however small, you can take. Resisting change is costing you. The longer you ignore your truth, the more time you lose and the more damage you do to yourself, your relationships, your business or career.

When you take control of change, you have agency and the ability to make choices. You're no longer at the mercy of what happens to you, forced to cope with whatever mess and personal distress the changes you're going through bring on. Isn't this a wonderful thing to know? That you don't need to suffer or feel the pain to change? Your breaking point doesn't need to be at the end of your rope. Your breaking point can be the moment you decide to change. When you finally say to yourself: "That's it, I'm done with this; I deserve to be happier, healthier, have better relationships with my friends,

enjoy my work more, be more creative, successful, and fulfilled in my life."
Your breaking point can be right now!

You can't stop change from happening

Change is always happening. As you're reading this, wherever you are, change isn't only happening around you; you are changing. The cells in your body are breaking down and being replaced. Your brain is creating neural pathways for the new information you're gathering from this book and everything happening in your life right now; all the while, the Earth is spinning around its axis, making its way around the Sun that keeps on combusting to eventually burn out. The Universe is expanding at an ever-increasing pace. There's no way to stop change. If there is only one sure thing in life, it's that everything constantly changes.

Still, we cling to things the way they are and insist on wanting everything to stay the same. Our fear of the unknown or that something might go wrong (read: get worse than what we currently have) often stands in the way of what we truly want, as does our need to hold on to things instead of letting them go – something we'll look at later in this step when we address impermanence – the true state of all things. We might be unhappy, frustrated, or angry at our current situation and still choose not to do anything. This is an illusion. Not choosing is also a choice, and often a terrible one. While you claim you want everything to stay the same, things keep changing. And the worst part: you have no control over it.

Luckily there are better ways to deal with change. Instead of waiting for things to happen to you, you can go out and make things happen *for* you. How you do this can be disorganized, a spur-of-the-moment kind of thing, or you can take a more practical approach. In this book, we'll look at the latter, at how you can become intentional about change, starting right now with a reflective exercise that changed my life and the life of many of my clients.

Prompt: Your ideal day[5] and your ideal life

Give yourself some time to do this exercise. Pen and paper are great, but just thinking about it, in this case, is a form of doing too.

Imagine an ideal day. A day out of your beautiful, happy and successful life. Not an out-of-the-ordinary day, so not a holiday, a day you run and win a marathon, or even your birthday – just a good, typical, happy day out of your ideal life.

When you have the image of this day in mind, start at the beginning when you open your eyes in the morning, and let the day run its course until you get back into bed at night. Walk through your day mentally and look around you. What can you smell? What is hanging on the walls (if anything)? What can you hear, close by and in the distance? Let your imagination take you where it wants to go. This is not the moment to censor yourself (you've done enough of that already!). This is the moment to dream big.

As you're making your way through your ideal day, ask yourself:

- **What are you doing?** What's the first thing you think about or do when you get up? Do you eat breakfast? If so, what's on your plate? Are you alone, or is someone with you? What do you feel? Do you stay in your pajamas or go straight to your closet to pick an outfit for the day? What happens afterward? How do you spend your morning? What do you have for lunch? What are you doing in the afternoon? Keep imagining your day until you go to bed at night, happy and inspired.

- **What do you see around you?** When you open your eyes in the morning, what do you see around you? In what kind of room are you? Is there anything hanging on the walls? When you step out of the bedroom or where you slept, what does the place you call „home" look like? Are you in a mansion, a house, an apartment? Are you sliding open the door of the campervan you're touring around the country with? Are you living in a cabin in the middle of nature? Are you lounging on a beach with a mocktail or sitting inside at a desk? How does your day feel? How's the weather? What do you hear in the distance? What's happening around you?

- **Where is your attention going?** What are you focused on? Are you working, writing, or on a video call with someone? Cooking something delicious for the kids who are about to come home? What are your thoughts? Is there something in the back of your mind, something you can't forget, like a birthday or a deadline for an important project?

- **How are you feeling?** How's your body feeling? Is there tension somewhere, or are you relaxed and chill? What emotions are you experiencing? How's your heart doing? How are your lungs? Are you hot or cold? Are you happy? Is there something you look forward to? If you had to pick one thing, what would you say is the most beautiful part of your day?

- **What about your ideal life?** Stringing beautiful days like the one you just imagined together creates an ideal life. What would you need to add to the day you just described to turn it into a life you could genuinely enjoy living? What should you have, do and be to live out your most beautiful life? How could you start gently adding some of that into your life today?

A note about trying to change others

Clients often share how difficult they find it to change. They tell me it's probably one of the hardest things they've ever had to do. I think it's true, don't you? When you've been stuck for a while, thinking about change can cause agony and despair. But here's the thing: if we know how hard it is to change ourselves, why do we insist on trying to change others? We all know it's impossible, yet we keep pretending that we can.

The boss who never listens, the co-worker who's always sloppy and never refills the coffee machine, the clients who are never satisfied, the partner who sucks at loading the dishwasher, or the friends who just don't get it. We've told all these people a million times how we want them to behave and treat us, and still they insist on ignoring us. Crazy, right?

This strategy doesn't work. Nobody will change their behavior because you tell them to. They might try for a while because they want to make you happy or avoid conflict, but they will remain the same internally. It's only a matter of time before their habits resurface and you get frustrated or angry again. So if you're staying stuck waiting for others to change first, it's time to change your strategy. What's a better way to deal with this? To get unstuck, you must rethink the person that *you* are. Don't focus on trying to change the people around you; focus on what you can do to change yourself (even if that includes removing some people from your life). It's the only thing you can control.

Chapter Five: How Does Change Happen?

"If we don't change, we don't grow. If we don't grow, we aren't really living."
– Gail Sheehy

Change can happen in two ways. You can wait for it, like most people do, until you reach a breaking point (or a magical unicorn comes and hands you fairy dust), or you can be intentional about it and take control of your life. The *Ideal Day and Ideal Life* exercise is the first step in doing precisely that: claiming back control. When I did the exercise for the first time many years ago, I'd been stuck for a while. Without consciously searching for something, I questioned every choice and decision I ever made. I never felt the itch as strongly as I did back then. When I put pen to paper, as you've hopefully just done, I had no clue what would come out. All I knew was that I wasn't happy and that something needed to change. At first, not much came out. It took me a few mornings of staring at a blank page to start seeing the contours of the life I wanted, to draw itself on the page. But you know what? Even though it was a tedious process that required patience and grace, the ideal day and life I imagined are the ones I'm living now: I wanted to help others, write, teach, and keep on learning so I could keep my overactive, creative brain happy. I wanted to learn new skills, be free, and be the only one to decide how I spent my time. I wanted to be inspired by the work and talents of others and continue to discover my talents. I wanted to be courageous and adventurous, to find my wings again and to explore the magic that is my life. I still have the journal in which I wrote all this down. In fact, I'm looking at it right now as I'm writing these words. I'm astounded by how much of what I wanted my life to be is now my life. This stuff works – if you're willing to do the work.

Now that you've seen and imagined a glimpse of the life you could be living, you have a starting point to make real change happen. As we've seen before, lack of direction is one of the most common reasons people get stuck. But that's not your case anymore because you finally know where you want to go!

Many of my clients still need clarification about what to do next when they've done this exercise. It was hard for me at first. Perhaps you're feeling that way too, and for a good reason. You've just imagined the most beautiful day and life possible; you've felt it as if you were already there. But now your inner voice can't stop whispering why it will never work, or that you're not good enough. "Ok, yes, I understand where you're going with this, Murielle, but what am I supposed to do now?" This is the question I hear the most when the fear of change takes over. If you're thinking this right now, don't worry, you're right where you're supposed to be! Let's diffuse that fear with another exercise.

Prompt: What do you want to do with the rest of your life?

We don't know what our lives will ultimately be made of or how long we'll be alive. This is a mystery and insecurity we must all live with. Many philosophers throughout history spent their lives trying to solve the riddle of a life well lived. It's not an easy nut to crack, and I don't claim I will do that here. But I firmly believe that you should not waste the precious life you've been given. Every day spent being stuck is a day you'll never get back. To get over the fear of change, it helps to remind yourself of how little time you have and how important the decisions you make are.

- **How long do you have left?** I'm in my forties as I'm writing these words. Going by averages for females living in Europe, I guess I have about the same number of years left as I've already lived. Forty-something years doesn't sound too bad, does it? At the same time, I'm more than halfway through, which, without wanting to sound morbid, is a lot. Of the 4000 weeks[6] I approximately have, I've already spent about 2400. This means I have 1600 weeks left. Luckily, the years I've lived have taught me many interesting (and sometimes painful) lessons. Hopefully, moving forward, I'll be smarter with my time and how I decide to spend it. How about you? How old are you? And how much time do you have left? When you've answered the question, stay with it for a few minutes and feel what that means to you and your dreams.

- **What do you want your life to look like from this moment on?** Go back to the *Ideal Day and Ideal Life* exercise and review your answers. When you're done, answer the questions below without too much overthinking. Just allow what comes up.

    - What do you want to experience?
    - What kind of person do you want to be?
    - How do you want to feel?
    - What impact do you want to have on the world?
    - Who do you want to be with?
    - What do you want to learn or know?
    - How are you going to live your life from this day forward?

Waiting for a breaking point to *finally* change is what most people do, often unconsciously, out of fear or other negative emotions. Maybe this is where you're stuck. I know how hard it is to get out of that place. It's not your fault; you're not confused or indecisive by nature. You're a product of your upbringing, environment, experiences, and beliefs. I see too many amazing creatives and entrepreneurs feel guilty or ashamed for not being able to decide precisely what they want. Let me repeat it: it's not your fault.

There's nothing wrong with you. Society makes you think you should have clarity about what you want to do with your life. It's the single most asked question throughout your life! What society fails to mention is that the more things you go through, the more people tell you what's best for you, the more rigid the beliefs and values you were passed down are, the harder it will be for you to figure that out.

Feeling stuck can be a byproduct of change in action

Take my client Mei. Her parents emigrated from China to Italy when she was a baby and her brother had just turned three. Mei's parents worked hard all their life to provide for their children. When they arrived in a small town about 30 kilometers (19 miles) from Florence in Tuscany, some 35 years ago, they had no choice but to take on the jobs the local folks were willing to offer them. They learned Italian on the job, although it never went further than just enough vocabulary to buy a house and put their children through school. After a few years, they moved from Italy to Germany, where Mei still lives. Her parents and her brother left Europe and returned to China almost ten years ago. It was hard for Mei to stay behind, but she knew in her heart she would not be happy trying to create a life in a country she didn't know. When Mei contacted me for career and business guidance, she'd worked in tech as a content manager for almost eight years. The money was good, but the pressure was horrible. Mei found some satisfaction in holding down a job so her parents wouldn't worry about her, but she wasn't happy. When Mei and I first connected, it was apparent she was on the verge of burnout. "Why can't I just like the stressful tech job? What's wrong with me?" Mei asked with visible dismay. "It would be so much easier if I just liked it." Mei is right, isn't she? It would be much easier if we just liked what society tells us to like. For some people this works; for others – especially the creative and entrepreneurial types – it often doesn't.

I learned the hard way that I was stuck in a box that was too small for me. I tried everything I could to make others happy: I built the businesses, had the house, the dog, the shoes, and the cars. It never made me happy; it kept making my life smaller. It took me years to get free. When clients come to me, it's often because they're starting to feel that the box pushing against their shoulders is making their life smaller too. Most, like Mei, know something is off but don't see the box yet, or aren't aware they're stuck in it. The telltale sign that they're starting to notice pressure on their shoulders is an intuition, a feeling. In Mei, it expressed itself through incessant inner chatter, anxiety, overthinking, and stress about her ideas and the steps she could take to make them work.

Even though Mei was stuck, she was also experiencing change in action. Letting go of the conditioning from her childhood and the culture she was born into was hard – as it is for everyone. Trying to listen to her creative impulses, her interests and passions, and the dreams she had for herself was equally tricky. Mei was at a crossroads – probably the most challenging one anyone can find themselves at.

While Mei was shedding old skin, the inner turmoil was painfully real. When so many impulses and forces pull and push at you, it's hard to take a step – in any direction. For Mei, it meant accepting that she wasn't going to be the perfect child her parents wanted her to be and that she wasn't the hotshot IT consultant they'd dreamt of her becoming. It also meant dealing with the guilt and shame that come when we finally choose ourselves and go after our own dreams.

Mei couldn't shake the feeling that she was doing something terrible and letting everyone down. After a few sessions and a lot of inner work, she realized it was fear speaking to her. She concluded it was useless to wait any longer for her to feel happy with her 9-to-5 job. One day, as we were in the middle of her series, she told me she had decided to give herself permission to like the things she really wanted and to live her life the way she believed she was allowed to. It wasn't an easy decision or process for Mei, but she did it. Once she accepted herself as herself (because that's really what this is all about), things changed quickly. Mei got unstuck and started moving toward the life and career she always wanted. Now she has her own creative business where she combines her love for crafts, personal development, and writing.

More than anything, the fact that she's free to live her life as she wants makes Mei enjoy every moment.

Dismantling the old so we can build the new

History recounts everything that ever was and no longer is or will be. It's a record of change in action. Not a story of peace and smooth sailing, but a recounting of destruction and reconstruction.

We build the future upon the ruins of the past. Cities are built on the remnants of older structures, technological advancement on ever-growing knowledge about the laws of nature, and scientific insight that cannot exist without the work of the people that came before us.

Each human experience is unique and has a starting point. Time eras are how we differentiate between generations. The fabric of life itself isn't different from one generation to the next; the evolutionary changes are too microscopic and slow to be noticeable, but what makes up those generational lives is often quite different. Because of the technological, social, cultural, intellectual, and artistic advancements (even though the idea that the direction we're going as a species is a betterment is often up for debate) that are continuously moving and never stop, one generation must, by definition, be different (better off?) than the next.

Nature and the universe have change built into them. As a product of nature, we cannot escape the laws that permeate everything. What is a human life if not constant change and transformation? Cells that divide even before birth, a heart that beats, grows more vital to give us life, and then one day stops, skin that sheds cells and renews every so many years. Everything about our bodies and mind is constantly changing until one day, the life force that made us conscious leaves us again. Even then, transformation doesn't stop.

Our physical bodies decay further until every atom we were made of is returned to the universe (the actual one, not the woo-woo version). Some particles find their way into the soil; some end up in the air or water. Others might become part of someone else's heart or end up as a strain of hair on a sweet-smelling toddler's forehead. The stuff we were made of ends up everywhere, but only temporarily. The soil, the air, and the water are constantly changing too. Perhaps you've heard the expression that you're made of stardust. This is true. Not only does about 15000 tons[7] of cosmic dust rain down on Earth every year (of which most is burned when it enters our atmosphere), everything that makes up the Earth and whatever is on it (that includes you) is made up of stardust. At the center of our solar system, the sun formed partly out of the dust of red giant stars; around it, gas and dust gathered out of which, slowly but surely, the Earth and the other planets emerged.[8]

After reading this, I hope you're as awed by this as I am. The nature of life, the universe, the Earth, and our bodily existence are all peppered with change and transformation. Even so, when it comes to our lives and our day-to-day experiences, we stubbornly believe that we're the same person as we were ten years ago, that we only differ physically from the child we once were, that we will still be "ourselves" when we're enjoying a vitamin-filled cappuccino on the deck of a cruise ship for our retirement. Following the same logic, we believe that other people are permanent too, that the way we knew them before is still who they are today. It's one of the reasons there's so much heartbreak in the world: we hold on to the picture of people the way we think they are without giving any thought to the changes they must have gone through.

Chapter Six: Impermanence Is the Only Truth.

"The root of suffering is attachment."
– Buddha

According to Buddhism and many other spiritual traditions, failing to see how we are always in transition is a source of suffering. Impermanence, as many call it, is something we must come to terms with as human beings.

Our sense of self, our wish to understand the world as it unfolds before us, intuitively works against the reality that nothing is permanent. Our mind loves giving meaning to the things we see and experience and constantly creates systems and structures of understanding. This is a great thing. It helps us live, set goals and achieve the things we want. At the same time, it tricks us into believing that we are somehow at the center of something. We know how things are just by looking at them, and we count on things staying the same. In a way, it's true. If you go to sleep tonight, when you wake up tomorrow, most of what was yesterday will still be true. Your bedroom, house or apartment, the pillow you slept on, and so on. They'll be the same. In the short term, change is mostly invisible. But that doesn't make it less true, it only makes it harder to grasp. Let's do a quick thought experiment to understand the implications.

Prompt: Does everything really stay the same?

For this thought experiment, take a few deep breaths, come into the present moment, and look around you for a few minutes.

- Take in what you see, what you hear, and what you feel. Look at the objects around you, what you're sitting or lying down on, and your clothes. Feel the textures surrounding you, the book you're holding in your hands, or looking at on a screen somehow. Now try to feel the permanence of this moment. Ask yourself the following questions:

- Will everything I see, touch, and hold in my hands still be here tomorrow?
- Will all of what I see around me still exist tomorrow?
- Will anything about me or what surrounds me be different when I wake up?

- Now project yourself into the future. Not a month, a year, or a decade, but fifty or a hundred years from now. Take a number that feels big for you. One you believe you won't be around to see. When you have that number in your mind, answer the following questions:
  - Will everything I see, touch, and hold in my hands still be here (your number) years from now?
  - Will all I see around me still exist (your number) years from now?
  - If I were to wake up (your number) years from now, would anything about me or what surrounds me be different?

Evolving identities

I was at a friend's dinner party about ten years ago, sitting across from Richard, a luxury car dealership owner, and long-time friend. A heated discussion was going around the table about the future of the automotive industry. Richard, a third-generation car business owner, was going on about how cars would never be sold online (I know) and how car salespeople were an absolute necessity for buyers to make the best car decisions and purchases. Alex, another friend, younger and working in e-commerce for a few years by then, was sitting next to me and listening quietly.

When Richard stepped off his soapbox to take a breath and eat the food on his plate before it turned cold, Alex offered his equally strong, but opposite perspective (don't you love dinner party discussions, everyone's always an expert). While chewing on a delicious piece of oven-baked stuffed tomato, he said: "Richard, I see what you mean, but we're already seeing people choose and buy expensive things online. Everything's going online; why would cars be any different? It's just a slightly bigger purchase, that's all." The discussion continued as Richard wasn't satisfied with Alex's arguments. "Statistically, we see an increase in online car configuration," said Alex. "Yes," replied Richard, "but they still come to the dealership to talk to someone and buy their car."

Like a game of ping pong, both of my friends passionately continued to defend their points of view without looking at the bigger picture. After half an hour, everyone at the table was ready to move on, including me. In the meantime, dessert was served. I took my chance while Richard and Alex were enjoying their warm apple pie with vanilla ice cream and said: "Ok, I get both of your points, but I think you're looking at this from too close. When you say *never*, Richard, what time frame are you thinking about? And you, Alex, when you say *soon*, how soon are you actually talking about?" They both looked at me. I could see them thinking while they were silently swallowing their delicious desserts.

"I agree that car dealerships will remain an important part of car purchases in the near future," I said. "I also agree that more and more purchases will happen online in the future." Now, everyone at the table was silent and looking at me. "So, we've covered what, the next five to ten years? Because with the advancement of technology, everything keeps going faster and faster, wouldn't you agree?" They both nodded. "But Richard, can you say with absolute certainty that there will still be car dealerships, let's say, 50, 100, or 200 years from now? I mean, will we even have cars in the future the way we're used to them now?" Richard looked at me, pensive. "Well, no," he said, "I guess in 50 years, there won't be. There might not even be cars anymore, at least not how we know them today." Alex nodded slowly. "I have to agree with Richard," he said, "technology goes so fast that in 100 years, everything about our lives and the world will be different, cars included." My point exactly.

Chapter Seven: Change Is Messy.

"All change is hard at first, messy in the middle and so gorgeous at the end."
– Robin Sharma

Richard and Alex realized through this Socratic questioning (a way of asking questions to encourage critical thinking and explore complex ideas) that things aren't static at all. Impermanence flows through all people and all things. It knows no borders, religion, or limitations of any sort. It just is.

It's fair to say that in 200 years, nobody alive today will still walk around the earth. Or perhaps some will, as this is what geneticists are trying to achieve. But if that happens, they'll still live in a massively different world than the one we live in right now. Most cities will look nothing like what they look today; language will be different, and social media will have gone through its millionth iteration (if it still exists). It's hard to imagine anything still being part of such a distant future. But when we think about our lives and ourselves, the only thing many see is periods with no change, followed by breaking points, and periods without change after that again.

We are naturally inclined to want to keep what we enjoy and like about our lives exactly how it is, while fear, negative expectations, and mindset blocks (among other things) work against us moving forward. This is what we call "being stuck."

We don't see change as a slow and gradual process because we're unaware of it most of the time. When change happens, we don't choose it. It happens to us without our will and outside of our control. Not because we can't control or decide the changes we want in our lives, but because we don't give ourselves the time and effort needed to change on our terms. When change happens to us, instead of us happening to it, change looks and feels messy. It's stressful, gives us anxiety, and turns our world upside down. Naturally, nobody wants that kind of change. Would anyone who's never run want to be at the start of the NYC marathon? Or would someone with no legal education want to be the first chair on a trial jury? Probably not. And there's a good reason for that. There's no scenario (except in Hollywood) in which it would end successfully.

Unprepared, change can feel like you woke up on the stage of *Dancing with the Stars* just when the camera starts rolling. You try your best to remember your killer dance moves from high school, but whatever you do, you fall short. Backstage you start to beat yourself up, thinking you could have won or at least not made such a fool of yourself. But could you have done better than your best without knowledge or preparation? Better than what you delivered? Probably not.

Accepting uncertainty

Nothing is ever certain. It's a hard truth for some and a freeing thought for others. It depends on how you look at it and what your circumstances are. When we hold on too tight, uncertainty can seem like the worst thing in the world. We don't want to lose or let go of what we have, so we do everything in our power to keep things the way they are. We've seen before how uncertainty and our difficulties in accepting change are evolutionary phenomena; it's in our DNA to dislike change because, in ancient times, it often meant danger. Although change isn't often life-threatening these days, our nervous system responds more or less the same way.

A real danger in life though, is that you stay stuck somewhere you don't want to be. A big step in getting ourselves out of the mud is developing the willingness to adapt. Our refusal to accept uncertainty is more dangerous than most of the curveballs life can throw at us. By accepting that you can't know or control everything that will happen to you, and by allowing life to unfold instead of trying to contain it, you're not just making it easier for yourself to navigate change; you're also giving yourself the gift that goes along with it. As I've addressed before, too often we think of change as something negative. But change and uncertainty are bringers of opportunity.

Think about it: if everything stays the same in your life, will you ever learn new things, meet new people, explore new parts of the world or get to truly know yourself?

To grow and reach our full potential, we must put ourselves in situations that are not familiar to us. I've witnessed this countless times in my coaching practice – and in my own life. When we try to have everything figured out before doing something, we usually do nothing. That's why I encourage you, dear reader, not to be too attached to the outcome you have in mind. Give yourself direction and quickly take a step. The unfolding of the process will happen before you and for you. You only need to keep going, one step at a time, and be open to what emerges as you do.

When things were hard with my ex-husband, I put together a vision board. Much of it was about intimacy, love and warmth, which we had lost in that relationship. Every time I looked at the vision board, I saw pictures of happy couples doing fun things together: dancing, kissing, relaxing while listening to music, cuddling, laughing and cooking together. Every time I envisioned them, I could only picture myself experiencing those things with him. It never happened. Instead, a few months later, while we were living in another country, on a Friday night, without warning, he packed all his stuff, loaded everything, including my dog, into his car, and left.

The separation was painful, mainly because I didn't (want to) see it coming – even though we weren't in a good place. I clung on too hard and couldn't let go of my vision for us. But here's the thing: after a few years of wanting to be single and figuring myself out, I met someone with whom I'm experiencing everything on my vision board. All the joy, warmth, and intimacy I so desperately wanted came true for me, not the way I envisioned it but better! I'm having the most wonderful time and so much fun with someone who values me and I enjoy spending time with. This is one of the greatest lessons in manifesting and getting unstuck that I've ever received: put out a vision for yourself, work towards it, but don't get too hung up on how exactly you think it needs to happen. If you do, you'll miss the magic of what the winds of change might bring.

Tolerating the pain of change

Does this mean that change is always fun and magical? Absolutely not. If it was, I wouldn't have a job. In the moment, change sucks and that's why we rebel against it. Between the moment my ex left and the life I'm living now, difficult times have passed. It took me about two years to build myself back up and to accept and feel blessed for the new life I'd been forced into.

Learning to tolerate the pain of change, accepting the discomfort of the liminal space you have to traverse to become a new version of yourself, is a superpower. The better you get at it, the easier it will be for you to achieve your dreams. *Being comfortable with being uncomfortable* is an incredible skill. Now, to get you fully ready for what's to come, here are some final thoughts on fear and moving from a mindset that holds you back to one that is open to change.

Believing in yourself

The best way to overcome your mental blocks and to let the fear go away is to take action over fear. Gradually you'll be less afraid of daunting things, and you'll start believing in yourself more and more. In my opinion, believing in yourself is the number one trait of people who go out and live full lives. It's also the number one trait of people with a growth mindset.

The growth mindset teaches us that there is an unlimited supply of knowledge and practice available to us that can help us change anything and everything about ourselves. Every day is an opportunity to show up as the best version of ourselves. Whatever our current abilities or circumstances, by learning and practicing, we can become experts at just about anything. Yes, anything! That includes getting unstuck or helping people get unstuck. Two things I never imagined I would be able to do but that I'm now proud to call myself an expert at!

Believing in yourself means standing in your power. It means reframing what you believe about yourself and the world. That is the work required to cultivate a positive mindset. In this way, believing in yourself is a radical act. It asks you to take a leap of faith and to trust that no matter what comes your way, you'll be able to handle it.

Believing in yourself means:
- Believing in a positive outcome, whatever the momentary situation.
- Saying yes to opportunities.
- Being disciplined and doing the work.
- Working your way through fear – always.
- Guarding your boundaries and going outside of your comfort zone.
- Being self-loving and self-caring.
- Showing yourself grace.
- Remembering that you can change your reality by changing your mind.

I know you've got this. Now it's time for *you* to know this, too!

In the next Step, we'll start looking at your options and how you can create possibilities for change in your life and work. But first, let's look at the takeaways of this first and exciting step of the MOVE method to help you get unstuck.

Summary: Step One – Mindset

This first step was about clarity: understanding what being stuck really is, and how change works because without change, you will not get unstuck.

In this first step, you learned:

- What mindset is and how what you believe and how you think creates your life.
- The difference between a mindset that expands (growth mindset) or limits (fixed mindset) your reality.
- What it means to be stuck and how people get (and stay) stuck.
- What it feels like to be stuck.
- The connection between being stuck and being afraid of change.
- The first step to getting unstuck: looking at life with a beginner's mind.
- What change is, and the breaking point most people need to reach to change.
- How feeling stuck can be a byproduct of change in action.
- That impermanence is the only truth: everything constantly changes.
- How to embrace the messiness of change.

Hurray! You're done with Step One of the 4-step MOVE method to help you get unstuck. By now, you should better understand how your mindset works and how it influences your life. You should also start to recognize what change is, how it happens or doesn't happen, and the truth you must embrace if you want to finally get unstuck: there's no need to fear change! It happens all the time – and that's okay.

It's time to move on to Step Two and figure out what to do with all that newfound knowledge, so you can finally see all the options that have been hiding in plain sight and all the possibilities you have in front of you. Let's go!

STEP TWO:
OPTIONS

"When nothing is sure, everything is possible."
– Margaret Drabble

In this step you'll learn:

- That the world is full of possibilities, you just need to see them for it to be so.
- That you're the leader of your life.
- What the tyranny of inherited dreams is and how it influences your life.
- How outdated ideas of success keep most people stuck.
- How our environment shapes our reality.
- That getting unstuck is not only about seeing, but also about creating new possibilities for yourself.

Chapter One: The World Is Full of Possibilities, We Just Have to See Them.

"Only those who can see the invisible, can do the impossible."
– Jeffrey Fry

Selena, a passionate and hard-working 25-year-old creative with a diverse cultural background, who desperately wanted a career change, came to me believing that she didn't have the power to change anything about her situation. When we first connected, she shared how unhappy she was as a social media manager for a company run by a bunch of "old, white dudes" (her words). Although she had two university degrees and had been headhunted for the position, her manager, who had no marketing or communication background, would systematically give her the lousiest jobs. She was never included in strategic meetings or decisions, even though she was constantly pressured to perform and clean up the mess of her manager's uninsightful decisions. "I don't know what else to do," she told me, crying out of frustration. "Whatever I try, they keep ignoring me."

I felt deeply for Selena. I had a capable and bright young woman in front of me whose talents and expertise were systematically being underutilized. I listened to Selena as she dried her frustrated tears and calmed down. When I felt she'd said all she needed to say, I asked her, "Did you ever think about telling the CEO about what's been going on?" Selena looked at me in disbelief. "I could never do that," she replied hesitantly. "Let's take it one step further. Did you ever think about telling the CEO you need a raise for all the work you've been doing for your manager?" I could see more fear and despair in Selena's eyes, but I also noticed she was intensely listening and making sense of what I was saying. "Have you ever thought about quitting if they don't give you what you want?" Selena was silent for a few minutes; then she said, "Well, no, I didn't think I was allowed to do that. Am I allowed to do that?"

You are the leader of your life

We've addressed *the myth of change* in Step One. That myth wants us to believe that change only happens when you reach your breaking point, when the nail is stuck so deep in your butt-cheek that you can't ignore it anymore. I hope that by now, you realize this isn't true. Even though Selena thought she had no options, that she had to wait it out until someone would come and change her situation (aka rescue her, thanks a lot Disney), she had the power all along.

If Selena doesn't change her situation, by the looks of it, nothing about her situation will change. But where does the idea come from that she has no power over her life? It's not because of a lack of agency. She's a free and experienced young professional. So what is it? Conditioning. We all have to bear the burden and pressure of rules and beliefs passed down to us through our upbringing, education, and culturalization. The main result of that programming is that it strips away our options. We're left with only what we think we should, or are *allowed*, to do. It takes away our power—and freedom.

In Selena's case, uncovering the beliefs that blinded her from the many possibilities she had wasn't hard. She had a strict upbringing, with a mother and father who had high expectations for their daughter and never allowed her to color outside the lines they had defined for her. Not to mention systemic oppression and the underrepresentation and unequal treatment Selena had dealt with since childhood. Then, she had turbulent years getting her degrees, not because she wasn't studying hard enough or doing her best, but because of undiagnosed dyslexia and ADHD. It had always taken Selena longer to read and write and to find focus, not because she didn't know what she wanted to say or wasn't a good communicator or writer, but because the letters, words, and ideas kept swirling around in her head and she had no idea why. While working together, Selena got her official dyslexia and ADHD diagnosis and found the support she needed. That alone was life-changing, but it's not the only way she freed herself. As we progressed through her coaching sessions, Selena learned how change works. Using my unique and proven methodology, I taught Selena how to take the necessary steps to achieve small goals first.

I remember how, the next session, she came back to me with a big smile and such joy. "I did it," she told me, "I did what we'd said I would do, and it worked. I feel so different. It's weird and great all at the same time." Selena went to her manager and told him that if she had to execute the plans discussed during the strategic meetings, she wanted to be part of those meetings. She had come to that conclusion, and coaching action, after we'd gone through her options again and looked at why she thought she wasn't allowed to ask for anything, and why she should be *grateful* she had a job. I've mentioned her strict upbringing and undiagnosed dyslexia and ADHD, but there was more. Selena had spoken up once in her previous (first) job, which hadn't gone well. She'd been fired on the spot, no reasons given except that she didn't have the right "attitude." All these experiences made Selena believe she couldn't ask for what she wanted or needed.

The problem with a belief like that is that it takes away your power. Waiting for someone else to do something for you, is like waiting for a frog to turn into the person of your dreams. Yes, that's right, that too only happens in Disney movies. In real life, though, you often don't need to wait if you don't want to – you have control. But you cannot use that power until you become aware of it, and that's precisely the problem. To realize that we have agency over our lives, we must first understand we've been programmed to forget that we do. It's only when we remember that we can stand up and claim what's ours, as Selena did. After a few months of working together, I had an entirely different Selena sitting in front of me during our sessions. Her entire life, people had told her what she was allowed to do and not to do, to think and not to think, even to dream and not to dream. She'd been so accustomed to listening to someone tell her who she was and what she was capable of that she had lost her ability to lead.

This is true for many of us, perhaps for you too. It definitely was for me. When I started my journey of self-discovery more than a decade ago, I felt like I had no control over my life. Yes, from the outside looking in, everything seemed great. I was building a business and climbing the ladder everyone had always told me I needed (and should be so lucky) to climb. On the inside, I felt miserable because I wasn't in charge of my life. I have been through intense life changes, healing, growth, and big and small moments of discovery about myself since then. All of which helped me find my way back to the wild and free human I was always meant to be and am today. Everything I share in this book has been instrumental in getting me here.

One event in particular, like Selena finding out she had ADHD, had an almost instant effect on me: being diagnosed as autistic. I'd never felt like I belonged, and there were many reasons for that: my difficult childhood, my creative brain, the limitations I had been born into, and the ones I had internalized. But even when I had come to understand and heal all those things, I still felt like something else was keeping me from being like everyone else. I'd often been called shy, introverted, and difficult, especially when I struggled with social situations or cues. After my divorce, I wanted to "finally figure out what was wrong with me."

It had never occurred to me that I might be neurodivergent. To me, like so many other eighties kids, autism equaled Rain Man.[9] One evening, when I felt particularly sorry for myself and was searching for answers to how I felt, I stumbled upon a comprehensive article about Asperger's Syndrome in women and a self-assessment test. Being diligent and a good student, I'm used to scoring well on tests. But I wasn't expecting a high score for this one! The test score and the article explaining how I felt almost to a tee motivated me to continue my search. I found a test center that didn't have too long of a waiting list (unfortunately, waiting times of a year or more are no exception in autism diagnostics) and went through the long testing process.

The day I received my official diagnosis, about six months after my first visit to the center, I could not stop crying. A weight lifted off my shoulders, and I finally had answers to many questions about myself. I could stop trying to figure out what was wrong with me because now I knew I was just different, and there was nothing I could do to change it.

The power of knowing who you are is incredible. You don't need a neurodivergent diagnosis for that; whatever your situation, following the steps in this book will help you figure out precisely that. But if you feel there might be something else, if you've been wondering what "might be wrong with you" the way I used to, seeking clarity and a diagnosis might be. It certainly was for me.

Since I've known I'm autistic, I've stopped trying to be what I'm not and embraced my unique autistic traits instead. I've maximized on my strengths and sought help for the aspects of my personality that I find challenging. Everything about my life has become so much better because of it. There is power in stopping trying to be what you're not and accepting who you are instead. That's how you ultimately get unstuck, whatever your brain is like.

The tyranny of inherited dreams

As a coach, I know a thing or two about dreams. I dive deep with my clients daily to help them figure out what they really want and how to get it. Together we define a new path for their dream career or business. As you probably guessed by now, a big part of that work is figuring out what keeps them stuck. Clients often come to me when they're at a crossroads in their lives: just like you, they've felt like something's off – sometimes for a long time – and they can't ignore it anymore. They're:

- stuck in unfulfilling careers,

- tired of the endless and exhausting cycle of overwork and productivity,
- torn between their ambitions and the needs of others,
- yearning to grasp why – while doing everything right – they still aren't happy,
- wondering what happened to them and how they got where they are,
- weary of the guilt and shame for wanting what they want,
- tired of their self-doubt and lack of self-confidence,
- afraid of never being who they know they're supposed to be,
- lacking a sense of meaning, purpose, and direction in their life.

When I started working with creatives and entrepreneurs, I noticed something incredible about them. Even though they feel stuck and sometimes have been stuck for years, they also have many talents and passions. They're:

- creative,
- hard-working,
- wholehearted,
- compassionate,
- ambitious,
- always willing to try,
- not afraid to do the work,
- smart and witty,
- with an insatiable hunger for knowledge.

I wondered: for anyone with all these fantastic qualities, why is it so hard to figure out what they want? It's the tyranny of inherited dreams.

A blueprint of success that isn't yours

Inherited dreams are those we pursue but don't choose for ourselves. They're a product of the world we're born into. A mix of social expectations, false (limiting) beliefs about ourselves and the world, pressure to conform, and unwritten rules we believe we must live by passed down to us in childhood. You're right if you think inherited dreams are related to a fixed mindset and the myth of change I mentioned before. They're a product of our upbringing, education, and culture, just like our beliefs and how much we think we can control our lives.

Often, we're not aware those dreams aren't our own. Even when we know it, it's tough to resist them. If we give in to them entirely – which we're all doing when we're not questioning our choices – we spend our lives not fully living, somewhat sleepwalking our way through it, estranged from our true nature, deepest desires, and our authentic selves.

When I was working hard at building a career for myself, I was following a blueprint that wasn't mine; I was following my own set of inherited dreams, ones I thought I wanted but that I never dreamt of for myself. From the day I started working as a freelancer to the day my parents passed away, almost two decades later, I tried to achieve a picture of success that had been given to me by society, my upbringing, the desires of my parents, and what they thought was good for me.

Like everyone else, I wanted to be successful. Who doesn't want that? I'm sure it's something you aspire to as well. The question is, what does that look like? Especially when you're not the one imagining it. In my case, I followed the capitalist blueprint. I wanted to dress in the nicest clothes, wear expensive watches, carry luxury bags, travel the world, and make a lot of money. As a result, I worked relentlessly – and burned myself out – for years, trying to build the career I thought I needed to achieve that dream. Even though the money was coming in and I bought the bags, the holidays were more exclusive, and I was now traveling first class instead of economy; I still wasn't happy. Ok, I'll be honest, traveling first class is a memorable experience. But even when the flight attendant was making my bed for a restful night 35,000 feet (10,000 meters) above ground, something was still missing from my life.

An outdated idea of success

The financial security wasn't enough. I also wanted to be beautiful. I wanted to look like the airbrushed models in the magazines: thin, youthful, tanned, smiling, hair and nails perfectly done, always put together. Even though there was nothing wrong with my weight, I constantly put myself on a diet. I also exercised excessively for a significant part of my life, but in the end, I was never satisfied with myself.

More than anything else, I wanted to be liked. That too, was part of the picture-perfect life that had been ingrained in me. I catered to everyone's needs, always trying to make sure friends and family had everything they needed, pleasing every need but my own. This, again, didn't make me any happier or more fulfilled. Instead of being the strong and capable human I knew I could be, in my day-to-day life I felt more like a pushover with no boundaries.

Don't misunderstand me. Wanting to be successful, beautiful, or liked, is all part of the primordial needs we have as humans: to be loved, to be fulfilled, and to have a purpose. But love, fulfillment, and purpose are not inherited dreams. They are the most profound connection we have with ourselves and each other. They are our life breath. Without them, we can never be truly happy.

Society tells us that we need to have a specific and narrow set of mostly material things and physical qualities to be successful. Inherited dreams add to that, by telling us who we must be to be loved, fulfilled, and purposeful based on other people's definition of success.

To Western society especially, success means money, status, power, and all the "perks" that go with it. The clothes, the travels, the sandy beaches, the private jets. It also means being ready to do "everything it takes," glorifying busyness, the *hustle* and the relentless pursuit of productivity. To the capitalistic world, beauty is a commodity; it means youth, thinness, and whiteness. It also means being ready to starve yourself, to exercise beyond injury, to accept the dangers of surgery, and to reject anything that doesn't meet the narrow beauty standards. In that same world, likability means politeness, not speaking too loud, being a good person, and saying "yes." It also means letting others cross your boundaries, putting yourself last, bottling up your emotions, and not being your true self.

Chapter Two: Coming Home to Yourself.

"You'll never know who you are unless you shed who you pretend to be."
– Vironika Tugaleva

Inherited dreams are a construct. Just like all the rules in the world, we – as a society – created them. Historical events, beliefs about the world, and value systems upheld and shared by those in power all contributed to the inherited dreams we have today. But it wasn't always this way, and it doesn't need to be. There's something else buried beneath our inherited dreams: our truest, most authentic dreams. Like inherited dreams, I believe we all have authentic dreams. The problem is that most of us don't know what we want because other people's dreams cloud our judgment.

After coaching hundreds of creative entrepreneurs, I've realized that finding your way back to your dreams means taking leadership in your life. Before we imagine what that can look like for you, I invite you to search for your authentic dreams. We start this process by going back to our childhood selves.

Prompt: Your Childhood Self

This activity will help you to remember who you are and what makes you happy. To do that, I want you to remember your earliest dreams and wishes. Find a quiet place to sit down and write, relax, take a deep breath, and think about the questions below and what they bring up for you.

Think back to your childhood memories. Quietly listen.
- What did you want to be when you were a child?
- What made you the happiest?
- What were you good at?
- What did you enjoy doing?
- How did you love spending your time?

What do you see when you think back about that little human and all that they loved to do and dream about? Who might you have become if your childhood self had followed their dreams?

Write down ten things you loved to do as a child. Next to each one, write down if you still love or would love to do that now. Then, for each item, write down the last time you did it.

Are these things still part of your life? Do you miss them? Do you want them in your life again?

When I do this work with my clients, it amazes me how everyone remembers what they wanted to be when they were younger. It might take a while to get there, but eventually, we can see a bigger picture – the dreams we used to have for ourselves before the world convinced us otherwise. This was the case for Linda, who came to me when her two, now adult children, had just left for college.

Linda had spent the last 20 years of her life caring for her family. A stay-at-home mom, she diligently provided her husband and children with food, love, and safety without ever taking a day off. Her husband, CEO of a multinational company, traveled six months out of the year. On top of ensuring everything was taken care of in the household, the day-to-day care for her children was Linda's responsibility. Linda never missed an appointment with the doctor or dentist; she ensured her children were always prepared for school and exams, organized the best birthday parties, and knew when to step up and volunteer as a parent at her children's school. All those years, Linda felt she was doing her part, modeling after her mother, who had raised not two but five children without the help of Linda's father, a factory worker who spent 12 hours a day, six days a week, on an assembly line with heavy machinery. Linda felt she was lucky. Even with his traveling, she saw more of her husband than her mother had ever seen of her father. When her two children left for college, Linda knew she had to brace herself for the empty nest they left behind. She knew it would be a massive change for her, even though she had no idea how it would feel.

I met Linda three months after her children had left. When she sat before me, Linda was silent for a while. "You know," she said after a few minutes of us smiling at each other, "I always thought raising my children was what I was here to do." I nodded as she changed positions on her chair while she was talking. "But now that they're gone, I wonder if this is it. Now that they're grown up and off to college, does that mean my life is over?"

I continued to make space for Linda and the thoughts she was organizing in her mind. "I mean, I thought I would feel relieved," she said after taking a deep breath, "and I did feel a burden fall off my shoulders at first, but now the only thing I keep thinking about is 'what's next for me.'"

I could see Linda was starting to feel more at ease; she'd found a comfortable sitting position with her back against the chair and her legs slightly crossed in front of her. Her breathing was slower, and she'd stopped fidgeting with her hands. It was time to start digging a little and see if we could uncover the dreams Linda might have buried within herself.

"I'm curious, Linda," I started, "if you never had any children," I asked her gently, "how might your life have been different?" I could see my question making its way deep into Linda's mind and heart. After a long pause, she looked at me with a smile. "Well, if I never had any children," she said, "I would have traveled the world and drawn maps of my favorite cities." Now I was the one smiling at Linda. "When I was younger, I used to draw all the time. I filled notebook after notebook with anything and everything. What I loved most was doodling and drawing maps. When I was eight, my father came with us on a weekend trip to the country. It was the only holiday we ever took as a family, him being so busy and all. But on that trip, we went into the woods, and my father, who had been a boy scout, taught me how to mark the path we were taking so we could find our way back. It was an amazing experience. That night, while my mother was preparing dinner for the seven of us, I sat at the kitchen table in our cabin and drew a map from memory of our route. I added the trees and all the other marks I could remember. When I was done, I showed it to my father. I could see how proud he was of my skills and memory. I still have the drawing and the notebook. After that first drawing, I started making other maps, mostly of our town and the places I visited. With school, we went to New York City for a day trip when I was fifteen, and on the bus back, I drew a map of Manhattan and all the cool places we'd seen. My art teacher saw it and told me I was talented and should do something with it. A few years later, Jeff, my husband, and I started dating. One thing that attracted me to him was how much he loved traveling. Before the kids were born and Jeff was promoted to sales manager, we used to take trips almost every weekend to local towns or big cities. Then, when I was twenty, I got pregnant with our first son. Jeff continued to travel for work, and I stayed home with the baby. We never went on a trip like that again, and it's been years since I drew anything."

Linda looked at me. I could tell something was brewing inside of her. After doing this work for so many years, I know when things are starting to shift. I hear it in my client's voices; I see it in the way they look at me. "You know," Linda continued, "now that I think about it, I'm going to go into the garage and find those notebooks. No, wait, I'm going to find those old notebooks, but I'm also going to buy a new one. Do you think I could still draw like I used to?"

Creating new possibilities for yourself is a process of unraveling, imagination, and transformation. It's not about having bigger or better versions of your inherited dreams. It's about dismantling them, about admitting your most authentic, truest dreams to yourself. It's about coming home to who you are – and always have been. It's about coming home to yourself.

After that initial spark, Linda needed a few months of coaching to figure out what she wanted to do and how. This is common. It's one of the reasons why my coaching packages are at least three months long. The dreams and desires we've ignored for so long need time to resurface and make sense to us. We need to work at figuring things out while transforming our mindset, breaking through the beliefs that keep us from going after what we want, and so much more. It's a process. A fun and inspiring one, for sure, but a process nonetheless.

Today, Linda is enrolled in an art class at her local college. She draws daily and has filled many notebooks with maps and doodles that she makes after she and her husband go on a trip together. When Linda shared her childhood dreams with Jeff, he remembered what a fantastic artist Linda was and how fun it was to go on weekend trips with her. So now, whenever he has to travel for work, if Linda isn't busy drawing a personalized travel map for a friend or client, she accompanies Jeff. The last time I checked in with her, Linda and Jeff had planned a trip to Rome. "I wanted to challenge myself," she said in our Zoom call, "US cities are easy, but what about a European city, I thought. Jeff is going to work during the week, giving me plenty of time to see what I can make of this complex and chaotic ancient city." If Linda had not followed the itch that there was something more out there for her, who knows where she would be today, but probably not on a flight to Italy.

Prompt: Tapping into Your Deeper Knowing

With this activity, I want you to tap into the parts of you that are often ignored. Because of the intensity of this exercise, your inner critic might show up. If this happens, know that it's not uncommon for your mind to want to protect you from your authentic dreams. They're the ones that matter most, so there will be some resistance. By staying close to your center – breathing deeply, remembering why you picked up this book, and focusing on how important it is for you to get unstuck, you'll be able to counteract those thoughts and move forward. Whatever your inner voice says!

Read through the questions below. Answer the ones that speak to you (remember: it's okay to skip anything that isn't right for you, leadership starts with making your own choices).

- What do you currently do, or have done, that makes you feel your happiest?
- If you had the right education or skill set, you'd definitely try ______________, because ______________.
- What personal attitude, skill, or attribute are you proud of?
- What was something (person, book, movie, quote, and so on) that inspired you in the last year? Why?
- Is your dream career (from when you were younger) different from what you're doing now? Does it look anything like what you thought it would? In what ways?
- Was there an event, moment, or feeling this past year where your gut, instinct, or heart spoke to you somehow? What happened, and what do you think it means?
- Was there an event or moment where you felt confident, happy, and joyful? When was it, and what were you doing?

After answering the questions, please read them, examine them from a place of curiosity and wonder, and highlight any themes, patterns, or thoughts that stand out. These themes point to what your childhood self (or true self) is trying to tell you.

Success is being true to yourself

I remember how, before becoming a coach, I was climbing a ladder but never questioning the wall it was leaning on. After losing my parents, I couldn't do that anymore. My picture of success had reflected this perfect human I thought I needed to be in order to be loved: hardworking, pleasing, always available, without drama or desires of my own. Just like Linda, I had to come home to myself. That process started slowly. When I began questioning the wall I was trying to climb; I couldn't find one thing, not one desire or dream that were my own. Everything I imagined was always for someone else. I'd been focused on other people's needs for so long that I'd lost the connection with myself, my core, and my intuition. Perhaps reading Linda's story or doing the exercise above, you've felt the same. If that's the case, know that it's not abnormal for someone who's spent a big part of their life catering to others to forget about their own needs.

When those around you have big dreams for you, it can be hard to realize that those are not your dreams. Everyone wants their children to be safe, have enough money, a family, and be happy. Even when they don't voice their dreams out loud, we still pick up on what they want for us. The problem is, in dreams others dream for us happiness usually comes last, not first. That's not to say that the people who care about us don't want us to be happy, simply that they've bought into inherited dreams themselves. Most people believe you need material and financial security before you can be happy.

And, yes, there's some truth to it. According to Maslow's *Hierarchy of Needs*[10], many needs must be met before someone can self-actualize. But once basic safety, financial security, and connections are present, what matters is to discover yourself and your dreams. Not a bigger house or salary.

According to science, we can put a financial number on happiness. Research has uncovered a sweet spot, an amount that, once you go above it, doesn't add to your happiness. In a 2010 study that questioned participants' sense of well-being, that number was about $75000 a year[11]. I will always be the happiest kid when flying first class, but does that matter for my happiness? According to the study, earning more doesn't improve how happy people feel. You need fulfilling relationships, a job with meaning, and good health to be happy.

Without happiness there can be no real success

After a long period of grief and introspection following the loss of my parents, it was time to step off the ladder, not climb any higher on it. Not only was it leaning against the wrong wall, I knew there was no endpoint to climb towards. The version of ambition sold to me was a relentless pursuit of something that didn't exist. Trying to find it was like hitting a moving goalpost with a soccer ball. It made no sense.

When I got to the bottom of the ladder and set foot on the ground, I was scared out of my mind. Not because I could fall or fail; I couldn't get any lower than where I was. I'd been climbing that ladder mindlessly for so long; I'd worked so hard that I had no clue what to do with myself when I wasn't working or taking care of others. I'd decided to sell my agency and do something completely different. The problem was, and this is why I was so anxious and stressed out, that I didn't know what I was going to do next or how to even get started.

So much has happened since I first sat at my kitchen table, wondering what I would do next with this new part of my life, asking myself what I wanted to do when I "grew up." Eventually, it all came down to seeing the opportunities available to me and not being afraid to create new ones for myself.

Today, I define success in terms of sustainability (can I do this for a long time without burning myself out or chipping away at my happiness?), self-care (is doing this good for my mind, body, and soul?), and overall well-being in my life and business (is this work meaningful, purposeful and does it have a positive impact on the world?). I define beauty through art, wonder, and curiosity instead of my body size, the wrinkles on my face, or how much I weigh. Most of all, I define likability by how much of my true self I can bring into my relationships, how much love I have to give and receive, and through authenticity, integrity, and respect for myself and others.

Does this mean I make no money or stopped enjoying the finer things in life? No, of course not. Are you crazy? A Chanel bag still makes my heart flutter, and a diamond around my neck or on my finger doesn't hurt either. I have businesses that feel right to me now, that I work on in a way that doesn't exhaust me, and with marketing practices aligned with my values. I still have a closet full of clothes. I like the VIP treatment I get when I fly business (first class is cool but so expensive!), but these material things don't define me. I certainly don't need them to be happy.

Chapter Three: Leadership Is Never Given, You Have to Take It For Yourself.

“I never dreamed about success. I worked for it.”
– Estée Lauder

To get unstuck, you must be willing to dig deep and see the mud sticking to your boots and preventing you from getting out of the wetlands. It’s called leadership. You must admit to yourself that you’re the one staying in the mire and that you have a role to play in getting yourself out of there. It’s up to you. Nobody’s coming to pull you out; no amount of thinking will magically lift you up and bring you to dry land.

Buddhists believe that we become what we think about and that our thoughts shape our reality. I must admit I believe this too. It’s like the red car experience: once you’re primed to see red cars, they seem to be everywhere on the street. The exciting thing about this is that these cars didn’t magically appear out of nowhere; they were always there. Only your focus and attention shifted, making you notice them. The same is true with everything in your life. If you believe bad things will happen, you will focus on spotting the moments in your day that aren’t great. If, on the other hand, you believe that good things are going to happen, even the most minor positive event will be a confirmation.

In the first chapter of this book, we learned that our minds and thoughts dictate our lives. We also touched on the fact that we can take control of our minds. We’re not our thoughts; we have control over what we allow ourselves to think, believe, and act on.[12] In this second step of my four-step MOVE method, we continue to build on those insights. Not only are you not your thoughts, but you can also choose your thoughts.

In 2015, while living in Sofia, Bulgaria, I gave a TEDx talk titled: “Don’t believe anything you think.” I remember how Tabby[13], the expert TEDx talk and speaking coach I worked with in preparation for it, asked me if I meant to say "everything" instead of "anything." I questioned it for a while because claiming that you shouldn't believe *anything* you think is a daring statement. By the time I decided to give a talk, I was already convinced that our thoughts are a product of our complex consciousness system, so I decided to go with the bolder statement – one of my favorite daily mantras. In my own life and the life of many of my clients, I've seen how adopting this idea changes things. Especially for someone like me, who spent a big part of her childhood and adult life anxiously worrying about pretty much everything, reminding myself that I should question my thoughts before accepting them has been a transformative force in my life.

When you create distance between yourself and your thoughts, personal leadership can emerge – something essential to living a full life. Leadership, both as a research area and as a practical skill, encompasses the ability of an individual, group, or organization to "lead," influence, or guide other individuals, teams, or entire organizations.[14] In that sense, personal leadership is about leading, influencing, and guiding yourself. It starts with you asking yourself what matters to *you*. It begins with you wondering what *you'd* do if you knew you couldn't fail or were loved unconditionally. It's about defining what purpose means to *you* and figuring out what *you* really want. Personal leadership is about examining your life and actions and questioning the rules you live by. It's about asking yourself where all your beliefs come from and if you want or can live by them without selling yourself out.

A lot to ponder, I know. You're doing great by the way! This work is important, but that doesn't mean it's easy. We're almost halfway there; how amazing is that? It's time to ask yourself those questions and look deep within. If you're ready, let's go!

Be a participant, not a bystander

Remember the story of the dog and the nail from Step One? Being a bystander of life means not getting up when sitting on a painful nail. Participating in your life is feeling the pain and deciding to do something about it or, better yet, anticipating the nails and ensuring you never sit on them.

Whatever our situation is, we always have a choice. If we can't get out immediately, we at least have the choice to change how we think about ourselves in the midst of what's happening. I've learned to see myself as the leading character in my life instead of the victim of my circumstances. It took me a long time to understand that I was in charge, but when I did, things changed dramatically. This is also true for many of the people I've supported on their journeys to get unstuck. There's a moment in a coaching series when things just "click."

One client in particular, Elsa, a bubbly 27-year-old who came to me feeling stuck about everything in her life – and I mean *everything* – had things *click* about two-thirds into her coaching series. It must have been her fourth or fifth session when she arrived in my virtual office with a big smile and a little bit of cheekiness in her eyes. "Murielle," she said as she settled into our time together and greeted me, "I've had a realization this week, and I still can't believe it." I looked at Elsa with gentle joy. "You know," she continued, "the process you've taught me, the way we're working on my goals and projects, I think I've figured out how it works. I think I can use it for all my goals in life." The mental shift Elsa had made was the transition from looking at her life and what happened to her from the outside, waiting for someone to make things better for her, to seeing her life from the inside out and realizing that she was the one in charge and able to make all the changes that she wanted. At that moment, she knew she was in the driver's seat.

A little later, when the firework dust had settled in that same session, Elsa understood the full extent of what she'd just uncovered. First, she let out a big sigh of relief. All good so far. Quickly, that sigh was followed by something that sounded more like a giant exclamation mark or frustration. I asked Elsa to describe what she was thinking and feeling. "Well," she started tentatively, "up until now, I've been so happy realizing that I have control; I have the power to change my life the way I want to." I nodded in agreement. "But now, I don't know; there's so much to do. And I've wasted so much time already!"

After doing this work for many years, as I mentioned, I've become used to certain ideas showing up at specific turning points in the coaching process, and Elsa was right on time. So, yes, when we finally understand that being stuck is a feeling – not a fact – and that we're the ones keeping ourselves feeling this way, excitement quickly makes room for stress and anxiety again, though now it has a different focus. We don't stress over not having any say in our lives. Instead, we get anxious because we understand we have every say in it! Although this newfound knowledge is liberating and exciting, it also makes us realize how often we gave that power away and let others rule our lives – or in Elsa's words, how much time has been wasted.

At first, most people go into overdrive, trying to make up for time lost and take on every project and change at once. This doesn't work, and I don't advise it. What you want to do with this new knowledge is to pace yourself: little changes over time alter who you are and change your life in a more profound way than bursts of action that you can't sustain. The only thing you have to do is to take.the.step! To make your dreams come true, tiny steps repeated over time do the trick.

In Step Four, we'll look at the "Seinfeld Strategy" and how "not breaking the chain" is one of the most important things to stop procrastinating on your goals. It's not about how big your steps are every day or how much you do each time; it's about repeating them. When Elsa started applying the Seinfeld

Strategy in her life and work, things shifted for her for good. Today, this bright and young creative has a successful online store selling digital products that she designs herself and travels to exotic locations. She enjoys long periods of living by the sea (something she wanted when we started working together), and she's working on building up her copywriting skills now that she has started her own agency.

Actively choose your behavior

The number one reason I see people get and stay stuck is that they give up. Even though Elsa is a poster child for how a coaching series should go, in the middle of our work together, she had a moment of doubt that almost caused her to give up on her dreams entirely. At that time, she'd managed to land two copywriting clients that provided work for one day a week. It wasn't enough for Elsa to live and travel from, but it was a start! Especially considering that Elsa had only been putting a few hours of work into finding clients on an online freelance platform.

"I'm so demotivated," Elsa told me when her session started, "I think it's going to be too hard to find the clients I need to sustain myself; maybe I should find an English tutoring job abroad and just do that." I asked how much time she'd spend looking for clients to find the two she now had. "A few hours a couple of weeks ago," was her reply. Elsa hadn't done any prospecting in the last month and was now thinking about taking on a full-time job instead of putting in some more hours to find the clients she needed to build her freedom business. I knew it was time for some truths and asked Elsa if she was open to me telling her my thoughts. She said yes. "Well," I started, "I'm wondering how you're doing the math here. If I understand what you're saying, you're telling me that you'd rather work full time than put in a few hours of work a day to find clients and build your own business?" Elsa nodded. "How long did it take you to find the ones you have now? A few hours, right? Why do you think it will be too hard to find more?"

Elsa looked at me for a while, then said: "I guess it's not that hard; I just don't feel like it anymore."

This is something that I often see in my work, people giving up when things start to work out the way they want. I know, it's crazy, right? It's also human. Often, we're more afraid of things working out than things not working out. We're back to knowing what we have but not knowing what we could get, which is one of the main reasons people stay stuck. Unconsciously, Elsa was afraid that this might work out. She could work from anywhere, travel abroad, and build a business if it did. But those were all things Elsa had never done before. Without knowing it, through her behavior, she was sabotaging her efforts.

You may recognize this behavior in yourself. Our behavior, the choices we make daily, are either actively moving us towards getting unstuck or actively keeping us stuck. There's no middle ground here. We're all – always – either doing or not doing something. When sabotaging ourselves, a part of our behavior is always unconscious. We make choices out of habit or fear, or operate on *autopilot* without thinking about the consequences of our repeated actions over time.

To get unstuck, you need to choose your behavior actively. It won't always feel great. In Elsa's case, it meant applying for copywriting jobs every day for at least an hour (a deal we made during that coaching session) and reporting to me about it. The fear of success was still there for Elsa, but she did it anyway. With every application she sent, she became more comfortable with feeling uncomfortable about achieving her dreams. Two weeks later, she'd found enough courage to increase her hourly rate and send a proposal to a well-known international copywriting agency. They're now one of her main clients, and she's writing for them from a sandy Greek beach.

Our environment shapes our behavior

One thing that made it difficult for Elsa to keep going was the lack of support from her immediate family and environment. None of her friends understood what she was trying to achieve, while her well-meaning parents wanted her to finish college and become a doctor or lawyer like her two older siblings. It's not that they didn't accept her choices; it's just that they didn't understand them, so it was hard for them to support her. They were letting her *do her thing*, so she could *get it out of her system*, waiting for the day she would see it didn't work, come to her senses, and finish her degree. Not an ideal environment for Elsa to thrive in, and something we addressed on a few occasions in her coaching sessions.

Be mindful of who you spend your time with, who you share your dreams with, and who you look to for support in your efforts to change and get unstuck. Your environment holds your identity together. Your environment will often be closed to the changes you want to make. The people in your life don't have the same aspirations you have; perhaps they're happy with how things are or not conscious enough to see that things could or should be different.

When working with people, I tend to return to what Jim Rohn, an American entrepreneur, author, and motivational speaker, famously said: "We're the average of the five people we spend the most time with."[15] From personal experience, I know that statement to be true. When I look back on the environments I was in at specific periods of my life and what I was doing, I see a direct correlation between the people around me and the decisions I made or the dreams I had. Growing up in a poor lower middle-class family, all I heard my father say was that money was bad, that you had to suffer to make it, and that someone was always looking to take it away from you. "There's only a fine line between being able to pay your bills and ending up in a gutter somewhere," he would often say.

My father had many problems, which had a lasting effect on my family and me, not just his money mindset. But none of those issues and ingrained beliefs were genuinely apparent as long as I lived at home. My unconscious negative beliefs about money became a self-fulfilling prophecy. Through my behavior, I allowed the idea that money is something other people take away from you or that you must work hard for to come true. I worked hard and made good money in my early entrepreneurial days. I also generously shared my hard-earned cash with romantic partners, family members, and even people I hardly knew. They didn't have my work ethic, but I assure you they enjoyed the fruits of my hard labor. Nobody forced me to give it away; I did it all on my own. It was what I'd always known, what had been imprinted on me. Long after I'd left my parent's house and lived by myself, the echo of those beliefs about money still rang true.

Your environment is like soup. If you, like a carrot, are swirling around in it with the potatoes, the onions, and the celery, you won't escape their flavors rubbing off on you. To change your life, you must choose a different soup.

Following Hegelian philosophy,[16] I believe other people hold your identity partly together. You, the self, are aware of your *self* because you're separate; you're a distinct identity from someone else – another self – and because you're seen through their eyes. In that sense, you not only become the people you surround yourself with, but those people also profoundly shape you. People always affect our identity and who we are; our interactions with those people partly create us. Nobody in your (inner) circles is neutral to you. You can be stuck because of the people in your life. Some of them, like Glenn, my therapist,[17] says, are positive sponsors, and some are negative sponsors. The positive ones are the ones that help shape a strong and whole identity; the negative ones are the ones that encourage or enable you into bad habits and thoughts.

Make your environment work for you

Because our environment so profoundly affects us, it's crucial to control it as much as possible. One thing you can do is surround yourself with people who show you who you can become instead of reminding you of the person you don't want to be. Another powerful thing to know about your environment is what James Clear talks about in his book *Atomic Habits*[18]: even though we all think we have complete control over what we do every day and the choices that we make, the author argues (and, with him, a plethora of scientific research) that a lot of the choices we think we make are made for us by our environment. We respond to the cues that surround us. That's why coffee shop counters are filled with sweets and cookies, why grocery stores have grabbable stuff throughout the check-out isles, and why it's hard to resist buying lipstick at the beauty shop when you only went in to try perfume. What is available around you is your default number one option.

Without realizing it, everything you gather around you influences your decisions, your habits, your identity, and your life. This is a good thing. It means you have another type of agency over your life that can help you get unstuck and achieve your goals. As James Clear continues: "By changing your surroundings, you can place a hurdle in the way of bad behaviors and remove the barriers to good ones. I like to refer to this strategy as environmental design."[19] What this means is that your environment can make it easier to make better choices for yourself and create new and better habits, so you won't have to use willpower (which, as we'll see later on in this book, isn't as great as it's cracked up to be) or control your behavior to get there.

Prompt: Design your environment for success

Look around you at home, work (or your home office), and think of the spaces you regularly frequent, like the grocery store, the gym, etc. Now consider your goals and answer the following questions:

- **Is my home environment supporting me in making decisions aligned with my goals?** Imagine you want to read more and watch fewer videos on demand in the evenings. Is your environment encouraging you to do that? How easy is it to turn on a show on your smartphone or television versus picking up a book and reading? How could you make your environment more encouraging for the good behavior or habit you want to have?

- **Is my work environment supporting me in making decisions aligned with my goals?** Think of your place of work, your desk, and how your work environment is organized. Is this environment helping you do your work positively, or is it making it harder for you to focus and do what you need to do? How could you change your environment so it encourages better work from you?

- **Are the spaces I frequent helping me to achieve my goals?** Let's say you aim to eat more vegetables and cook one meat-free meal every week, but this is a challenging lifestyle change for you. Is your grocery store of choice placing a hurdle between you and the behavior you want to change, or is it encouraging it? How could you change that, so it becomes easier to stick to your meat-free day once a week?

Once you've reviewed the spaces you spend time in regularly, come up with three things you can do to make your environment work for you. Remember: your environment must align with your goals – if it isn't, you'll have to use willpower to get anything done, a finite resource that you'd better not bet your dreams on.

Chapter Four: What Do You Really Want?

"Clarity precedes success."
– Robin Sharma

Anyone who wants to work with me can schedule a free 30-minute coaching session online.[20] This session is an excellent opportunity for the potential client and me to see if we're a good fit for each other and to start imagining what coaching could do for them. If you'd like to experience this, I invite you to schedule your session with me. You'll find the link to do so in the endnotes of this book.

I'm not mentioning this to get you to sign up (although it would be cool to learn more about you and your dreams!) but to share something unique that happens regularly. In that first, no-strings-attached session, clients often tell me precisely what they want, in most cases as a seemingly insignificant side note to the story they're sharing with me. Then, as quickly as they mention it, most people brush it off and move on to other things they'd like to accomplish.

Take Catherine, a wonderful young woman building her first company with a co-founder, who came to me exhausted and at her wits' end. Because we were both in the same city, we decided to meet at one of my favorite coffee bars in town instead of connecting online. I was already sitting and enjoying the taste of a dark roast blend when she walked in and waved at me with a big smile. Catherine is one of those people that, when you meet her for the first time, you immediately fall in love with her personality. She's a bright 28-year-old with a massive ambition to change the world and make good money doing it. We hit it off right away. After she'd taken some sips of her coffee, a spicy Chilean daily brew, she almost immediately told me, "If I'm really honest with myself, I know it's time for me to move on to other things. The company I've built for the past five years is doing great, we keep expanding and attracting new and bigger clients, but things don't work with my co-founder anymore." I sipped from my coffee in silence to give Catherine space to continue. "I've been thinking about it for a while now, and I want out."

Even though she had come to me because she felt she needed support in her day-to-day business activities and wanted a business mentor to help guide her, the reality was that Catherine felt stuck. She didn't know how to get out of the partnership and didn't feel like she was allowed or ready to take that bold step. Because she had addressed it, I asked her to tell me more about her co-founder. "We're absolute opposites. I do all the work while she imagines the company's future. I loved this about us when we just started, and I didn't mind being the one keeping everything together, but now that we've grown so much, I resent her for not doing more." Catherine paused. "You know, I think maybe I need to learn to communicate with her better. Maybe it's me, and maybe I'm just not getting through to her."

This precise moment is when the clarity about what she wanted to do made way for a smaller, less drastic, and scary idea. Even though deep within herself, she knew she didn't want to work with her co-founder anymore, Catherine downplayed her needs and desires. As we've seen in Step One, this is something many of us do when we're afraid or what we want feels overwhelming. It's natural to try and make the mountain in front of us into an ant hill so it feels easier to climb.

Catherine was sitting on a nail that wasn't hurting enough yet. She wasn't taking complete control or leadership over the situation because, even though it was becoming harder to stay with the pain, it was still bearable. Having that coffee together was a decisive first step for her to take charge, but as we've seen, this is a process. We grow into leadership; it requires self-knowledge and an understanding of how change works. We did the work. Because her true desire to leave the partnership and start her own thing was too big of a mountain at first, she decided to work on her communication skills, boundaries, and time management skills. Even if it wasn't clear to Catherine then, all these goals had one common denominator: her co-founder. Working on her communication skills was to try and get through to her in a positive way; building stronger boundaries was to make sure she could protect herself from the many ideas her co-founder would have at all hours of the day and dump on her to work out the next, and bettering her time management skills was to try and find balance again in a work-life that was all about doing the work her co-founder should have been doing, and not enough about enjoying her life.

In a way, we all know what we want. We might not have all the specifics or details aligned and straightforward, but we know what direction we want to take and certainly – if we're honest with ourselves – what we don't want anymore. Let's try this out now. Use the quick-thinking prompt below to capture your true desires.

Prompt: What do you really want?

Close your eyes and take a deep breath. Think about your life, work, relationships, and yourself… Feel into who you are and what matters to you most. Get to the core of your being; touch your soul. Stay there for a few minutes and be open and curious about what wants to come up. Then ask yourself the following questions:

- What do I "know" I want to do or should be doing to be happy?
- What would I "like" to do but think I won't be capable of?
- What have I "always wanted" to do but keep telling myself won't work out?

Reflect on these questions for a few moments, so you can hear what your intuition and gut are telling you before your inner critic takes over. Take a (mental) note; we'll return to this later.

PS: If you can't come up with anything, don't worry. At this stage, it's not abnormal for your dreams and desires to be blocked, especially if you've been following other people's dreams for a long time. If this is you, I invite you to lean into the idea that "the goal might just be to have a dream." It's a great starting point to help you get unstuck.

At the end of our work together, Catherine left the partnership and started her own agency. In only a few months, she built it out to be one of the best agencies in the country. I often see interviews of Catherine in well-known publications, and she's a sought-after consultant and keynote speaker. She still comes to me for sessions sometimes when she needs a sparring partner or someone to see what she cannot see, but she has transitioned into a leader who takes control of her life and work. She knew what she wanted to do from the start and eventually jumped, but she needed to build her mindset and self-confidence first to allow herself to do it.

What Catherine went through is a personal transformation. She became the person she needed to be to be able to leave a partnership that had become toxic. Understanding this is important when you're aiming for any change.

Change yourself, and the rest will follow

There are two sides to personal transformation: an internal one and an external one. The external one is easy to spot: goals you achieve, a number on your bank account, the size of your house, getting promoted, starting a business, going to the gym consistently... they're all external goals and subsequent achievements. That's why we're so focused on those expressions of life because they're easy to measure. We *see* when a goal is achieved. But that's only half the story – if even that much.

I shared before about the TEDx talk I gave a few years back. Stepping off that stage after delivering the talk I'd spent weeks preparing, I felt weird and sad instead of excited and great. I dealt with these negative emotions, known to dance and theater performers as the after-blues, for quite a while. In my mind, I'd achieved a significant milestone in my life and career, but I didn't feel it in my body. I was waiting for something magical to happen, for things to be different, but after a few days, I realized life was going on the same as before; it was back to reality with all of its responsibilities and work. Only after I'd integrated the journey that got me on that stage did I feel like I'd accomplished something. I realized I'd brushed over that period way too fast. To this day, I regret it. I would have felt better if I'd taken more time to enjoy how I was transforming myself by learning, rehearsing, feeling the fear, and doing it anyway to get on that stage. Because I was so externally focused on delivering the talk, the pleasure of the transformation process passed me by.

I know I'm not alone in this; maybe you've experienced it too. You aim for something and work hard to achieve it, only to find that it doesn't change how you feel when you're finally there. I get it; it's hard to focus on the journey when you want to reach a destination. We all know that the journey matters most, but because it's elusive, we tend to focus on what we can measure: a clear goal.

The problem with focusing on goals rather than the journey is that the change you're creating isn't lasting. We can fool ourselves into thinking we love running and force ourselves to get up in the morning to go out for a while. Still, if nothing changes about our relationship with running (aka if we can't stop hating it for forcing us out of bed in the morning), eventually, we'll give up. This is true for any goal you set yourself without considering whose goal it really is or why you truly want it.

We're back at mindset. But this time, I'm talking about something other than developing a growth mindset so that you believe you can achieve your dreams. We did that in Step One. In this second step, I invite you to start using your growth mindset to imagine other possible versions of *yourself*. We already know that we have to claim leadership and that nobody is waiting to hand it to us. The same is true of the person you must become to achieve what you want.

A growth mindset might make you feel better or worry less about crappy people or situations, but it won't magically change your career, bank account, or relationships. This is where the manifestation gurus lack clarity. For years, many have been proclaiming that you only need to visualize your dreams and desires for them to appear, or that you only need to change your mind to change your life. Some of this is true, as we've seen in Step One: without powerful mindset shifts, you stay stuck. But this is not where the story ends. You must also rethink the person you are and allow yourself to dream your true dreams. Let's explore this a little more as we look at Paulien and her journey to give herself permission to let go of her inherited dreams and follow her true dreams instead.

Allow yourself to become who you want to be

When Paulien approached me for career coaching a few years ago she had been unemployed for a while. Following her sister's advice, who'd successfully made a career switch from employee to freelance consultant while working with me, Paulien scheduled a free session with me online. A few days later, we met on Zoom (unknown to most people then, but already an indispensable tool for my international coaching practice). Paulien started talking about the job she was looking for: an office job, preferably in the fashion industry, with the security of a fixed income. It wasn't long before she admitted that sitting at a desk in front of a computer for long hours terrified her. "But my sisters want me to have a steady job so much; I don't know what else to do." Paulien had two older sisters and the sister I had coached. All three liked security, and a fixed income was top of their list. Pauline was different. She loved adventure, far-away travels, writing, art, history, and discovering new cultures. She was sensitive and artistic and had a nose for fashion trends. Because my coaching is integrative, I always start with the person. In Paulien's case, I asked her if she would be okay not looking for an office job for a while but instead going in search of what she really wanted. This question appealed to the adventurer in Paulien. She enthusiastically accepted the challenge and went home with several actions to take, including writing out her "ideal day," like you've done in Step One of this book.

This exercise is a classic for a reason. It's also one of my favorites because it lets you look closely at your interests and creative brain. If you notice that your ideal day doesn't look much like your reality, it's good to slowly begin to think about why that is because that's probably where some of your "stuckness" is. We'll begin looking at solutions to get you unstuck in the next step of the MOVE method when you create a vision for your future.

Dare to dream (and don't censor yourself)

With the ideal day exercise, Paulien, the 28-year-old adventurer looking for an office job to please her sisters, discovered not one but three ideal days within herself that had nothing to do with her life at the time. You may have also realized you had a few ideal days in you when you did the exercise. If so, don't worry, this happens often, and it's not a problem. It gives you more options to work with and a richer life to create for yourself!

This is what Paulien wrote about her ideal day(s):

1. *"My ideal day starts with a breakfast meeting with my business partner to go over our goals for the week and discuss what we need to do to manage the company. We're also taking steps towards launching our clothing line. For this, we will travel to Milan this week. We're working on a new event that will delight a great group of women with a unique experience. I feel that our workshops make a difference and contribute to the happiness of these women. I received a note from my business partner that a women's*

magazine wants to write an article about us. I feel great in my own skin and look great. Back at home, I can count on the support of my partner, and we enjoy a nice meal together with a glass of delicious, chilled Chardonnay."

2. *"I wake up at the ranch and get to work immediately. I enjoy getting up in nature. I get the horses out of the pasture and start training with them. Later in the day, I accompany a group of travelers on a trail. I meet people from all over the world and enjoy the adventure that every day brings. My partner, like me, loves nature and horses, and we enjoy going on long rides and picnics together. For us, it's not about material things but finding happiness in the small things. After a hard day's work, I feel fulfilled and enjoy a big meal with ingredients from our vegetable garden. In the evenings, my partner and I relax on the rocking chair on the porch, sipping on a large cup of herbal tea."*

3. *"I arrive at the office and am welcomed by a top team. I'm going to work with great energy to promote the new show we're working on. We're going on tour soon, and I'm helping with the preparations. This afternoon, there's a roundtable in which I participate and where I represent our company. In the evening, I go to watch the rehearsals. I connect with the artists and make sure I know 100% what message they want to convey. I look forward to all the busyness and healthy tension that comes with this. I feel proud to be part of something meaningful, and my network is growing too. I come home and share my excitement with my partner, who supports me completely and who I always look forward to coming home to."*

During Paulien's following coaching session, she was nervous and elated at the same time. "I couldn't choose. By doing the exercise, I realized that I have different ideal days and lives," she told me with tension in her voice. "But I know one thing for sure: an office job is not for me." The assignment was successful. The uncertainty that Paulien had struggled with for months in search of a job that would make everyone except herself happy, disappeared instantly. Even if she didn't know precisely how her ideal days would become a reality and how she would put her interests into practice, she now had a direction. Above all, she had reconnected with her true self and knew she wanted to remain faithful to her many passions.

The "Ideal Day" exercise never ceases to amaze me. It's so simple yet so powerful because it offers a direct way into desires and dreams we might otherwise not even dare to admit to ourselves or that we've forgotten about. By painting a vision of what we believe our lives could look and feel like, we're allowing ourselves to see beyond the borders of the lives we're currently stuck in. This is precisely what this second step is about: creating opportunities for ourselves. Let's see how that turned out for Paulien.

Chapter Five: Opportunities Show up When You Make Room for Them.

"Don't sit and wait for opportunities to come. Get up and make them."
– Madam C.J. Walker

In the sessions that followed, Paulien and I came up with jobs that could be both meaningful and inspiring for her, in which she could express as much of her interests as possible to get closer to living out her ideal days. It soon became clear that Paulien would be the happiest by combining things. She preferred to put as many interests as possible in one *portfolio*[21] career in which she could be financially secure, find meaning in her work, and enjoy variety in her days.

When Paulien discovered the type of career that would suit her best, she could finally give herself permission to pursue her interests. In the end, her love of adventure, nature, and horses got the upper hand. But she also didn't want to let go of her creative side, her entrepreneurial spirit, and her desire to do something meaningful for others.

After more thinking and trying things out, a career with horses began to take shape for Paulien, with a ranch in the background, making a difference in people's lives, and a business that she could develop along the way. During her last session (a journey of only three months), Paulien and I celebrated! She had found her first job as a trail guide on a horse ranch in Hungary, which she would travel to only a few weeks later. This was a couple of years ago. Today, Paulien continues to add ingredients to her career. Recently, she took her first steps as an entrepreneur in the world of equestrian sport, a logical next step if you know the courageous road she's traveled. But during the first conversations we had, nobody could have imagined the beautiful life she would be living now, especially not Paulien, who had never allowed herself to dream about it.

Getting unstuck is not only about seeing, but also about creating new possibilities for yourself

The life Paulien is living now was available to her all along, just like the many other lives she could be living. It's not that somehow – magically – this life materialized for her out of thin air. Even though Paulien transformed her situation in a record time, she worked hard for it. To work hard though, first, she had to know where she wanted to go. She needed to take off the blindfold that was keeping her stuck. That blindfold is what I like to call *opportunity blindness*. A lot of people are wearing it. Either that or their eyes are wide open to only one possible path or alternative. Unlike the blindfold, where you're stuck because you don't see the many options in front of you, seeing just one option keeps you stuck between a rock and a hard place.

Seneca (and Oprah) famously said that "luck is preparation meeting opportunity."[22] When you prepare to see red cars, those cars eventually show up. Opportunities to change your life work the same way. We're used to seeing what we're accustomed to; it's hard to imagine something else might be available.

Prompt: Look at your life with new eyes

To see new opportunities, you need to remove the blindfold. A good starting point is to look at your life with the eyes of a beginner, someone who doesn't know anything about your life or who you are. Imagine you're someone else, someone you appreciate or that you look up to. Now, look at yourself through that person's eyes. Take the facts, look at what you see around yourself, and start there.

- What are you doing?
- Where are you?
- Who's with you?

- What are you famous for?
- What options are available to you?

Take some time to reflect on your answers. What new opportunities emerge when you look at yourself from the outside this way? Write them down.

Sometimes, you'll need more than the beginner's mind. What I believe Oprah meant when she talked about „preparation" is knowledge – if you want more options, you need to be aware of more things. Looking at life and the world with wonder will help you take some steps, but after that initial high, you'll need something more to keep going.

The magic trick is this: you need to understand that there's a mountain you've created in your mind between where you are right now and where you want to be. That mountain seems insurmountable from where you're standing, knee-deep in the slush. Because you've created that mountain with the limited set of options you believe are available to you, to climb the mountain (or make it disappear) you need to dismantle the beliefs that created it.

Be wary of your interpreter

I've been practicing TM (transcendental meditation) for more than a decade, and that helped me to overcome my constant anxiety and worry. One thing you learn in TM is that you shouldn't make decisions based on thoughts that arise during meditation. When you meditate, stress stored in the body is released. This stress could be anything from childhood trauma to something trivial that happened and that got stuck in your body. When your analytical brain feels that this stress is being released, it will try and give meaning to it. The neocortex does this every time you have a bodily sensation because its purpose is to understand what's going on with you. Unfortunately, it often misinterprets the signals.

I remember one of my first TM sessions many years ago. I was sitting with eyes closed with a small group of practitioners. After about 10 minutes, when I was settled in my meditation, I could feel the tension leaving my body. A tingling sensation ran from my shoulders down my arms into my fingers. I could feel my neck and back stiffness soften, and my spine relaxed. Almost at the same time, I started having thoughts about a friend I had lost touch with over a silly fight. The more I calmed down and felt the stress leave my body, the more negative the thoughts about my past with that person became, to the point that I felt the emotions of our difficult goodbyes again as if it had just happened. The prevailing thought was that I'd been wronged, never defended myself properly, and never had closure or a final conversation. You can imagine how I felt by the end of the meditation. I wasn't relaxed; I was all worked up and ready to grab my phone and send what I felt was a long overdue text.

The event wasn't painful, and it was a long time ago. I can see now how I had my share of responsibility for what happened. But not after that meditation. Luckily, a teacher was present in our group because I was still in the early days of my meditation practice. I told him what was happening, and he helped me to see that it was a misinterpretation of the stress I was releasing that got me into that state, not the story from my past. When I'd calmed down enough, I knew he was right. As soon as I got into my day, I forgot about it and never felt any of those emotions about that experience again. Since then, thoughts of all kinds have come into my mind during meditation. I've learned it's normal; it's what happens when you give your consciousness and body a break. I also learned it's not the time to make decisions because those thoughts are not a reflection of reality but of something deeper going on.

Most of us don't realize that we often make decisions in moments that we shouldn't. TM is just one example. It's easy to understand why it is not the best idea to base one's actions on your brain's interpretations during meditation. However, many of us make decisions when stressed, under time pressure, tired, hungry, angry, frustrated, or sad. That's because our brain doesn't only like to *give meaning* to why we're feeling what we're feeling; our brain also loves to provide us with reasons for *why we do what we do.*

Dr. Michael Gazzaniga, a professor of psychology at the University of California, Santa Barbara, and a leading researcher in cognitive neuroscience, has devoted a significant part of his career to understanding the brain through split tests between left and right brain hemispheres. In particular, Dr. Gazzaniga did extensive research with test subjects who had undergone split-brain surgery where the corpus callosum – their right and left brain hemispheres – had been partially or entirely split to stop epilepsy seizures. The study showed that meaning, aka interpretation, is a right-brain activity. When shown images of things, the left hemisphere can draw pictures of them but can't give them meaning without the help of the right hemisphere. The right hemisphere is where interpretation happens, even when both hemispheres aren't *talking* to each other. For instance, J.W., onc of Dr. Gazzaniga's subjects, was shown two words simultaneously: BELL + MUSIC. „Bell" was shown to his non-speaking right brain, and „music" to his speaking left brain. When asked to point to a picture of what he saw with his right brain, he chose a picture of a church bell, out of four images of which the three others depicted musical instruments. When asked why he chose that picture, J.W. told the researchers it was because the picture reminded him of music, and he told a story about a bell he heard right before the experiment.

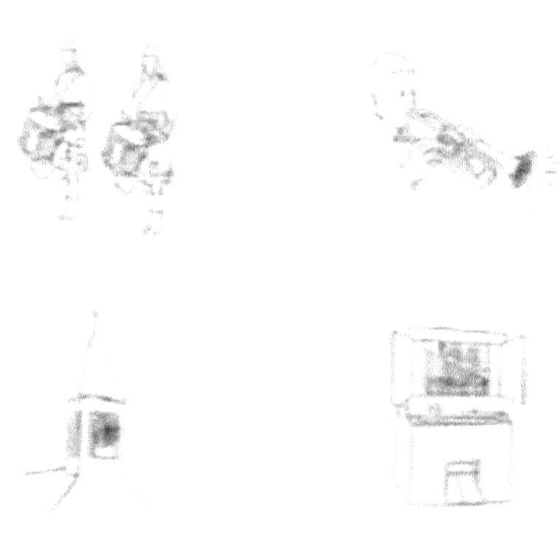

Image from one of the 2009 Gifford Lectures given by Dr. Gazzaniga at The University of Edinburgh.[23] The picture J.W. chose after being shown the words BELL + MUSIC is the bottom left picture of a church bell; even though his right hemisphere didn't see the word "bell," it still tried to make sense of why J.W. chose it.

What does this tell us? The right hemisphere is excellent at analyzing and perceptual grouping, organizing complex patterns into meaning. The left brain hemisphere loves to interpret and synthesize information into a common narrative that relates to us, the person, as a whole. When the left hemisphere picks up a visual or language cue, the right hemisphere will look for its meaning, even when it doesn't have all the information available or hasn't *seen it*.

"The interpreter," located in the left hemisphere, "is only as good as the data it gets," as Dr. Gazzaniga says.[24] Knowing about this highly developed ability of our brain is important. If our brain constantly tries to make sense of the sensory inputs it gets, all reality is virtual. Depending on the information we get, our brain will interpret what is happening around us and to us by continuously creating meaning and structure as we move through life and our experiences. One might wonder what would happen if a virtual world like, let's say, the Metaverse became so sophisticated that it would trump reality in how real it feels to us. Would our brain be able to tell the difference between actual life events and those happening in that virtual world? Would it matter? What would *real* mean by then? What does it say about the world we are living in right now?[25]

We feed our interpreter flawed or incomplete data all the time. We're continuously filling in the gaps and not seeing our blind spots. As we're doing so, we're constructing a version of reality that feels complete to us, with rules and ways that things are or can be – including ourselves. The problem is that by the sheer nature of how the brain works, it's impossible not to process at least some wrong or incomplete information, and so also flawed beliefs about what we are capable of in that reality. To change, we must be willing to question the world as we see it.

Chapter Six: Real-Life Experiments to Activate Change.

"Most people don't see their beliefs. Instead, their beliefs tell them what they see. This is the simple difference between clarity and confusion."
– Matt Kahn

One thing I love to have clients do, above all else, is real-life experimentation. To get unstuck, you must go out and do things, try things, and experience things. You cannot think yourself out of that annoying place where nothing moves; you must take action.

Let's recap because I know I'm throwing a lot of stuff at you right now:

CIRCUMSTANCES > become > EXPERIENCES > become > BELIEFS > become > THOUGHTS > become > BEHAVIOR > become > YOUR REALITY

If your experiences have taught you that you cannot do something, your behavior will reflect those experiences through your unconscious beliefs and the thoughts that will emerge from them. If we go one step further, we could say that your circumstances (certainly when they are negative) will influence your experiences and, therefore, everything that happens because of your circumstances: what you believe, what you think, what you do, and eventually what you see as reality.

Many studies have shown this to be true. One such study looked at the gender biases of teachers and parents regarding mathematical studies for boys and girls.[26] The study found that stereotypes about boys being better at math than girls, or mathematics not being a „girl" field, affected girls' performance. Overall, if not excessively, it was lower than the performance of boys. The study also found that the girls and their mothers, who otherwise denied stereotyping, had less confidence in the mathematical abilities of girls than boys! And it's not only the girls or mothers who have ingrained beliefs about the differences in mathematical abilities between genders. Fathers do, too. But unlike the mothers, they admitted to being biased and somewhat believing in the stereotypes.

It's not a coincidence that the traditional intelligence test for the Theory of Mind[27] – the ability to attribute mental states to oneself and others such as beliefs, emotions, desires, intents, and knowledge – is a false-belief test used to assess the understanding a child has about the false beliefs other people can have about the world. One such test is the Sally-Anne test, in which someone leaves an object in a location (a toy in a basket) that is moved to a different location while the person is outside the room. In a 1985 test, Simon Baron-Cohen, Alan M. Leslie, and Uta Frith used the Sally-Anne test to investigate whether autistic children could understand false beliefs.[28]

The test goes like this:

On a table, two dolls (Anne and Sally) are placed facing a closed box and a closed basket. The child being tested is sitting at the table. (The doll) Sally puts a marble into her basket and then goes away. When Sally's gone, (the doll) Anne takes the marble out of the basket and places it into the closed box in front of her. The experimenter now asks the child where Sally will look for the marble. To pass the test, the child must point to the basket. Being able to do this means they understands that, although reality had changed since Sally put the marble in her basket, Sally doesn't know the marble moved, so she has a false belief that the marble is still in the basket because she didn't witness it being moved. If the child points to the basket, it means they understands how beliefs work, separate from actual reality. It means the child knows Sally has her own beliefs about the world that differ from hers: Sally doesn't know where the marble is, while the child does.

It's hard to fight against beliefs, especially when everyone around you claims their truth. In a world where everyone thinks the marble is in the basket, you'll have a hard time being the one saying it's in the box. Ask Copernicus,[29] he knows.

In a way, what I want you to do, is precisely what Copernicus did so many centuries ago: examine your worldview, debunk your false beliefs, and review the theories and rules that you distill from them and live by as a result.

Prompt: The beliefs that keep you stuck right now

With this final activity of Step Two, I want you to look deeper at your beliefs. It's a continuation of the inner critic exercise you did earlier, but it's different. Previously, you uncovered the negative thoughts that keep you stuck. Now we want to take it a step further: we want to dig up the beliefs about yourself and your situation that keep you stuck.

Take a deep breath, and either on paper or in your mind, reflect on the following questions:

- If I'm honest with myself, what is the #1 thing holding me back right now?
- What do I believe will happen if I do what I know deep down I want to do?
- What doom scenarios am I making up in my head when I think about this change?
- How much of this doom scenario might actually come true? How do I know for sure?
- Do I care what other people will say if I do what I really want to do? What do I think they will say?
- What is so wrong with what I want to do that I'm not allowing myself to do it?

These questions are tough, I know, so take your time. Once you've uncovered the beliefs that keep you stuck right now, I want you to ask yourself the following two questions:

- How much of myself am I denying by staying where I am because of these beliefs?
- What will my life be like five years from now if I let myself be guided by these beliefs?

Desensitizing yourself from your current worldview

Moving forward, I want you to start trying things out and experimenting. Only then can you train your nervous system to believe in different outcomes and create new neural pathways in your brain for new beliefs to take shape. You must realize that your circumstances are not permanent, that your experiences are just that, experiences, and that you can change what you believe, think, and do. You can change your reality.

It's all about reprogramming your central nervous system and rewiring your brain. Throughout your life, you've been conditioned to think a certain way, act a certain way, and even want things a certain way. That programming doesn't only happen in the neocortex, the thinking part of your brain; it also occurs in your reptilian brain and your nervous system, a complex wiring of nerves and pathways that process the information coming from your brain. If you only think about the changes you want to make in your life, without ever trying anything or doing something about it, there's a big chance you'll stay stuck for a very long time (if not forever). You are not just a mind; you're also a living, breathing body. Mind-body experiences are essential to effect lasting change. It's not just your beliefs you have to reprogram or your mind you must convince; you need to tell your body that what you want to do will be ok too. If not, you'll keep activating the fight or flight response, and you'll feel resistance towards what you want, in many cases, without even being conscious of it. You'll label it "doubt," "lack of clarity," or "procrastination" when in fact, it's your body reacting to something unknown that feels scary.

I invite you to look for small experiments you can do every day.[30] The idea is to allow yourself to feel that there's no real danger when you do what you're thinking about doing but are too afraid to try. Think of it as micro-dosing, but for your nervous system. By exposing yourself to little moments of fear and excitement, you're giving yourself a chance to learn that nothing terrible happens when you do. Whenever I have a new, big goal or project I want to go for, I start reprogramming my nervous system this way. It makes it much easier to go after what I want by expanding my comfort zone little by little to fit the things I'm excited about but also anxious and stressed to do.

Here are some examples of experiments that created effective change and helped clients reach big, scary goals and dreams:

- **Build stronger boundaries.** Say "no" to little things you don't want to do, like going to that party you don't feel like attending or helping someone paint their apartment. Build up from the little "no-s" until you're capable (and maybe even comfortable, although that's not a prerequisite) to say "no" to the bigger things. Practice daily, and you will see results fast. The most important thing is to give your nervous system a chance to experience that nothing terrible happens when you protect your boundaries, that the people who matter still like you, and that everyone else will start to respect you more.

- **Speak up about your needs.** In situations where you usually would go along with whatever someone else proposes, speak up and state what you want. Again, build up from the little things until you can voice the big stuff. I used to go to the movies weekly with my ex-husband, and even though I was the one who suggested going and said what movie I wanted to see, he always managed to make me pick another movie at the last minute. I usually went along with it, but I hated myself for doing so as soon as I realized I had to endure watching a movie I didn't care about for two hours. I don't let myself be talked into something I don't want to do anymore, and it all started with baby steps and sticking to my movie choices.

- **Stop overthinking.** Chronic overthinking is one of the reasons many people get and stay stuck. Because of brain plasticity, forming a habit of munching over every choice happens without us realizing it. Add a dash of the nervous system to it that feels as if danger lurks every time a decision needs to be made, and you have a recipe for disaster. The way to get out of overthinking is by training yourself to make quicker decisions without giving them much thought. Again, you want to practice on little things first, like the clothes you'll wear today or the coffee or sandwich you'll order at Starbucks for lunch. Practice making quick choices daily and gradually work your way up to more complex situations and options.

- **Keep perfectionism in check.** Another reason why so many people are stuck is perfectionism. Whatever they're doing needs to be perfect, or it shouldn't get done at all. Perfectionists will either take an excruciating amount of time to do something or will only start if they know they can deliver it the way they want. As with all things, there's childhood programming, fears, and insecurities, and sometimes trauma behind this way of thinking and approaching life. To start rewiring yourself into someone who accepts "good enough" as a standard instead of "perfect," find small daily ways to be imperfect. Deliver the report, even if you want to add two pages of additional research to it; invite friends and family over for dinner, and don't spend a day cleaning your place before they come or do things that you would usually fret over for days or weeks in a set time frame. When the time is up, so is your work: send the email, publish the article, stop the research. Finish the thing!

- **Move past the fear of failure.** The fear of being wrong or making mistakes is not only related to perfectionism; it's often another solid pull for staying where you are instead of trying to change your life. The type of failure that keeps us stuck is a fallacy. It's a construct we take with us from childhood, often given to us by caregivers or teachers. Since so much of our growing up centers around learning to play nice and avoiding mistakes, when we finally reach adulthood, we have it drilled into our core that taking any misstep is dangerous. To reprogram your nervous system into knowing that nothing terrible happens when you fail – and that failure is simply part of living and achieving your dreams – you can start with little experiments with friends, family, and loved ones. Forget the condiments next time you set the dinner table and go, "Oops, my bad," if anyone notices, misplace your mom's glasses and see how she reacts when you tell her about your "mistake," go to a restaurant and order something you don't want and change your mind when it arrives. You get the point.

Whatever the challenge, think of instances to expose yourself to it in small ways. Every time you do, however insignificant you might think the effort is, you'll give your nervous system, brain, and mind a chance to learn that it's safer than you think to color outside of the lines society has defined for you. The more you practice, the bigger your comfort zone will become. Every experience will expand on the previous one, which is more than enough to grow.

Change happens over time, not all at once

You've come a long way. You're almost halfway through this book. Can you believe it? Massive growth and change are already happening within you. The fact that you've worked your way through the material and exercises I've suggested has already changed you forever. Here's the thing: we often start before we think we do. Because we only see change as the result of a grand gesture and life-altering experiences and decisions, the daily steps we take or ideas we have go unnoticed when in fact, it's those small acts that create change over time.

By now, I'm sure you know that getting unstuck is a bit like Jim Carrey waking up on the Truman Show and realizing that the life he's been living isn't real. First, you need to understand that most of what we do in life is conditioned and unconscious. Then you can start to make decisions for yourself and take the lead.

In the next section, we'll take this new knowledge and dive even deeper into what it means for you. Envisioning, above all else, will be at the center of what we'll do in Step Three of the MOVE method. We'll look further at the fabric of reality and how we make sense of the world. We'll question whether what we see in front of us is real or not. Does our mind play tricks on us? And if so, how can knowing this help us get unstuck? But first, let's look at the takeaways of Step Two.

Summary: Step Two – Options

This second step is all about options: understanding the limitations our mind creates when shaping our reality and learning to see through that shadow into a world of limitless possibilities.

In this second step, you learned:

- That the world is full of possibilities, you just have to see them.
- That you're the leader of your life.
- What the tyranny of inherited dreams is and how they influence your life.
- That leadership is never given; you must take it for yourself.
- How our environment shapes our reality.
- How opportunities show up when you make room for them.
- Real-life experiments to actively change.

Well done! You're through with Step Two! Woohoo! By now, you should have a better understanding of how your mind operates, how it influences your life, and how your worldview limits your reality and the opportunities you see as a result. You should also understand how you can expand your reality by taking on different – Copernican – viewpoints, and how opportunities will show up when you make space for them.

You're now ready for Step Three, in which we'll discuss the fabric of reality and what is real versus what is not. It's time to dive deeper into the agency you have over your life and work and what that means to what is possible for you. Let's break things open and push the limits of what you believe to be true. I can't wait! Are you ready? Let's do this!

STEP THREE:
VISION

"Find out who you are and do it on purpose."
– Dolly Parton

In this step, you'll learn:

- That it's ok to be different, and how to turn your difference(s) into an advantage.
- Why breaking promises to yourself will keep you stuck.
- Why real impostors don't feel like impostors.
- Disruptive strategies and how they can help you get unstuck.
- How we make perceptual judgments, and why most of them are false.
- How to change and influence your reality.

Chapter One: Who do You Want to be When You Grow up?

"It takes courage to grow up and become who you really are."
– E. E. Cummings

When Anna stepped into my office, she was full of expectations. She wanted to find a quick answer – and solution – to the questions that had plagued her for years. What should she be doing with her time? What was her passion? What kind of work and life would make her happy? Anna had been to many coaches, and even a few therapists, with her questions before, but never got a satisfactory answer, at least not one that stood the test of time. Sometimes, she went home with some new insights about what she could potentially do, but every time, after a while, the good ideas faded into the background, leaving her with the same empty feeling she had carried with her since college. "I don't know what's wrong with me!" she exclaimed while sitting down in front of me. "I've been doing this patchwork of jobs for years, but I always seem to lose interest or feel like something's missing, and then I give up and I quit."

Anna is a wonderful 42-year-old creative with a passion for books and vintage furniture. In her spare time, she loves to wander around thrift shops looking for rare finds, or visit libraries, "because books never disappoint." Anna had been a bartender, kindergarten teacher, bookkeeper, in-house help for an elderly couple, event organizer on a cruise ship, and even a flight attendant for a private charter company. Her bubbly personality and curiosity made her an open-minded, fun, and likable person. You'd think Anna had it figured out and was happy with her life and choices. Yes and no. Anna was delighted with the freedom to do what she wanted; the problem was she didn't feel as though she truly knew what that was – or who *she* was. After so many years, she still hoped she'd figure it out and finally find what she was supposed to be doing. Even though from the outside it looked like Anna wasn't stuck at all, on the inside, she felt like she wasn't moving forward or knew where she was going with her life.

Anna isn't alone in feeling this way. A lot of the suffering burdening my clients and people who feel stuck is invisible. It looks like we have it all together on the outside, but on the inside, it's pure agony whenever we think about what we should be doing with our lives. I know how painful this can be; I was there for many years. It's one of the reasons I was feeling like such an impostor (more about that later in this chapter) because how could I be proud of something I'd accomplished when inside I felt like such a mess?

It was only when I gave myself the gift of genuinely looking at my situation and coming up with different options than the ones I'd always gone for that things started to shift. The same happened to Anna. She'd never given her choices the attention they deserved. She would often decide on a whim what to do next, feeling in the moment that it was the right thing to do. For a while, it worked that way. But then the dreaded *ennui*, the familiar boredom, set in. That's when Anna inevitably felt the itch, again and again, to go out and look for something else. "When I start doing something, I'm always so excited and inspired," Anna told me on her second visit. "But then, the love affair fades, and I'm left with this empty feeling again. When that happens, I know it won't bc long before I quit and move on. I've been doing it for years, making me feel ashamed and guilty. Why can't I pick something and stick to it like everyone else?"

Anna kept looking for the problem within herself. During her second session, she talked about all the times she'd started something new, only to leave it hanging in mid-air, sometimes long before the finish line, or at least what her friends, family, and coworkers considered to be the end. Because of this mismatch between when she felt she was through with something versus what society considered the end post of her endeavors, Anna felt like a loser. "I've been trying for so long; I've given up on finding something that'll keep me interested." Perhaps you've felt like Anna before, or you're feeling like her right now. If so, what follows is for you.

Are you a creative generalist?

My sweet spot is to help creatives and entrepreneurs get unstuck. I've been doing it for almost a decade, and it's been one of the most rewarding experiences of my life. It's also been the most outstanding way to learn the intricacies of my own mind and behavior.

One of the things that emerged from my work, and something I recognized in myself many years ago, is the concept of creative generalists (also known as multi-passionate creatives, polymaths, or multipotentialites[31]). Although I've used the terms interchangeably for many years, in the last few, I've mostly been using "creative generalist" to talk about this special breed of human. I even wrote a book about it[32], and I'm working on a second, more in-depth one – there's just so much to say! I'm mentioning creative generalists because many of the people I see who feel stuck fall into that category, so perhaps you do too.

When working with clients, recurring themes invariably come up. The frontrunner, though, is this: spending years trying to fit in, doing what's expected of them, sometimes with great results but in almost all cases without the desired feeling of fulfillment or happiness. Even the most successful of my clients (by society's standards) feel misunderstood, out of place, and never good enough.

Before we can free ourselves from those negative feelings and replace them with positive and inspiring insights, we first need to understand why so many people feel this way.

The pitfalls of the creative and entrepreneurial mind

Do you ever feel like life is passing by too quickly? You look around, and the only things you see are a bunch of ideas and projects waiting to happen, problems that need solving, and significant challenges in the world that you'd like to tackle. But at the same time, you struggle with self-doubt, stress, and feeling like you're pretending to be someone you're not, even though people think you're smart and capable. It's gotten to the point where you've lost the inner drive that used to push you to learn and discover new things. Instead, you lack confidence and have a history of starting new things and failing to stick with something and making it work.

In my first book for creative generalists, I shared the story of the ugly duckling because I've used this folk tale in my practice since the day I started coaching. What many creative generalists experience in their life is like that story: the duckling who had to survive and make it on his own amid a family that looked nothing like it. Because no one had ever told the duckling it was different, it kept trying to fit into a world where it didn't belong.

What's unique about this story, and perhaps applicable to you, is that we focus so much on belonging that we don't see the differences between ourselves and the group we want to be part of. Under social and economic pressure, we make desperate efforts to become like everyone else, believing this is how we succeed. We hope that by just trying a little harder, we'll finally want the same things as everyone else, and we'll be happy with that type of life. But as long as we keep trying to be something we're not, real happiness won't be possible. It's only when we accept that we're different that positive change can occur, and a vision of the life that is meant for us can emerge, allowing us to finally feel liberated and *good enough*.

There's nothing wrong with you. You've been misdiagnosed!

At the end of the fairy tale, it turns out that the ugly duckling is not a duck at all but a swan. When the duckling didn't know it was a swan, it believed everything the ducks said about how it should be and what was wrong with it. When it was a duckling, its brothers and sisters made fun of it because its feathers looked different, its neck was bigger than usual, and its feet looked weird. The duckling swam differently, and nobody understood its sounds when it tried to communicate with them or call its family.

Since it was the only duckling that looked different, it felt like something was wrong with it! Sometimes the others teased or laughed at the duckling, but most of the time, they ignored it. It was never invited to play at the lake and couldn't fly like the others. The loneliness of being so misunderstood was excruciating. To avoid feeling so alone, the duckling was willing to go through a lot. That's why it tried so hard to fit in and belong.

Almost all the clients I welcome in my (virtual) office can relate to this story. I can too (that's why I always check second-hand bookstores for old editions of this story). For the longest time, I felt like the ugly duckling, not knowing what was wrong with me or why I could never feel like I belonged. It took me decades to understand and accept that I was different and that my brain needed more. It needed other things than just one topic to focus on for life – or even just a moment. It took me years to accept that I needed variety in my work, that I'm easily bored when I do the same thing for too long, and that I'll always have a wide range of interests fighting for my attention. Ring a bell?

Although I'm a proud swan today, I was once a lost little duck who felt out of place, lonely, and anxious. Through my work, I've learned what I believe are the three most common difficulties and negative emotions, which are a natural result of the lack of recognition of who you really are. I want to emphasize the "natural" aspect of it. Just as the duckling can't help it and doesn't understand why it feels terrible around its brothers and sisters who look nothing like it, neither are you responsible for the mismatch between the demands that society has placed on you and the way your brain is wired. In other words: there's nothing wrong with you!

Prompt: Are you someone with many ideas and interests?

The more I do this work, the more I realize there are a lot of creative generalists out there: people with many ideas and interests who don't fit into the tiny box of specialization that the world is trying to put them in. The questions below can guide you to figure out if you're part of that fantastic crew of incredible swans (the fact that you're still with me tells me that you might!).

- Do you get bored quickly when you figure out how something works, how to do it, or if you must do the same thing too often?
- Do you enjoy learning, researching, exploring, and developing new skills or insights?
- Do you keep changing your mind about what you want to do with your life? Are you still wondering what you'll be when you „grow up"?
- Is it difficult for you to explain to someone what you do?
- Do you often daydream about everything you "still" want to do or will do „someday," both professionally and personally?
- Do you start many things but often only finish a few of them?
- Do you feel like you need to be more focused?
- Do you have trouble choosing for fear of losing something?
- Is there a rebel living inside of you that hates authority and can't stand injustice?

If you answered „yes" to three or more of the questions above, there's a good chance that you're a creative generalist.[33]

Chapter Two: The Burden of Being Unconventional.

"The most damaging phrase in the language is:
'It's always been done that way.'"
– Grace Hopper

If you recognize yourself in the above, if this *is you*, I have great news for you: Welcome! Up until this point, you simply didn't know. But now you do!

There is absolutely nothing wrong with you!

On the contrary. You've simply been misdiagnosed or created a wrong image of yourself. What you think is a flaw may well be one of your superpowers. Your brain is unique. It makes connections where others can't, something that quickly converts new information into meaningful neural networks. The only bad luck you and your extraordinary brain have is that you've been born into a world that isn't quite made for you (yet).[34] You live in a world that doesn't understand how you operate. And this is where things get tricky. If you have no clue about how you're put together, there's a risk that you'll agree with what the world around you thinks of you. This puts a damper on your creativity and problem-solving skills, makes you feel frustrated, and can even lead to what is now known as burnout or, often worse for creative generalists, *boreout*.

This all ends right here, right now. I want you to give yourself permission to stop trying to fit into the tiny box society wants to keep you in and, instead, fall in love with the unique brain that you have and the person that you are. First, let's look at some common burdens you might be carrying.

#1 Shame and guilt

Someone recently referred to a game of snakes and ladders when describing their career to me. The game's ups and downs symbolize the twists, turns, and unforeseen circumstances that shape your professional journey. I like this metaphor because it perfectly captures a non-linear career's unconventional – and unpredictable – nature. Like in the game, you may encounter unexpected setbacks (the snakes) that can divert you from your intended path (if you even know what that is). You might also stumble upon opportunities (the ladders) that push you forward and open new doors. If you're like me and many of my clients, your professional track record is atypical, to say the least. It reflects the uniqueness of your brain, passions, and interests. There may be gaps or a line-up of seemingly disconnected jobs or work experiences. There might also be *a lot* on your resume, temporary jobs here and there, over extended periods. Or you've diligently worked your way up a ladder in the corporate world, and your professional journey looks linear; the problem is that you don't feel that way. There's so much more to you that isn't on the page. Whatever your situation, if your stomach cringes every time someone asks you about your work experience or what it is, precisely, that you do, I hope you know by now that you're in good company.

Creative generalists tend to twist and turn their way through life instead of going straight forward. But like specialists (a denominator for people who don't have many passions in life but instead happily focus on or become experts at one thing), creative generalists are going somewhere too. Only they do it in such a way that no one, often themselves included, realizes where their choices lead. As a result, many are confronted with prejudice and misconceptions about their paths and journeys. These discriminations can damage their self-confidence, create limiting beliefs, and cause emotional wounds or even trauma. Unfortunately, as we've seen, that's a recipe for getting and staying stuck.

Shame and guilt are emotions we feel when we're comparing ourselves to some standard and find ourselves wanting, but failing to meet it.

Befriending your emotions

All our lives, we hear that we must specialize, that we have to choose and turn one interest into a career. But if there's one thing we can't do, it's precisely that. Remember that as long as the ugly duckling doesn't know it's a swan, it feels ashamed. The same is true for us. We must realize that it's a fallacy, a trick our mind plays on us because of the world we're living in.

The solution is to turn the situation around and give new meaning to our feelings of inadequacy. Rather than seeing shame and guilt as negative or as a sign that you're not doing the right thing, use those feelings as clues that you're doing something important. As Gabor Maté[35], a Hungarian-Canadian physician and author, and one of my favorite people when learning about trauma (something we'll talk more about in Step Four) explains, shame and guilt often arise in childhood as a response to a desire thwarted by caregivers. A child wants to do something, but a parent or caregiver is not allowing it, so the child is shamed into not wanting to do it anymore.

Without going into details about the neurobiological and psychological consequences of our upbringing, I want to point out how the systematic thwarting of childhood desires becomes ingrained in us: shame and guilt become our means of self-regulating what we want and don't want to do, what we're allowed to dream and what we aren't, and ultimately what we do and don't do. Still following Gabor Maté's insights on this, shame is the opposite of authenticity, the state of being that we all naturally strive for. In this state, we allow ourselves to be who we naturally want to be and express our creativity freely.

For our survival, it's important to bond with our caregivers as best we can when we're children, and listening to them is essential. The feelings that helped you do that were useful tools growing up, such as the shame you felt when you were caught eating your sister's brownie or the guilt when you saw the disappointment on your parents' faces coming home with a bad report card. Back then, those feelings ensured that you learned to adjust your behavior to the world around you. You were *good* when you did what was expected of you and *bad* when you didn't follow the rules.

Meanwhile, you're a grown-ass adult who can take care of him, her, or themself. Yet we often continue to struggle with the same feelings. When situations today feel like echoes from our past, shame and guilt resurface, ready to control our behavior like they did when we were children. What was once a helpful strategy has become a detrimental one. The shame that kept us from eating all the brownies is now holding us back from pursuing a life or career we've been dreaming of for years. There's no reason for shame to show up, but it's become an automatic response to a trigger. When we're triggered, we react the way we've been taught. We take the triggers with us from childhood and never question them again, often because we're unaware of them to begin with.

Imagine a desire you have but systematically fail to act upon. It could be a career switch or starting your own business. You may feel like traveling around the world or buying something for yourself. In the dream, you see yourself in the spotlight, on a stage, or on a beach stretched out in a blissful lounger with a palm tree as company and a mocktail in your hand. It doesn't matter what your desire is, just focus on something you don't seem to be able to do or have. You want it so badly, but something is holding you back.

What if you paused and asked yourself why you're reacting this way to a desire or dream that you have? If you take a closer look at the dynamic, you'll often conclude, as I learned from Gabor Maté, that those icky feelings indicate that you're choosing something for *yourself*. For that alone, these feelings deserve to be celebrated and embraced. Diffuse your shame and guilt by being proud of them: they're proof you're working to get yourself unstuck.

#2 Lack of confidence

When Carla first came to see me, she didn't know what to do. She bit on her lip in an attempt to save her nails and looked around with fearful eyes. "I don't know what's wrong with me," she said quickly, gasping for air. "This is the umpteenth time I'm giving up; I can't tell my parents anymore."

Carla was 32 years old and lived in Lisbon. As an Irish woman, she had opted for the sun and warm ocean of the Portuguese capital a few years ago. Before settling, she had traveled for a long time. For four years, she had visited just about every corner of the planet and immersed herself in as many cultures as possible. Carla loved to experience and discover the world. She had graduated from a prestigious film academy for a reason. Long before she knew how to operate a camera, she looked at the world and the people around her in a unique way.

After her film studies, Carla made some beautiful short and feature films as a director. In the world of alternative cinema, she'd become a well-known name. She'd also co-written several successful screenplays and created high-performing films and acclaimed plays. But that's not all Carla did. She had also earned her spurs as a photographer. But even with all that, she still felt like a failure. After the last success she'd had with a small exhibition of her work, the people around her had become so enthusiastic that they had pressured Carla to go all in as a photographer. The film world is unfamiliar territory for most people, so no one had ever commented on her career choices in that field. But after Carla won a prestigious prize with her beautiful photo, everyone suddenly had an opinion about her professional life.

Carla's career had always been one of switching between and circling around her various interests. She'd been trying to make the most of her photography business for a few years, but she was tired of it. She missed the creative flow that writing and directing gave her. Although Carla knew what she no longer wanted, she was still stuck. The direction she'd chosen because of all the positive pressure she'd gotten from the people closest to her turned out not to be the right one for her anymore. She had lost all confidence in herself. Even though her clients praised her, she earned good money and was allowed to work on beautiful projects around the world. She was widely recognized for her work, but for Carla, it was over. An emptiness had taken hold of her.

It's not a lack of self-confidence, it's a lack of insight

Like Carla, many people get stuck at some point in their lives. The difference between Carla (and you, perhaps) is that she'd already tried many things, going from one thing to the next on the waves of trial and error, disappointments, and interests she thought she would never lose, but that kept on fading. While there can be many obstacles why people get stuck (as I'm sure you know by now), in the case of Carla and many creative and entrepreneurial souls like her, there are two main reasons: they've had to start a professional life with too many interests or possibilities without knowing how to make them work together, or they realized after being professionally active for a while that what they chose (or were pressured into choosing) was not the right choice after all.

In both cases, a lack of self-confidence is keeping them stuck. If you've been told time and time again, "What?! You're starting something new? But you haven't even finished the other thing yet!" Or if you're stuck in a nine-to-five job that your parents are proud of but that brings on jealousy and frustration every time you hear your friends talk about what they do, know this: you're not alone.

Perhaps a voice in your head keeps reminding you how little focus you have. A voice that's also invariably ready to offer all possible counterarguments every time you've found some clarity about what to do next with your life.

I'm familiar with this voice, and if you're a creative, an entrepreneur, or a generalist, you probably are too.

The root of this is by no means a lack of self-confidence but a lack of insight into how you're put together and how your creative brain works. The problem is that as long as we think we're a duck and act like one, we deny our own needs and fail to see the beauty of being a swan.

Breaking the promises you make to yourself

We all have good intentions that turn into promises to ourselves, and although they sound different for everyone, most of them have something in common: we rarely keep them!

"In the morning, I'll start planning better and things will finally work out."

"If I try a little longer, maybe I'll like my job."

"I'll start tomorrow."

What do we do when tomorrow comes? Nothing. We eat chips on the couch while watching Netflix, scrolling through TikTok or Instagram. Without much effort, we quickly break a promise we made to ourselves, only to make the same promise to ourselves again later in the day or further into the week when we suddenly remember all that we want to accomplish and the dreams we want to achieve.

When you get into a cycle of promising yourself you'll do something and then failing to make good on that promise, you lose trust in yourself.

Creative generalists – but this applies to anyone with many ideas – often have a long list of things they want to do. Looking at mine, here are some of the things I'm currently working on or can't wait to get started with: creating a "Get Unstuck" coaching certification, getting a new consulting business off the ground,[36] outlining my next book, drawing, studying philosophy and neuroscience, genealogy research, volunteering, launching a new start-up (so exciting!) to help diverse and underrepresented talents find meaningful work,[37] painting kids' faces just for fun, screen-printing my own t-shirt line, creating a new online program and so much more.

There was a time, ten to fifteen years ago, when I had plenty of those dreams too. I would think about everything I wanted to do every day; I would tell myself that I'd "start tomorrow," but when the morning came, I wouldn't act on any of my goals. By the time I realized I was stuck in a never-ending cycle of procrastination, I'd been doing it for years. Years! It was hard to accept that I'd been dreaming about all those passions and interests but never did anything with them. That's when I unconsciously decided to make *getting people unstuck* my life's mission. I'd wasted so much time thinking about things instead of doing something about it that I wanted to save others from having to endure the same pain and suffering.

What I know now is that there is a way out of procrastination, out of feeling lost, out of being stuck, and despairing that it will always be the case. I experienced it in my own life, and I see it daily in my coaching practice.

A broken promise is broken trust

When we're stuck, what keeps us where we are more than anything else is doubt. And that's perfectly understandable: who wouldn't start to doubt their abilities when you've tried things so many times but never really found what feels right? Or when you've told yourself you were *finally* going to do something about your situation but continue to procrastinate or do busy work instead of focusing on what could push you forward. It seems harmless to tell ourselves something one day and then not see it through the next.

After all, we've learned to keep our promises to others, but we've never been told the same is true for what we promise ourselves.

The problem with this habit is that you undermine your self-confidence every time you make a promise to yourself and then break it.

Imagine that a friend has already promised to drive you to the doctor three times, but each time she comes up with an excuse as to why she can't at the last minute. Now she offers to take you for the fourth time. What does your gut feeling tell you? Do you still believe her? Or have you made other arrangements? Are you starting to doubt whether you will ever get to the doctor with her? Or do you book a taxi?

Although we often don't realize it, the same is true when we promise ourselves things we don't do. If you tell yourself every night that you'll go for a run at 7 am the next tomorrow, and then you just snooze your way out of it, or if you put self-care on your calendar but then skip it as soon as someone else needs something from you, you're breaking promises to yourself – and putting yourself last in your life!

There's absolutely nothing wrong with changing your mind, choosing a different path, or getting tired of something. It's also fine to go all-in for a job that you think is perfect for you and then realize after a few months that you're bored or made a mistake (it's called shift shock, and it's perfectly normal!).[38] The problem lies in what you say to yourself in the meantime. A broken promise to yourself is broken confidence that you'll do what you say you'll do. In turn, this leads to you not really trusting yourself anymore, eventually undermining your belief in your ability to make your dreams come true.

My advice is to be very careful and scarce with what you promise yourself. Only promise yourself what you know you'll actually do, and when you do make a promise to yourself, keep it at all costs! Promises to yourself deserve the highest priority!

#3 Impostor Syndrome

Maya Angelou, famous American poet, activist, and author, once said, "I have written eleven books, but each time I think, Uh-oh, they're going to find out now. I've run a game on everybody, and they're going to find me out."[39]

Impostor Syndrome is real and a burden for many creatives and entrepreneurs. At its core, it's about not being able to internalize your accomplishments; whatever you achieve, whatever your successes, you simply don't allow yourself to see or feel it. Why is it so hard for so many of us to accept that we're good at something? To appreciate our successes? To believe that we are capable?

The answer is complex, but for many people, it's rooted in the need to be accepted by others. Not feeling good enough as we are is part of this; we compare ourselves to those around us and feel like we're constantly falling short. We don't realize that we're only seeing a curated version of everyone's life. We hardly ever see the struggles, fears, and insecurities of others, so we feel even more like impostors when we see other people's successes. We constantly strive to meet certain expectations of what success should look like or feel like, and if we don't fit that idealized version of success, we conclude that we suck.

Another thing that I heard about impostor syndrome recently comes from Shahroo Izadi. In an interview with Steven Bartlett, the host of the podcast *Diary of a CEO*,[40] she had two interesting ideas about where impostor syndrome and not being able to internalize your accomplishments come from.

The first one is shame and guilt (how surprising!). Shahroo is an anti-diet advocate and someone who has overcome an eating disorder and works with people suffering from addictions. People with mental illness, addiction, or an eating disorder, have a lot of shame and guilt about their behavior. Because of this, it's difficult for them to acknowledge their professional accomplishments because many feel ashamed about so many other things that they won't allow themselves to internalize their capacities.

Real impostors don't feel like impostors

We all have things we're ashamed of and feel guilty about. These can be small things – something we do, how we think about ourselves, how we talk to ourselves, and what makes us feel guilty when nobody else is around. The promises we don't keep. It could also be trauma, things we've done and now regret, mistakes we made in the past. We carry these secrets with us, and sometimes even if on a superficial level we've achieved a lot, and everything looks great, inside, it's hard for us to accept our successes. Just remember that real impostors don't feel like impostors. It doesn't mean they're perfect or have no secrets, only that they're not affected by them like genuine people are.

The second thing I got from Shahroo Izadi's interview is a trick she shared. She said that when you give yourself permission to find what is difficult for you, difficult – even if it's super easy for other people, something extraordinary happens: it tends to have a significant impact on your impostor syndrome. She said to find something difficult that others find a no-brainer, accept that it was hard for you to do, and feel proud about it.

There's a lot of truth to this. In my own life, I've worked hard to become better at things and to accept my creative generalist nature in a world of specialists. Using my own measuring tape for what is hard for me –

irrespective of what is hard for someone else – has made me feel prouder and less like an impostor over time. It's a process; success is clearly not the cure for impostor syndrome, but using your own version of it will help.

I used to compare my academic successes to that of others, friends and partners mostly. I know I'm not alone in this. Many generalists suffer from what I call the *degree collection trap*. We believe that if we *finally* get the degree or certificate, we'll *at last* measure up to specialists and stop feeling like a fraud. I would define my capabilities, knowledge, intelligence, and my worth based on the degrees I had earned compared to those of other people. Because of the unconventional career path I've been on my entire life, I would also, systematically, compare myself (and feel like an impostor) to the job titles of my specialist friends who were moving up the corporate ranks. Every so often, I would go online and spend an evening researching college degrees, certain that this time I would go back to school or I would get lost in the vortex of online job boards looking for positions that could match those of my friends.

I know better now, but at the time I thought that my different way of building my career and how I wanted to live my life (not sitting in a golden cage waiting to be set free at retirement), was a failure on my part. For most of my life, I thought that anything someone else was, and I had trouble being, was a flaw in me. I had to work hard to break that thought pattern and recognize that many things come easy for some people but not for others. In my case, with all my interests and passions pulling at me from a young age, climbing the same corporate ladder for many years was hard. There was just too much I was interested in and wanted to learn! Admitting this to myself was difficult, but such a relief. When looking at specialists and their career paths, I was comparing cupcakes with jelly beans. But I didn't see it that way; I could only see what I couldn't do or the choices I couldn't make, not what I had built for myself.

There are no fixed success or achievement standards – it's whatever works for you. It can be brave to accept what is difficult for us and give ourselves credit for the effort we put into doing it despite our fear or anxiety. It can also be so liberating and fun to decide not to do it. This can make a huge difference in how we see ourselves and conquer impostor syndrome.

The things we tell ourselves shape what we believe is possible

We addressed what we say to ourselves in Step Two when we talked about mindset. What we're going to look at now is a deeper layer and understanding of how the things we tell ourselves influence our behavior and keep us stuck.

The more negative self-talk you have and the more you care about what others think of you, the smaller your vision of what is possible for you. In this step of the process, that's what we want to focus on: your vision for your life.

To get started, here's an exercise that will help you take stock of the limits you place on what is possible for you.

Prompt: The limits you place on yourself

First, find a quiet place and make yourself comfortable. Take pen and paper if you like. Once you feel centered and calm, answer the following questions:

- Have you ever felt like you didn't belong? When did it start? What beliefs did it create in you? Are those beliefs still influencing your life? If so, how?
- Do you feel shame and guilt at times? Are these feelings holding you back from doing things you want to do? In your personal, professional life, or both?
- Think about keeping promises to yourself; what comes to mind? Do you sometimes break promises to yourself? How could you deal with what you promise yourself in the future? How might that impact or change your life?
- Do you sometimes feel like an impostor? Do you have a strong urge to prove yourself? When do you feel like an impostor the most? And what exactly do you want to prove? To whom?
- When you think about what you want, what's the voice in your head telling you? How is what that voice says impacting your vision? Is that voice keeping you small or helping you grow?
- What would you do if you allowed yourself to dream? If you felt okay with being unconventional or different. Who would you be? What would you change about your life?

What's holding you back? What's keeping you stuck? Be honest with yourself, nobody's watching. It's just you, so be brave and give yourself the gift of absolute truth.

Stop bullying yourself

While researching this book, I rewatched Sean Stephenson's TEDx talk "The prison of your mind," given at the Ironwood State Prison (California, USA) in 2014.[41] Although I've seen it numerous times since, every time I do, I get something new out of it. Sean Stephenson was one of my favorite and most inspiring American motivational speakers. He was also a therapist and self-help author. Sean Stephenson passed away in 2019 after living a full and courageous life with osteogenesis imperfecta (also known as brittle bone disease). This genetic disorder caused his bones to break easily. Although he was only three feet tall, experienced numerous bone fractures throughout his life, and used a wheelchair, Sean was a bright, funny, energetic, vibrant, and ambitious person who decided early on that his life wasn't going to be defined by his condition, something he achieved without a doubt.

In the talk, Sean explains how much of our suffering happens in our minds. He says to "never believe a prediction that doesn't empower you." He means that you should never mold yourself into what others think of you or tell you about yourself. But there's more. Besides these outside voices that keep us small and not living up to our full potential, the inner chatter goes on in our heads. The worst, he says, is not what others tell us about ourselves but what we say about ourselves *to* ourselves every day. He calls this *bullying* and says we must *stop bullying ourselves*. I agree with him. Just because your inner voice tells you something doesn't make it true.

Many of our negative feelings result from our upbringing. Much of how we see ourselves is based on what others have told us repeatedly to be true about who we are. That's why I'd like to share with you some interesting philosophical concepts and theories to help you look at yourself differently. Because the biggest hurdle isn't what others say about us or what we're internalizing to be true about ourselves but the fact that we cannot see past that point.

Chapter Three: Disruptive Strategies.

"You are always one decision away from a completely different life."
– Mel Robbins

Disruption has been winning terrain for a while in business and technology. Especially since the rise of Silicon Valley startup giants and the technological revolution of the last decade, "being disruptive" has become a buzzword that sells or, in the case that you're the disruptor, can potentially make you a lot of money. But that's the more visible macroeconomic aspect. Below the surface is where it really gets exciting.

Disruption isn't a new concept. Even the Ancient Greeks, Socrates in particular, practiced the art of disruption. The Socratic Method, a form of cooperative argumentative dialogue between individuals, based on asking and answering questions to stimulate critical thinking and to draw out ideas and underlying presuppositions,[42] is a disruptive strategy. From the Socrates Method, the Socratic Dialogue is the most popular form. In such a dialogue, participants choose a question. Following a loose structure, they then try to find out if what they believe about the question is true and the value that that truth holds. The investigation is based on past personal experience or the experience they can have or imagine during the dialogue. Each participant tries to understand the viewpoint of the other participants without necessarily aiming at a consensus. In many cases, a Socratic Dialogue will be successful when exposing the complexity of the question being asked rather than answering it, which often results in new understanding for the participants. That new understanding is the result of the disruption caused by this method.

Plato, Socrates' student and advocate, and one of the most famous Greek philosophers, continued the use of the Socratic Dialogue in his work and writings. His "Platonic Dialogues" gives a stage to Socrates, who often begins by claiming ignorance (aporia) about the subject matter being discussed. The dialogues often have the name of the person being questioned by Socrates. Socrates asks questions to look at the problem from all angles. This form of questioning is also known as "dialectic reasoning," a part of logic in philosophy that focuses on subjects that aren't necessarily certain but where one aims for the highest possible degree of probability.

In my opinion, the most exciting and intriguing part of the Socratic Dialogue is that, while you're asking questions and engaging with other participants to understand the topic, eventually, you come to a place where you can experience what it is you're looking at in the present moment through the discussion. In *Latches*[43] for instance, one of Plato's Dialogues, the participants are trying to figure out "What is courage?" In their questioning, there comes the point where they conclude that they cannot answer the question without considering how courageous it is to ask the question in the first place.

Socrates: And now, Latches, do you try and tell me in like manner, "What is that common quality which is called courage, and which includes all the various uses of the term when applied both to pleasure and pain, and in all the cases to which I was just now referring?"

Latches: I should say that courage is a sort of endurance of the soul, if I am to speak of the universal nature which pervades them all.

Socrates: But that is what we must do if we are to answer the question. And yet I cannot say that every kind of endurance is, in my opinion, to be deemed courage. Hear my reason: I am sure, Laches, that you would consider courage to be a very noble quality.

Latches: Most noble, certainly.

The Socratic Dialogue doesn't simply aim to answer questions about the world; it also – and perhaps even more so – wants to get the participants to look inward and learn more about themselves. Therefore, the effect of the questioning is that participants gain more self-knowledge while investigating concepts seemingly external to them. Socrates wasn't just a philosopher; as it turns out, he was one of the first life coaches!

It's only true as long as it isn't false

Back to modern-day disruption. Take science and the falsification theory, which I was introduced to in my first year of university as a philosophy student and has stayed with me ever since.
The "Falsification Principle," proposed by Karl Popper, an Austrian-British philosopher, academic and social commentator,[44] is built on the belief that all scientific knowledge is provisional – it's the best we can do at any given moment. The idea behind it is that something might be true right now, but that doesn't mean it couldn't be debunked later when we've acquired new insights or knowledge. It might not sound like much but believe me; it's world-changing! Before Karl Popper, scientific research mostly attempted to support theoretical hypotheses: you thought something was true and did some experiments to prove it. Popper proposed to attempt to disprove a theory – falsify it – rather than continually trying to find confirmation of its truth.

According to the falsification principle, only falsifiable hypotheses can be regarded as scientific precisely because you can test them and prove them false. This means that for a theory, proposition, statement, or hypothesis to be considered scientific, it must have the capacity to be proven wrong. This is called "falsifiability." Proving it wrong requires testing, hence why falsifiability and testability are sometimes used interchangeably or considered synonyms. A famous example of a falsifiable theory is "all swans are white." Observing a black swan can falsify this statement (or a duck that thinks it's a swan).

Non-falsifiable theories, because it's impossible to prove them false (either because of technological limitations or because of subjectivity), can't be considered scientific. An example is, "Cookies are always better than ice cream." Because of the subjective nature of that statement, it can never be proven false.

A theory is or isn't scientific based on its capacity to be proven wrong, not because it has been proven right. This has a significant and shocking effect: it's never possible to prove that a hypothesis is true! Anything we believe to be true (according to the scientific method) always has the potential to be falsified. I know, mind-blowing. It gets better!

Wisdom and its development

Science is about what we believe to be true (for now). But how does one gather wisdom? How do we understand more about life, the world, and our place in it in a helpful way that moves us forward and gets us unstuck? According to Igor Grossmann, associate professor at the University of Waterloo (Canada) and researcher in the fields of Wisdom, Experimental Philosophy, and Cultural change, disruptive strategies are relevant for bringing about wisdom.

In an article in European Psychologist[45] Grossmann advocates for a constructivist (vs. essentialist) model of wisdom. "From the constructivist perspective," he states, "wisdom is neither an innate property of the mind nor is it passively transmitted to individuals through experience. A constructivist account suggests that wisdom and wisdom-oriented learning are grounded in a socio-cultural context. Expression of wisdom in reasoning varies across situational and cultural contexts, which have the power to sustain or inhibit it."[46] What Grossmann means is that wisdom is something organic that is developed through social and cultural influences, shaped by the people and the world around you, not something that you're born with.

Why is this important? How can it help you get unstuck?

For one, I believe we should look to philosophy more often to help us understand the problems we face. Thinking about those problems and trying to come up with theories about what living a good life means and how to live it is something philosophers have been doing for more than two thousand years! But that's not all. It's essential, especially in this third step of the MOVE method, to get a broader perspective on how you integrate knowledge and experiences into wisdom.

After my parents' passing in 2010, while I was clearing out the home I grew up in, I stumbled upon a stack of books my mother had kept, still wrapped in plastic. These were self-help books, focused on living one's true life and pursuing one's most authentic dreams. The one that struck me most was by Wayne Dyer called *Your Erroneous Zones: Escape negative thinking and take control of your life*. Holding that book in my hands I cried tears I'd never cried before. For the loss of my parents, of course, but also for the lives they had failed to live.

Finding those books made me sad as I realized my mother had never pursued her aspirations; instead, she had served her family and always put everyone else first. This sparked a profound shift in my perspective. I believe that it was the first step that eventually led me to the life I'm currently living.

My mother's unfulfilled dreams haunted me so much that they helped (forced) me, after a long period of grief and self-reflection, to embark on a transformative journey of self-discovery. As I've shared before, this meant breaking free from societal expectations and personal limitations; I began to explore my creativity and passions, what I was truly made of, in search of what I really wanted. Writing, teaching, learning, exploring, helping others, and being brave became my guiding principles. That stack of books made me realize my mother had the same dreams I had but never acted on them. It confronted me with the fact that – even though I thought I was *so different* from her – I was on my way to becoming just like her and saying no to my dreams. Understanding this shifted my perspective dramatically.

When thinking about creating a new vision for your life and work, it's important to realize that you might have been looking at the problem in the same narrow way and from the same tiny angle for a long time. Thinking about it more this way isn't going to help, and it certainly isn't going to produce new and powerful insights. To get unstuck, you must step outside the limited perspective that you've been operating by.

To study the expression of wisdom in everyday life, Igor Grossmann and his colleagues synthesized aspects of cognition in a "framework of wise thinking."[47] They include intellectual humility or recognizing the limits of one's knowledge, appreciation of perspectives broader than the issue at hand, sensitivity to change in social relations, and compromise or integration of different opinions. See the figure below for a schematic representation of this framework.[48]

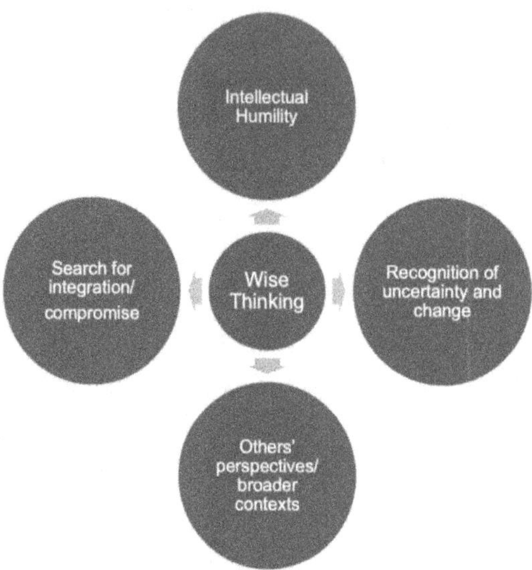

Schematic representation of Igor Grossmann's wisdom framework.
Grossmann, I. (2017) Wisdom and how to cultivate it: Review of emerging evidence for a
constructivist model of wise thinking: University of Waterloo.", p.8.

Wisdom seems to be cultivated through a mix of non-ego-driven and, therefore, potentially challenging mental and emotional traits and characteristics. Being open to other people's perspectives, accepting change and uncertainty, being humble in what you believe to be true, and actively aiming at finding common ground. Those are the traits that lead to wisdom (and great leadership, as we'll explore more a bit later in this book).

Creative insights and the Eureka Factor

In their book *The Eureka Factor*,[49] John Kounios and Mark Beeman explore when and how we experience creative insights and aha moments. Most eureka moments, they say, come when we're relaxed, in a fuzzy state of thinking, and doing things that don't require much brain work.

What's interesting about aha moments is that they include a moment of feeling stuck right before the insight strikes. If we look at the characteristics of these types of insights, we see they follow a pattern. It feels like the solution appears suddenly, there's a strong emotional response, and it's almost immediately perceived as the right solution. When creativity strikes, you might not have thought about the problem at all; it just came to you while you were doing the laundry, walking your dog, or relaxing. This is also one of the reasons why people often can't explain how they solved the problem.

To have eureka moments about a subject, you need to have a deep level of knowledge about it. I'm not a marine biologist, so without years of intense study into the topic, the chances of me getting creative insight into a problem about the communication skills of orcas or the natural GPS of turtles are almost nonexistent. You need immersion and practice to gain the necessary knowledge to have those moments. However, you don't need to focus on a particular question or problem. So, for a marine biologist wanting to crack the orca communication nut, it's unnecessary to have sleepless nights over it. Sometimes, the insights strike about problems you didn't even know existed. All it takes is to be surrounded for long enough by relevant information about the subject. Creative insights can be spontaneous; that's what's so cool about our brains; they work in the background while we're doing other things. It's why aha moments appear when we've not engaged analytically with a problem, when the workload for our brain is light, and we're in a state of calm or flow.

If you're trying to solve a problem in your life or career, if you feel stuck about something and have been contemplating your options for a while, chances are you're enough of an expert about the subject to have eureka moments. But to achieve those moments, it pays to stop thinking about the problem and let your brain step up and do what it does best: solve the problem for you.

Here are a few tips that can help spark more aha moments in your life:

- **Do your creative work when your brain is still waking up or when it's a little misty.**
  Don't try to be your most creative self right after you've spent time thinking about an analytical problem or when you're reaching peak focus time. I do my best writing in the morning, about thirty minutes to an hour after I've woken up. My brain is not working at total capacity yet, which is what I need for ideas to come more easily.

- **A positive mood enhances creativity.**
  The more relaxed you are, the more creative you'll be. You become more analytical when you're anxious, stressed out, and working around the clock to reach a deadline. It's not impossible to think creatively under those circumstances, but it's harder. When I'm fretting or feeling anxious over something or procrastinating on a task with a fast-approaching deadline, I can't write or do creative work. My brain is so focused on what I should be doing or what I'm stressing about that there doesn't seem to be any space left for creative thoughts.

- **Creative thinking is expansive, so it thrives better in expansive environments.**
  We need space to think. You won't get your best creative ideas in a broom closet! Aha moments ask for high ceilings, vast landscapes, skies filled with passing clouds, and disembodied experiences. When your visual attention or bodily sensations expand, your conceptual attention follows. I have my best ideas when walking in nature, on a massage table, or in the shower.

- **Take breaks, do something else for a while, let it go.**
  When faced with a problem that doesn't seem like it wants to be solved, there's a point where thinking about it has no point anymore. This is the moment when a lot of clients come to me. This is also where the *forgetting fixation theory*[50] comes in. This theory, also known as the set-breaking theory, gives procrastination a new perspective as it goes against most problem-solving approaches. Instead of encouraging a problem solver to continue to focus on a problem until there's a breakthrough, the problem solver is encouraged to stop doing the thing altogether. It's counter-intuitive and takes some practice, believe me, but taking a break from unproductive work is one of the most liberating things you can do. And guess what? It's often then that clarity strikes!

- **To have better creative ideas your brain needs to be rested and fresh.**
  To achieve this, you need decent sleep. Neuroscience has proven that the brain recharges itself when we sleep.[51] It goes through the day's events and organizes them. While the brain is consolidating its memory like that, it also gets rid of the toxic waste byproducts from its activity throughout the day. When I lack sleep, I lack creativity. It's that simple. Writing is hard when I wake up after a short night. The ideas won't come, and time passes much slower. I'm in a brain fog. When I get a good night's sleep, I often wake up with new ideas or concepts. The things I've been thinking about before bed that I had to „sleep on" tend to make sense in the morning. That's a result of the reorganizing and consolidating power of the brain. While sleeping, my brain archives and labels the events of the day to draw interesting, creative, or logical conclusions in the morning. If you have trouble sleeping, let this be your sign to not wait and do something about it.

What about intuition?

Intuition, it's said, is a form of knowledge. This elusive sense has something in common with aha experiences or eureka moments; just like when the answer to a seemingly unsolvable problem strikes, intuition is a stroke of insight in the moment. This "gut feeling" or sixth sense, as it's often referred to, is the ability to gain immediate understanding about something without consciously thinking about it. You just "know."

As with aha moments, when you're distracted by thinking, your mind cannot be intuitive. It doesn't mean we can only be intuitive when we're relaxed. Intuition also appears when we're sensing impending danger or an exciting opportunity. But it won't show up when we're breaking our heads over a complex problem.

Intuition and eureka moments are both parts of a spectrum, where intuition comes as a knowing beforehand. The eureka moment is the confirmation of that knowledge with a straightforward solution to a problem. "I sense there's something more here" is your intuition talking to you, while "see, I told you there was something" is your aha moment celebrating finding what "it" is.

In the Western world, scientific fact and knowledge take precedence over intuition and eureka moments, even though many scientific breakthroughs would not have happened without the latter two. Take Albert Einstein for instance, who believed there was a link between the intuitive mind and the rational one. According to Bob Samples, Einstein "viewed the intuitive mind as a sacred gift and the rational mind as a faithful servant, but we've created a society that honors the servant and has forgotten about the gift." [52] Whenever you step into your car or use the maps app on your smartphone, you engage with the legacy of Einstein's intuitive and groundbreaking discoveries.

Many years ago, when I first enrolled in a coaching course,[53] my coaching buddy spoke to me about intuition and its importance to her. At that time, almost a decade ago, I was still in "robot" mode, not in tune with my body or what I wanted to do with my life. Living happened in my head; everything from the neck down was unknown territory. One time, when we chatted about the course and our goals, I remember telling her that I didn't think I had any intuition. "I'm not sure what intuition is," I said hesitantly, "I don't think I have it." She looked at me with compassion but also with a little bit of worry. For someone like her, who was skilled at listening to her intuition, what I was saying must have been mind-boggling. Today, it's mind-boggling to me too. I remember what it felt like only to use my mind and analytical thinking to try and solve every problem in my life. It was often painstaking and one of the reasons I was stuck in the first place.

Consciously trying to solve a significant life or work question by only using facts without tapping into the vast knowledge bank that is unconsciously available to you is like trying to climb Mount Everest with some Home Depot rope and a kitchen knife. When faced with a non-acute problem – you're not going to fall off a cliff if you don't immediately decide – tapping into your intuition requires a calm mind, room to breathe and think, and a bit of letting go – just as aha moments do.

Prompt: Tapping into your intuition to help you get unstuck

Make yourself comfortable. When you feel centered and calm, bring what you're stuck on into your mind. Stay focused on it for a little while and look at it from different perspectives:

- How long have you felt this way or thought about this?
- What have you tried in the past?
- What do you believe about this?

- Where/how do you feel stuck the most?
- What would success look like for this?

Feel into what this problem (question, decision, change you want to make, or anything else that's keeping you stuck) does with your body:

- Where in your body are you feeling the stuckness?
- What sensations are you experiencing when you're thinking about being stuck?
- What is happening to your heart rate, breathing, and skin?

Once you're in tune with your mind and body, close your eyes and let your intuition take over. Make sure not to analyze, question, or invalidate what comes up. That's how we're trained to let our analytical mind silence our intuition:

- What images and symbols come up? Let yourself dive into them fully.
- What concepts, ideas, and options feel right in your body?
- What do you feel, sense, hear, and perceive? Allow all of it.
- If you've been pondering a yes or no choice, what feels right in your body?

When you're thinking about what you could do to move forward, do you have an open or closed sensation in your body? Open is your intuition, a feeling of *I want to*, while closed is often fear, ego, or any other limits you place on yourself from the realm of *I have to*.[54]

The Solomon Effect

Let's go back to wisdom for a minute. One thing Grossmann says we get wrong about wisdom is that most of us think it's something that, when you possess it, you're able to apply it in any situation. You're either wise, or you aren't, something like that. According to him, wisdom doesn't work that way. It's the exact opposite: wisdom varies across situations.

Think about a problem that you're currently stuck on. Chances are this issue will involve other people, either directly (your decision affects others) or indirectly (your decision affects what you think others will think of you). However long it's been on your mind, I'm sure you've described the problem in your head, thought about it, and tried to come up with solutions. The question is: from what perspective have you done this?

When faced with a problem, we usually describe and look at it from our egocentric first-person viewpoint. We're not doing this on purpose; it's the way we're wired to look at the world. That first-person egocentric[55] perspective allowed us to make it as a species up until this point. Without it, our nervous system wouldn't have known when it was time to fight or flight. Evolutionarily, we're doing what we're built to do. Unfortunately, just like the fight or flight response now causes so many of us to feel stressed out and exhausted, fighting spreadsheets or a toxic boss as if we were still in the savanna chased by lions, our first-person perspective is often what keeps us stuck.

Grossmann calls this Solomon's paradox. King Solomon, also called Jedidiah, was, according to the Hebrew Bible and Christian Old Testament, a fabulously wealthy and wise monarch of the United Kingdom of Israel.[56] People came from far and wide to seek the king's council and wisdom. He was famous for being just and fair in his judgments and helping others come to the truth. Based on this description, I would be the first to seek his counsel if Solomon were alive today. Wouldn't you? But that's only one side of

Solomon's story. According to the biblical account, Solomon had 700 wives and 300 concubines.[57] He didn't just love collecting wives; he loved amassing wealth too. But after Solomon's death, his son ruled as a tyrant. How ironic. Even though he was such a wise king, he failed to teach his son to follow in his footsteps.

The wisdom he showed for non-personal matters didn't seem to exist in King Solomon's private life. Was it just him, or is there more going on?

Taking our own medicine

An example Grossmann gives is a set of studies where people, all in long-term romantic relationships, were asked to think about situations concerning their partner (their *self-centered condition* in the experiment) or comparable situations concerning their friend's partner (called their *non-self-centered condition*).[58] Imagine the following scenario. Your partner admitted being unfaithful. You've been in a serious relationship for 7 years, and now you suddenly learn your partner is no longer happy and has been having an emotional affair with another person. Now think of this scenario. It's not your partner, but your best friend's partner who admitted to being unfaithful. Your best friend has been in a serious relationship for 7 years, and now they suddenly learn their partner is no longer happy in the relationship and has been having an emotional affair with another person.

In the studies, after participants were given these scenarios, they were asked to reflect on the future development of the relationship through questions related to wise thinking. Results show (not surprisingly) that participants could reason more wisely about situations involving friends rather than themselves. If you think about it, we all know this is true. We're good at offering sensible advice to others, but when it comes to taking our own medicine, most of us have difficulty swallowing the wisdom pill.

Let's get back to the problem you're currently stuck on. Instead of looking at it from the first person, the egocentric "I" perspective, re-describe the problem from the third person perspective. What happens? Most probably, now that you're breaking frame with the limited reality you're operating in (like we all are!), you realize there are many ways in which you could be addressing the problem that you haven't thought of before. Often when I ask clients to do this, they will have a new insight into how to solve the problem, like Sarah did below, when she stepped outside her perspective to think about what career shift she could make.

When I first met Sarah, she came into my office wearing a beautiful light blue summer dress with tiny pink and white flowers patterned on it. Sarah was a single mother of two, divorced only months earlier, and looking to go back to work after a break of six years being a stay-at-home mom. Lucy and Felix, Sarah's children, meant the world to her. She didn't regret making such a gap in her CV to stay home and care for her children, she told me during her first session, but now that she'd separated from her partner, she wanted to secure her financial future and that of her children. Before, Sarah would never have believed anyone who told her she would be a single mother. Now that it had become her reality, Sarah didn't think she could be a single mother and have a fulfilling career.

However hard they may be, breakups are an excellent example of how people (are forced to) break frame. I know because I've been through it. My divorce was hard because I was unprepared. More importantly, in the reality I had constructed for myself, there wasn't any room for the possibility of my partner and I ever separating. Even though that separation was the best thing that ever happened to me, my initial – and natural – reaction was to try and keep the frame together.

Without a complex mix of internal and external forces tearing through our constructed reality, most of us would rather hang on to that construct than endure the pain of seeing our reality morph into something else. People often talk about their life *falling apart* when this happens because that's what it feels like. Change, especially the one you're not controlling, causes pain and suffering. But, after thousands of hours helping people get unstuck, I've concluded that the anticipation of change is often worse than the change itself. This, more than anything, is why we're blind to the other realities we could be living. It's a systematic error: we look at the problem from our small and limited perspective.

When I asked Sarah about the career paths or types of jobs she'd been interested in, she told me that she had always wanted to be an air traffic controller. "But," she immediately added, "I could never do that." Before I had a chance to ask her why she gave me ten reasons why it didn't belong in her reality, from being too old, not being good at math, to being afraid of not fitting in. She said, "Some things just aren't meant to be, even when you want them badly."

For Sarah to see a path toward what she wanted, she needed to step out of her one-person perspective and take an outside look at her reality. "What if your best friend said this about her situation to you," I asked her, "or one of your children?" Sarah looked at me pensively. It didn't take long before she answered, "Well, I would tell them to go for it and that the excuses they put forth are just obstacles they have to overcome, not blocks they can't move past." I looked at Sarah with a slight smile on my face. As a coach, I try to remain neutral in all situations, but sometimes I'm just so happy and proud of my clients. When that happens, a smile might escape; oops! Sarah didn't notice; she was deep in thought. After a moment, she added: "You know, when I think about it, I always say I can't do something before trying, especially when it's important to me. I've talked myself out of many fun and interesting things throughout my life. If my kids did the same, that would make me very sad. I truly believe they should chase their dreams." I agree with Sarah.

We cannot think ourselves into a new career or life; eventually, we must go out and do it. To *go out and do it*, you often need to look at things differently, let go of what you think is going to happen or what you believe, and take on a new perspective.

If you stay in the tunnel of stuckness, chances are, even if you try, you won't find the exit because you'll only notice closed doors. This is called *confirmation bias*,[59] a natural tendency to look for confirmation of what we already believe. More about that shortly. First, let's identify how you talk yourself out of your dreams.

Prompt: How do you talk yourself out of your dreams?

This is an important question, especially if you've felt stuck for a while. In Step Two, I asked you to think about the beliefs that keep you stuck. This exercise builds on that. Feel free to revisit that exercise before moving forward with this one.

When you're ready, take a deep breath and think of how stuck you feel right now. Picture what or who you believe is not allowing you to move forward. When you have that picture, go through the statements below. For each, ask yourself if you've ever had or currently have comparable thoughts or feelings regarding your situation. Be specific.

- If this happened to someone else, I would know what they should do, and I would tell them! But when it comes to me, I simply don't know what to do.
- I've tried everything. I've also thought about everything. But whatever I try or think, nothing ever gets me unstuck. I've been feeling like this forever.

- There's so much I could do; the problem is, I don't know what to do precisely. From all the options that I have, what is the project I should pick?
- I have no choice. I've tried to get out of this situation, but there's just nothing I can do about it.
- Everyone I meet wants to help me with advice. The problem is, that advice might work for them, but it certainly won't work for me.
- What if I make the wrong decision? I know what I have now but not what I'll get. Whenever I think about doing something, I get scared I will end up in a gutter somewhere.
- Everything looks too big. It's so overwhelming that I feel completely paralyzed and don't know where to start. I want to do something, but I just don't know what.

Take note of the statements that sound familiar to you. If these or similar ones pop up in your mind regularly, you might be suffering from a mix of confirmation bias (see below) and the opportunity blindness we talked about in Step Two. It's not that you don't have options to choose from; you're just not seeing them. Let's fix that, shall we?

Chapter Four: Confirmation Bias and Motivated Reasoning.

"Confirmation bias is twisting the facts to fit your beliefs. Critical thinking is bending your beliefs to fit the facts."
– Adam Grant

We're back to seeing red cars. As we've seen before, thinking about them "magically" makes them appear. As I hope you're starting to understand, our reality is not an accurate representation of the "reality" of the world as it truly is. Our senses filter the world we create in our awareness; it's selective, subject to change, malleable, and often (if not always) biased. This phenomenon is part of what is called "confirmation bias" and "motivational reasoning."

We all have confirmation bias. It's a natural, unconscious tendency to interpret and look for information in ways that confirm what we already believe. Like confirmation bias, motivated reasoning[60] means actively looking for why we're right and rejecting facts and research that don't fit our beliefs. These two psychological mechanisms are one of the reasons why fake news easily convinces us or why we must be wary of the dangers of AI algorithms on social media. They entangle us into vortexes of similar bits of information that may confirm what we believe but might be entirely false nonetheless.

A great example is football games (or any other group activity or game you like that involves a level of competition). Depending on the team you're rooting for, you'll see more fouls committed by the other team than yours – guaranteed. You'll also be more likely to let some apparent mistakes from your team slide and might even come up with a rational explanation as to why it wasn't a mistake (of course it wasn't, it's the Yankees!). You're not doing this out of malice or because you lack fair play or integrity. It happens because you're a very complex human being affected by many things, including your desires and motivation when processing visual information.

My Wife and My Mother-in-Law

Another example is visual illusions. Maybe you've seen the popular clips on social media or YouTube. Someone shows you an ambiguous drawing and asks you what you see. Depending on what you're seeing, the person in the video will share something about your character or beliefs. Oddly enough, they're often right. Take this famous drawing from 1915 by American cartoonist William Ely Hill.[61] It was first published in *Puck,* an American humor magazine, with the caption, "They are both in this picture – find them." Although there are earlier versions of this illustration, the one by William Ely Hill is the most famous because it was later introduced to psychologists and has since been the subject of many studies.

My wife and my mother-in-law, William Ely Hill, 1915.

One such study from Flinders University in Adelaide,[62] South Australia, found that what you see in the picture determines how old you are. If you see a younger woman first, you're probably more youthful, while if you see an older woman, you're probably older. What did you see?

How do we make perceptual judgments?

It all starts with our eyes. But from there, the information we're gathering travels to our brains to be processed by the primary visual cortex. In this "translation," a hypercomplex clew of interpretation, recognition, and representation (based on everything our brain can do and the information stored in it) happens until we see or understand something. In that knot of neural pathways, there are things like the patterns we've learned to recognize and focus on, the experiences we've had that have taught us things about the world (oh, look, there's another lion, we'd better get going!) but also our desires and goals. Our brains' plasticity is constantly allowing us to mold our brain into a recognition machine, and that's a fantastic thing, but what it chews on – the input we give it – is what it is shaped by. The world we see isn't the world as it is; it is the world we have experienced. We have created a reality that is practical, not accurate. Or, to say it in the words of one of my favorite French writers and artists Anaïs Nin:[63] "We don't see the world as it is, we see it as we are."

Does objective reality exist?

This question has kept philosophers wondering since the beginning of time. Does objective reality exist, and can we interpret it correctly with our human senses? To physicists, objective – external – reality must continue to exist without any observer to witness it. But does an apple still taste like an apple if no one is there to taste it?

Today this problem is still debated in science and philosophy, but other disciplines, like neuroscience, are shedding some new light on the question: is reality an illusion?

Remember that scene in The Matrix when the guy gets bribed by the men in black with a juicy steak? While chewing on a big piece, he says: „I know this steak doesn't exist. When I put it in my mouth, I know that the Matrix is telling my brain that it is juicy and delicious. After nine years, you know what I realize? Ignorance is bliss."[64] I don't know whether we are in a simulation[65] or not but what I do know is that our brains are like the Matrix.

The idea of a constructed reality goes back to both Western and Eastern philosophical traditions, from Plato's "cave allegory" to Zhuang Zhou's "butterfly dream." More recently, even Elon Musk stated that: "The odds that we are in base reality is one in billions."[66] When we're eating a steak, a crunchy carrot, or an apple pie, the taste of what is in our mouth is not a property of the object in external reality; it is what our senses and our brain make of it. It's a subjective experience and perception. If not, we would all have the same taste, and everything would be the same for everyone. Think of cilantro. To me, it tastes like soap (thank you dominant genes!). To others, it's the most delicious seasoning in the world. We all know this to be true, but still, we insist that we have a grasp on reality in an objective way, separate from ourselves. We don't.

Tastes, smells, and colors, do they exist? Yes, but not in objective reality. You could say they are real to us; they are our *real* experiences. But they're not universally real. This truth has important implications. The world we interact with is real. However, the information and knowledge we gather from that world are subjective and don't represent reality as it is, but as we make it. Some philosophers, like Immanuel Kant, argued that objective reality exists but that we cannot know anything about it directly. If we're looking to get to the absolute truth of our world, we will fail since we only have our senses to help us get there.

There's something all around us, the thing we live in and are part of. It's just that we don't see it as it is. We can never see it as it is – at least not entirely. Our senses are limited, so the information passed through them can also only be limited. From an evolutionary perspective, our senses have been trained to process information in a way that will keep us alive, help us find food and shelter, and allow us to see what is meaningful to us – and dismiss much of the rest.

Someone who has never seen a whale or the sea will not know what they are looking at standing on a beach in front of a giant, stranded beluga. Not because the brain is deficient but because there never was an input of such sort. On the other hand, for someone with an interest in and love for whales, the chances of that person seeing whales in every rock formation in the sea or on the beach are much more significant.

When I was studying for my Master's in Philosophy, during a class about the nature of reality and quantum physics, our professor at the time shared a thought experiment that is so powerful that I go back to it whenever I start believing that my construct of reality is the only true reality there is. The story goes like this:

Imagine a two-dimensional being that only knows height and width but not depth. Tell that being to start walking the Earth in Antwerp and to not stop until it's back in town, at the exact spot where it left. When it's back, ask the being what it learned about the geometry of the Earth during its journey. "Well," the being might say, "I don't know, I just walked in a straight line and landed back where I started." Without the dimension of depth, this being cannot imagine the Earth to be round, so in its perception he just kept going straight ahead.

In a way, we are like this two-dimensional being. We construct reality based on our limited senses, and on what we know, want, and are afraid of. In short: we see what we can see – and mostly what we want to see. Our dreams, goals, fears, and desires influence not only our thinking, our emotions, and as a result, our behavior, but also – and much more than we want to believe – reality as we experience it. We would love to think that the reality we see is the true, objective reality because we want to be able to make judgment calls based on that truth. Unfortunately, that reality will always remain hidden from us. Just like our being will never know what a sphere or ball is. As Donald Hoffman[67] says, "We have to take our senses seriously, but that does not entitle us to take them literally."

Can we change or influence our reality?

If our senses and brain create reality, is it possible for us to change it? We can, and that is one of the critical pieces of insight I want you to take away from this chapter. If reality as we experience it is subjective, if it's only an approximation of absolute reality, it is prone to errors and can be improved! The subjective reality you're living in is a product of your senses and brain, experiences, past, sensitivities, and so on. Especially in interaction with other people or with things that matter to you, a lot can go wrong in the "interpretation phase."

Trauma survivors, for instance, often experience this unconscious misinterpretation. Daily, simple events can trigger emotional reactions that force their nervous systems into overdrive. The sensation they're experiencing is overwhelming, even though they might just be talking with a coworker by the water cooler. If you looked at this objectively, you would conclude there is no danger or reason to feel the way they do. Still, if their complex thoughts, memories, and deeply forged neural pathways firing off in the brain aren't altered, this is the reality of the trauma survivor.[68]

We must always be cautious with how we interpret the world. What we believe to be true might not be. If it is, it might still only be valid for ourselves.

Other perspectives also hold some truth. What this means is that the entirety of the world can't be filtered down to one viewpoint or experience. To get closer to the truth, you must be willing to entertain different perspectives and accept that together they – hopefully – form a better understanding of the world.[69]

Knowing that other people have different biographies, desires, and beliefs, and thus different perspectives about the world than we do, should help us get unstuck. If I'm looking at something and you're looking at something, and we're both seeing something different (which is often the case, just think about the difficulties the police encounter when trying to gather congruent witness accounts), what does that say about what I believe to be true? I can only ever hold "partial truth" about the world, and I can never achieve absolute truth.

Prompt: My perspective versus that of other people

Think about what you're stuck on and think back to the answers you gave in the previous exercise: *how you talk yourself out of your dreams.* Take a few moments to ground yourself, then answer the following:

- What is my perspective on being stuck?
- What is the view of someone that loves me that I've spoken to about this problem?
- What is the attitude of my family members?
- What would the perspective of someone I admire be on why I'm stuck?
- What would the perspective of my favorite high school teacher be?
- What would the view of my least favorite person in the world be?

Once you've answered the questions above, combine them into a broader and more encompassing perspective about your situation. Go back to the second prompt from Step One: *How stuck do you feel right now?* and review what you wrote.

- Is there anything that pops out?
- What is now true about why you're stuck that wasn't true (or visible to you) before?
- What new perspectives and/or opportunities have emerged?
- How can this help you get unstuck?

What about science?

Science, quantum physics, particularly, more and more points toward an independent reality that exists outside of our understanding, while at the same time gaining awareness of how our perception of that independent reality bends it into our subjective version of it. The most notable examples include the measurement problem[70] in quantum mechanics. This problem raises the question of whether reality exists before it is observed. Measurements are not independent of the observer, which goes entirely against the classic scientific method we addressed before, based on a hypothesis that must be confirmed through observation – in which humans or our consciousness play no influencing part. But that's not all. The world of quantum physics contains objects being in multiple places at once, communicating faster than light, or experiencing different timelines simultaneously that are somehow (magically?) connected. I know, it's amazing!

Disruptive science

In quantum sciences, a more disruptive approach to research is used. Instead of looking at old theories and trying to confirm them (remember the confirmation bias we talked about before), disruptive science introduces new methods and new and different questions, often adjusting old theories instead of merely confirming them. It's done by introducing disruption into the system because, guess what, like Albert Einstein said,[71] it's only by doing something else that you can arrive at a different result or conclusion!

A former partner, let's call him Liam, had the annoying habit of never putting on his seatbelt when driving. The German model car he had at the time didn't like that and started making a repetitive (and annoying) pinging sound as soon as he sat down and turned the engine on. It didn't seem to bother him. When I would say something about it or gently ask him to put his seatbelt on, I would invariably be met with a growling sound and rolling eyes while he reluctantly reached for the seatbelt and finally made the car shut up. This kept happening, no matter what I tried until one bright day we picked up his father to drive him to an event he needed to attend. I was sitting in the back of the car when Francis sat in the passenger seat next to his son. Unlike Liam, Francis immediately buckled himself up. In the meantime, the engine was on, and because Liam had not put his seatbelt on, the car had started to ping. As soon as the vehicle began to move, Francis said: "It's you," to which Liam, without saying a word nor looking at his father, with no complaints and no hesitation, put his seatbelt on! I couldn't believe that it could be so simple.

Everything I tried to get him to stop the car from pinging had failed. But what if I had finally found the answer? The next time Liam and I stepped into the car, I was eager to test my theory. As always, while we were exiting the parking spot, no seatbelt for Liam and a pinging vehicle for me. Then, with a bit of an anxious pitch but a lot of resolve in my voice, I said: "It's you." Without a peep or even looking at me, Liam put his seatbelt on – and that was that.

Disruption is important for science and for the advancement of technology. But what does disruption mean for you? How can you benefit from it to help you get unstuck?

One way is to introduce new options into a system, like with Liam and his seatbelt. I clearly needed a different approach. Francis was the one who introduced disruption into the system and gave me the solution I was looking for.

You can find an interesting example of this in the field of AI. The way AI "learns" is through improvement, a self-optimizing process. I remember an old AI test I saw in a documentary at least a decade ago where a computer was equipped with the "intelligence" to make out if a picture showed a man or a woman. The computer was shown random images and was programmed to tag each photo as male or female. The AI had a built-in feature to "learn" from its mistakes. At first, it was shown easy examples with classic differentiating pictures. The more it progressed, the more ambiguous the images became, showing a man with long hair or a woman with more masculine features (I apologize for the lack of gender neutrality in this example, it's from a different time). The AI made mistakes but then corrected. With each new picture and learning, it built an internal database of subtle differences on which it could depend moving forward. The computer needed randomization to be introduced into its artificial intelligence neural networks to learn. Without this noise, entropy, and randomness, there would be little to no learning, at least not outside the patterns of what is considered average and "normal" in the world. It looked like science-fiction at the time!

In artificial intelligence neural networks, you need this introduction of chaos to prevent the neural networks from overfitting the data or algorithmic bias.

Because AI doesn't possess our natural intuition and complex human nature, it can easily pick up on patterns too tightly in the sample given without giving any attention to the bigger context of the world. In other words: it can only learn from the data we feed it, and if it's given too much of the same thing, it's going to think the entire world is like that. Machine learning can and does often reinforce prejudices and biases. An example of this is the prejudicial errors made by the COMPAS[72] recidivism system in the US when deciding the likelihood of reoffending by former prison inmates. A study revealed that the AI system was twice as likely to incorrectly predict that a black person would reoffend as opposed to a white person.

But that's just one example. Discrimination and bias in artificial intelligence exist across all underrepresented groups. Take facial recognition technology again, not what AI did in the eighties, but what it's doing today. Studies have shown that facial recognition algorithms have higher error rates when identifying individuals with darker skin tones, particularly women. This bias can lead to discriminatory outcomes in various domains, such as law enforcement – again – where misidentifications based on race can have severe consequences.

Another area where bias and discrimination exist is in the hiring process. AI-powered systems that assist in candidate screening and selection may inadvertently perpetuate discriminatory practices. The algorithms can learn and reinforce those biases if the data used to train these systems reflect biased hiring decisions or if it's missing critical data about a large portion of the population which, unfortunately, is historically the case. This can result in adverse outcomes for marginalized groups, such as women, ethnic minorities, and people from economically underprivileged backgrounds. It's terrifying to imagine that the people who already face barriers to entry into the job market may encounter even more obstacles because of biased AI systems. As I mentioned before, helping to remediate this problem is one of the main reasons I'm currently working on an app to help underrepresented talent find meaningful (and well-paying!) work.

These examples highlight the importance of disruption on all levels, whether in your life and career or addressing and mitigating bias and discrimination in AI systems to ensure fairness and equity for all. Efforts such as diverse and inclusive data collection, careful algorithm design with an eye for internalized biases and discriminatory beliefs, and ongoing monitoring of the output of such systems can help minimize the negative impact of AI technology and promote more equitable outcomes across all domains.

Again, this is true for you as well. Be generous with the data you look at to decide what is right for you to do, identify and be weary of your limiting beliefs, and keep monitoring what you tell yourself and believe you are capable of. You too are biased and discriminatory towards yourself. The more you're aware of it, the smaller the impact this will have on you, opening you up to a world of possibilities.

Chapter Five: Correcting our Mental Biases: Disruptive Strategies.

"If there's something you really want to believe, that's what you should question the most."
– Penn Jillette

From the Solomon Effect, how wisdom is achieved, and the inherent flaws of our perceptual judgments, we know that humans tend to look at problems with a narrow, egocentric view, especially when the issues are about themselves.

In my coaching practice, many clients come in when they've been staring at a problem for a long time without finding a solution. They end up thinking in circles, getting stuck in thoughts or ideas about what they're facing instead of taking any action or stepping forward.

As I've mentioned in Step Two, real-life experiments are one of the things I love to have clients do. When I started designing these experiments a few years back, I used them on myself (yes, like the mad scientists from those action movies). The experiments intended to push me out of my comfort zone so I could reprogram my nervous system by going through new and different experiences.

The first I ever tried on myself was a "rejection experiment." For the longest time, with roots going back to a challenging childhood, I've been terrified of rejection. I became a people-pleaser and perfectionist at a young age and developed a very loud, scared, and anxious negative inner voice. Whomever I met and whatever I did, my focus was always to make sure they liked me. This is an untenable way of being. However challenging and dehumanizing, I managed to keep it up well into my adult life. I shared before that my parents passed away in 2010, and what a decisive moment it was for me. I was in my thirties, and it was only then that I started to question the self-harming and toxic way of being that I'd taken on for so long. If I'm honest,

I never was my authentic self with anyone at that time. I was so caught up in trying to be the person I thought everyone around me wanted, that I'd lost touch with who I was. When grief took over, there was no way to pretend anymore.

I was showing the world how I felt for the first time. I barely had enough life force to take care of myself; there just wasn't anything left for my brand-new husband or anyone else who'd been used to me being available to care for them. The result? I was forced into a gigantic experiment of another way of being. At first, I couldn't do anything, but as time went on and my grief became bearable, I didn't immediately return to my previous self. Somehow my unconscious had picked up on things, and so did my nervous system. I wasn't as nice or compliant as before. Through my bereavement, I was forced to take stock of how I'd treated myself until that point. I couldn't ignore my reality anymore. That's when the journey of transformation started for me, eventually leading to this moment, where I'm writing the words you're now reading.

This awakening was subtle at first, and much of the change went unnoticed (as it often does). I remember a moment when things started to shift. I was back at work full-time after a few months of trying to keep up with the demands of my business in the turmoil of grief. One of the people I worked with came up to me complaining about a project that had been slacking. There wasn't much wrong with the project; she just hadn't done the work she was supposed to do. Somehow, I'd always been a bit afraid of her. She reminded me of the bullies that I'd dealt with as a child. Whenever she was around – although she worked for me, it was my company, and I paid her! – I could feel my anxiety soar. But this time was different. When she tried to dump the responsibility for the work she hadn't done on me, I simply said no.

I remember the exact moment it happened because it almost felt like an out-of-body experience. It was as if I was looking in disbelief at myself while standing up to her. She probably had an out-of-body experience too because she looked at me, ready to say something but not a sound came out of her jaw-dropped mouth. "Ok, so that's settled then," I eventually said as I opened the door to my office to lead her out. I closed the door behind her and sat down at my desk. Adrenaline was rushing through my body into my fingertips, but this time it wasn't because of anxiety, fear, or stress. I'd used my voice, spoken up, and taken a stance – a pivotal moment.

When I started to notice changes in myself, especially around my fears, inner chatter, and anxiety, I wondered if I could take it further. I'd been forced to change because of the enormity of what had happened to me. But could I take control in some way and change even more? Facilitate the process somehow? Perhaps even change my mind about what was possible for me?

Introducing disruption to the "system" that is your life

My parents passing was the most disruptive event of my life. It was unexpected, extremely painful, and its effects are still rippling through my life today, although thankfully not as forcefully as they did before. If I could go back in time, I'd want my parents to still be with me today but by the same token, I would also like to go through this bereavement again. Maybe not exactly as it happened, but certainly with the same impact and result it had on me.

In a way, disruption is the thread that runs through this book. Now that you're nearing the end of Step Three, I hope you're starting to see how all the thoughts and strategies laid out here can help you get up from the nails you're sitting on. Either you wait until the pain is unbearable and you have no choice but to move or you get up now and do something about the pain before you reach that breaking point.

When we spoke of changing your mindset, what we were really saying was: disrupt your thoughts! Now you're ready to take it one step further. To get unstuck, changing your thoughts is important, but so is changing your actions and the way you've always done things.

I quoted Albert Einstein before, who (probably) said that insanity is doing the same thing over and over again and expecting a different result. Being stuck looks very much like insanity. You think about something you want and without leaving the comfort of your home, sitting quietly on the couch Netflix and chillin', you think yourself out of the idea for the millionth time. It always starts the same way, you dream about the wonderful life or career you could have, and it always ends with all the reasons why it will never work, or you shouldn't even try. You keep going at the problem with the same mental routine, the same inner chatter, the same thoughts and perspectives and, hey, what do you know? ... you always end up at the same conclusion: "I'd better not. It's a bad idea!"

When a client comes to me stuck in an overthinking loop like this, I know that my job is to help them see things from new perspectives. In fact, I want to argue that the main role of a coach is to help clients disrupt the mental, physical, and emotional systems that are in place in their lives. You can't make an omelet without breaking some eggs, just like you can't change your life without disrupting some of the (often invisible or unconscious) systems you live by. Believe me, we all have them. Life is a balancing act. We create order out of chaos. Our brain loves structure and will try to come up with some version of it for literally anything. Again, most of this is unconscious, so we often don't know we operate within these limits or that there's a way out of them. We simply accept them to be true.

Disruptive experiments

When I realized I had changed and discovered this new and fiercer voice inside of me, I wanted to know if I could somehow control the change process. It's not a great strategy to wait for a terrible thing to happen before your life can change. I needed to figure out how to do it on my own, how to get up from the nails I was sitting on as soon as they started to itch.

I've touched on experiments in Step Two. Let's explore them further now that you know how disruption can help you get unstuck. It allows you to see things from new perspectives so you can come to different conclusions. Experiments help you to assess problems or questions differently and keep you from falling into the dreaded overthinking loop. Finally, disruptive experiments help your brain make better, deeper connections and solve problems you would otherwise still be chewing on.

Consciousness is where you create your reality, and where you can alter it. For your life to change, your actions must change. To achieve this, first your thoughts must change, but your thoughts can only change if you have new ideas. That's why mindfulness and daily meditation, like the transcendental meditation I've been practicing for many years, are a form of disruption too. Training your brain to achieve calmer and more conscious mental states is a way to increase the variation of the processes you're activating in your brain: to create new and different thoughts. By improving your awareness and training your brain, you're introducing disruption into your mental system.

Shaking things up like that is good because you can get more awareness of what's invariant (what's fixed and unchangeable) in the systems that you live by. The more you vary what you're doing, the more you become aware of what's not changing. Take dating. When I was newly single after my divorce, a friend recommended I try dating apps. I was initially reluctant, but eventually, I gave it a try. My first dates were with copies of my ex; it felt like I wasn't getting anywhere. I wondered why I kept attracting the same kind of people until I realized I was the common denominator. I began changing my approach, and soon I found myself on much better dates. The disruption had shown me how to identify the invariant in my dating choices – me! – so that I could start making other choices.

When you start practicing disruption, you'll notice two kinds of invariants: good ones and bad ones.[73] The good ones will teach you a lot about the world: they're the underlying laws of nature, for instance, truths about how people interact with each other or insights about how your creative brain works. With experimentation, you'll start to pick up on more significant patterns that aren't changing and are real in the world, so you get a little closer to reality and what is happening around you and in your mind. The bad invariants happen when you stay stuck: you're introducing disruption into a system, but you're not getting free. You keep trying to solve a problem but fail to change the thing you need to solve it. Like your choice of dating candidates, or dots, like in the classic example described below.

The nine-dot problem

As John Vervaeke,[74] award-winning professor of psychology, cognitive science, and Buddhist psychology at the University of Toronto, explains in his inspiring online lectures, the nine-dot problem, also known as a "Gestalt-problem," is a well-known example of how pattern, convergent (non-disruptive, non-creative) thinking can keep you from solving a problem. The problem gained traction in the 1970s and the 1980s when psychology – particularly psychological experiments – became popular to a broader audience. It was so popular that I remember when I was about ten years old, my father took a piece of paper, drew the problem on it, and challenged me to solve it.

For this problem, participants are presented with nine dots arranged in a 3x3 grid. They are challenged to connect all nine dots without lifting their pen or pencil, without backtracking, using a maximum of four straight lines. My father was always adamant about this: "don't go back, and don't lift your pencil from the paper!" It made the pressure almost unbearable for my ten-year-old brain!

Before we move on, I want you to give it a try. Copy the diagram below onto the middle of a piece of paper and try to it. Don't worry, I'll wait.

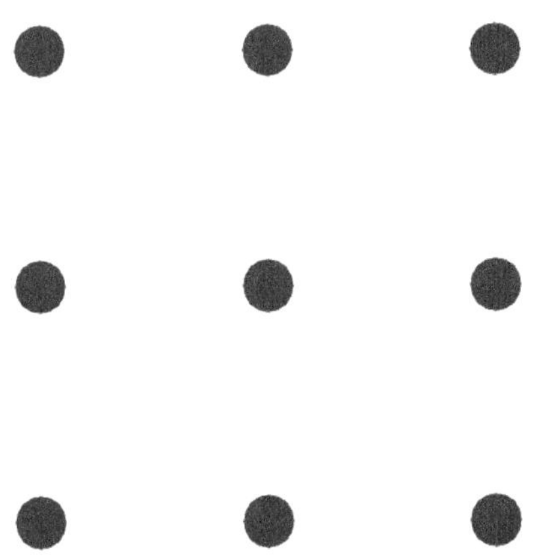

Nine dot problem. Try to connect all the dots without lifting your pen and in as few straight lines as possible (maximum four).

Did you solve it? After how many tries? What did you learn in the process? If you haven't solved it yet, read on; we're getting to that.

When presented with this challenge, most people keep trying to solve the problem without changing what needs to be changed. They formulate the problem – *frame it* – in a way that blocks them from figuring it out. The most common limitation that people self-impose is the restriction that they cannot extend the lines beyond the square outlined by the dots. Nowhere in the rules does it say that you must stick to the boundaries of the dotted square, still, almost everyone trying their hand at the problem will unconsciously do this. But there are other things keeping participants from eventually solving the riddle. Even when they're told it's allowed to extend the lines outside the square, many still fail to find the solution because they keep the lines short or don't see the full spectrum of what they can do with those lines. Here's one way to solve the problem.

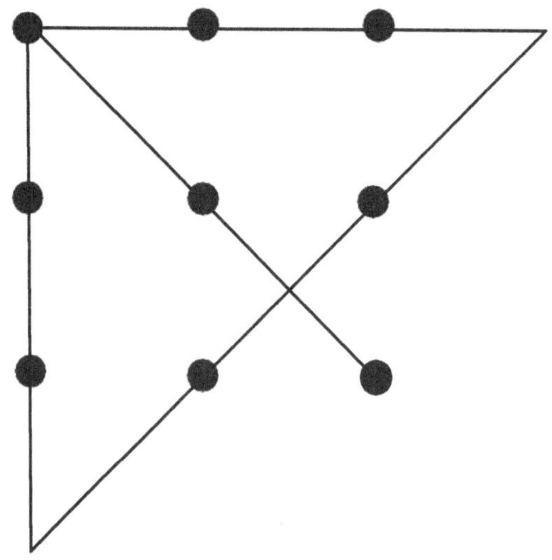

Here's one solution to the nine-dot problem.
To solve this problem, you must draw (and think) „outside" the box your mind creates around the dots.

The nine-dot problem is called a Gestalt-problem because it needs to be to be perceived in all its complexity in order for it to be solved. The Gestalt[75] approach to problem-solving states that finding the best solution to a problem requires an appropriate definition of the problem itself. You don't immediately try to find a solution to a problem when it's posed. First, you make sure you understand the system (the shape or form) you're looking at, that you have the correct definition of the problem so you can gain understanding into the structure of that problem. The key to solving problems lies in representing the problem in your mind. In other words: if your representation is wrong, limited or incomplete, you won't be able to solve it.

One way to gain more insight into the structure of a problem is to what? That's right, introduce disruption! But very often, what we're *not changing* is precisely what we need to change. Like the type of people you swipe right on in a dating app. Knowing this can help you break through the incorrect framing that keeps you stuck. It can be challenging, I'll admit. You need humility for it, and wisdom. You need to be willing to pay attention to your failed attempts and to remember your failures, so you can learn from them and apply this knowledge to new situations and problems.

Chapter Six: Insights, Enlightenment, and Getting Unstuck.

"If you change the way you look at things, the things you look at change."
– Wayne Dyer

Disruption provides insights that can eventually lead to enlightenment – a type of clarity where everything finally makes sense, and you intuitively know what to do next. By being open to the various solutions to the problem in front of you, you finally "see through the illusion that kept you stuck" and step into what is real – or at the very least real-er for you.

Prompt: What do you really want?

Now that you've learned so much about how we create our reality, don't see solutions because of our inclination for patterns and order, and trick ourselves into flawed thinking, it's time to go back to your dreams.

In Step Two, I asked you to reflect on what you really want. Go back and read your answer. Considering what you've learned, answer the question again: **What do you really want?**

Certainty vs plausibility

Before moving on to Step Four, I want to end with an important distinction that is so often overlooked: even though we'd love to, most of the time, we cannot base our actions on certainty; we must be ok with plausibility.

At the beginning of this book, I stated that "being stuck is a feeling, not a fact." It's a mental fallacy, an error in thinking ingrained in us through socializing and education. "Are you sure this is what you want?" is a question asked repeatedly to both children and adults. The question holds some merit regarding its educational purposes: you want children to think before they act and make choices that hopefully reflect their wishes. However, one can never know for sure if what one wants is forever, or the thing one wants right now, as is somehow implied in the question.

We learned in this step that nothing is certain, that we can never get to the absolute truth, and that reality, as it unfolds, is colored by who we are. How then, could we ever make claims of certainty or wait for it to appear before making a decision? We ask for certainty in a world that is all but one thing: certain. The simple fact that our lives happen as we live through them makes it impossible to know what tomorrow will bring. Waiting to do something, to decide, to act and move forward until you feel *ready* keeps you stuck. Your chances of winning the lottery are higher than your chances of waking up feeling absolutely sure of what to do next. That's just the way it works.

This is where the concept of impermanence shows its true power. Remember: you cannot *think* yourself into a new career, life, or anything. Eventually, you must go out and *do it*. The unknown must be trusted, otherwise you'll never take a step forward. That's precisely what Step Four of the MOVE method is about.

In the next and final section, we're going to roll up our sleeves and get to work. We'll use the new perspectives you gained to create a plan of action. Execution, above all else, will be at the center of what we'll do in Step Four. Not by working out a traditional plan but by working out exactly what you're going to get started with. To do that, we'll tap into your unbridled and unlimited creativity – something that might feel icky, especially for those who don't consider themselves "creative." Trust me, you are, and I will show you how to use this incredible superpower. But first, let's look at the takeaways from this step of the MOVE method.

Summary: Step Three – Vision

This third step is about seeing the world for what it truly is: understanding how our minds shape reality according to who we are and how to introduce disruption into our thinking to create new possibilities for our lives.

In this third step, you learned:

- That it's ok to be different, and how to turn your difference into an advantage.
- The pitfalls of being a creative generalist.
- Why breaking promises to yourself will keep you stuck.
- Why real impostors don't feel like impostors.
- How the things we tell ourselves shape what we believe is possible.
- Disruptive strategies and how to use disruptive experiments to change your life.
- Accepting plausibility instead of certainty.

Well done! You're now officially through Step Three. There's only one step left, you're almost there! By now, you should have a clear picture of what keeps you stuck and what you want to do as you move forward. If not, don't worry; by the end of Step Four, I promise you that you will.

STEP FOUR:
EXECUTION

"All progress begins with a brave decision. Action comes before the courage to act. Action generates motivation."
– Marie Forleo

In this step, you'll learn:

- That trying everything is as bad as trying nothing.
- How to not get overwhelmed by the choices that you have.
- The power of valued living versus achievement-based living.
- How you might be using every excuse in the book to not change.
- The truth about fear and how to not let it stop you from doing what you want.
- The impact of trauma and childhood wounds on being and staying stuck.
- What your glue is and how you can use it to make sense of your life.
- The myth of willpower and the paradox of choice.
- Three strategies to stay unstuck.

Chapter One: If You're Looking For Flaws, You'll Find Them.

"Instead of looking in the mirror and focusing on your flaws, look in the mirror and appreciate your best features. Everyone has them."
– Demi Lovato

You always start before you think you do. And you, my friend, started a while ago. When you picked up this book and decided to read it, that's when you set things in motion to get unstuck. You probably started even before coming across my book. When clients sit down in front of me in my (virtual) office, coaching is rarely their first attempt at figuring things out. When I see them for the first time, they've felt lost, confused, and stuck for a while, sometimes months or even years. They've often thought long and hard about everything they could do, but they've also thought themselves out of all those options. They might even have tried a thing or two, but according to them, nothing ever worked. Sounds familiar?

Perhaps you're like Dalia, a client who came to me feeling completely lost and not knowing who she was or what she wanted after caring for her three children, one who required extra care, full-time for eight years. The first thing Dalia said was, "I don't even remember what it was like to have dreams." She started crying. I could see big tears making their way onto her beautiful face and cheeks and disappearing into her hijab. Dalia had been trying to understand why she wasn't happy caring for her children. "I'm just a mom," she told me when I asked her about her interests and the things she loved to do. "It's the only thing I've done for so long that I lost touch with the fire inside me. I used to be so focused. I would set goals for myself and achieve them no matter what. Now, the only thing I can think of at night is what I must do for the kids in the morning. It's like I'm not even living."

Dalia had tried to come up with options for herself, she had thought about so many things that she could do to change her life, but every time she found a flaw in the idea and let it go. As I'm sure you know by now, finding flaws in everything is often just fear trying to stop you from taking a step forward. Sadly, as Dalia experienced firsthand, it's one of the best tactics our nervous system and brain must convince us not to step out of our comfort zone and try something new.

One of the surest ways to talk yourself out of anything is to look for what's wrong with it. Invariably, you'll find something if you look long and hard enough. If you keep having ideas but don't do anything with them, talking yourself out of everything might be the issue.

At the end of her first coaching session, I gave Dalia exercises to reconnect with herself and her deepest desires. By the second, and especially the third session, a list of things she liked and cared about besides her children started to emerge. At the beginning of that session, I could see how proud and happy Dalia was when I asked her if she wanted to share her list. "I didn't know I had so many ideas in me," she said, smiling when she was through her list. "So," I asked, "is there anything in particular that speaks to you and that you'd like to move forward with?" Dalia paused. I could see her thinking. After a few moments, she nodded, "No." I waited longer, knowing she was going through her list and processing my question. Eventually, she said: "I don't think so. None of the things on my list are doable for me. I'm just a mom. I have no education. I don't have time. I wouldn't even know where to start." When she was done, I looked at her and asked: "But, Dalia, didn't you tell me that the things on your list are the things you really want to do in your life?" After a short pause, she nodded a slow but determined "yes." "And," I continued, "didn't you tell me it would be sad for anyone to not go after what they want, to not listen to their desires?"

Dalia looked at me in a way I'm all too familiar with in my practice. I call it *the big reveal.* The moment when a client sees what's been going on inside themselves, like the lights going on and the curtain lifting on a theatre stage. It's often the first time this happens so vividly for them, so that moment of insight tends to hit them on the head as one of the biggest ahas of their life. It certainly did for Dalia.

Talking ourselves out of our true desires by finding flaws in them is something we all do. The life we're living when we're not aligned with them cannot be our best life; it's simply flawed thinking (as we've seen in previous chapters) to believe so. Why would you feel stuck or want change if everything was the best way it could be?

Dalia talked herself out of her dreams and never tried anything to change her situation. Thankfully, through our work together, she figured out what she wanted, put a plan in place, and got unstuck. It took time and effort, but today Dalia is not "just a mom," as she used to say; she's also a successful entrepreneur with her own sustainable children's clothes line and big dreams for her future.

Trying everything is as bad as trying nothing

Not everyone talks themselves out of doing things. I have many clients who, when they first come to see me, have been in constant action, trying things out faster than I can follow. Take Ben, for instance, who came to me when he started his yoga and reiki practice.

When we connected, I could see Ben was stressed. He'd just launched a new marketing campaign on social media, hoping this would bring in the clients he was desperately waiting for. When I asked Ben about his work and life, he immediately told me everything he had been trying to get his business off the ground – creating flyers and distributing them all around town one week, reaching out to a couple of influencers the next, organizing an opening night for his friends and family, trying to find partners to promote his business, even giving out free sessions to passers-by in a desperate attempt to make some sales. Ben took a breath. He was jittering so much that I could almost see his legs move through the computer screen that connected us. "They all sound like good actions to get the word out about your business Ben," I started, "but how long have you been doing all of these activities?" He looked at me, pensive. "Well," he said after pondering my question for a moment, "I did all of these things for a little while, but they didn't work, so I moved on to the next thing, which didn't work either. That's why I'm so stressed, I don't know what I'm doing wrong, but nothing seems to work."

What Ben shared is something I often see. People who are willing to try anything to get out of the rut. Unlike those who get overwhelmed by too many options and do nothing, these people pick and choose randomly from the options available to them and try everything. The problem is they're not sticking to anything, and they're usually not working on the deeper issues that got them stuck in the first place. Just like you don't get stuck overnight, you need patience to get unstuck. More than that, you need a plan and the perseverance to follow it.

Lack of consistency, looking for a quick fix, impatience. They're human traits, so nothing's wrong with them; the problem is they're not how you get unstuck. Moving from one thing to another too quickly shows that you need a clear plan or don't know precisely what you want. You need to remember that creating the life and work of your dreams is a lifelong process, and each step taken consciously will guide you closer to that goal. Don't rush it. Instead, plan it out, be instrumental about your actions, have some patience, and give your efforts time to sprout and blossom. More than anything, pick a strategy and *stick* with it.

Don't get overwhelmed by the choices that you have

In Step Two, we talked about all the opportunities that you have. In Step Three, you opened your eyes to a new reality and realized any vision for your life is doable: you have almost as many opportunities as you make yourself out to have. This is amazing, isn't it? You can do anything! For some people, though, and maybe you're one of them (I know I used to be), having too many choices can be paralyzing. "I could do all these things," clients will tell me during the first sessions of our work together, "but how do I know what I *should* be doing? How do I know what to *choose*?"

There are patterns in how people think about their dreams and desires. As I mentioned, clients often tell me precisely what they want during a first session, but they won't hear it themselves. Most will need a few months of working together to arrive at their initial desires, now in the form of a conclusion. It's normal and part of the coaching process. I'm not supporting my clients to do what I think is best for them; I'm supporting them to realize what they already know to be best for them. Sounds simple, right? Why can't we do this for ourselves then?

Because what we truly, madly, deeply want is hidden under layers of programming, limiting beliefs, stories we tell ourselves about what we can or cannot do, expectations we take on from others, fears and anxieties that we have, and so much more. Most of us (myself included) need help to crawl out from under the burdens weighing on our dreams.

Prompt: How did you try to get unstuck in the past?

Here are a few questions to help you filter out successful strategies that helped you achieve your goals in the past. On paper or mentally, take some time to review them and answer them as truthfully as you can (remember, nobody's watching, just be honest with yourself).

- Think of your successes and failures. What was different about how you chose the goals you achieved and those that you didn't? What was different in how you tried to achieve them?

- Were you clear on your desires? How did it affect the success or failure of your goals?
- What would you do differently now to try to change something about yourself, your life, or your work?
- Did you choose your goals freely, or were you going after inherited dreams? How did this affect your progress and success?
- Anything else you think influenced your success or failure?

Valued living versus achievement-based living

When many things pull at us, it's hard to figure out what we want. First, we need to weed out the noise. One thing that can help you do that is by relying on your core values. Values differ from goals or dreams in that they're not something you achieve; they're something you live by. You can't achieve "being a good friend," for instance; you must continually work at it and evolve with your friends to remain one. If goals are a destination you're trying to arrive at, values are the compass directions guiding you. Acting in agreement with your values is an ongoing process, not an outcome of some task or action. Living in accordance with your values will never end as long as you are alive.

The big difference between a life where you feel stuck and try to avoid the unpleasant feelings and experiences that go along with it and a life motivated by the pursuit of your most important values is the intrinsic gratification and sense of fulfillment that comes from valued living, whatever your external circumstances are.

Valued living isn't new. It dates back to the ancient Greek philosophers (them again!) who spent much time thinking about and debating what made life worth living. Most of them agreed that to live a good life and be happy, one needed to be virtuous. Eudaimonia (happiness) and aretē (virtue) were the two central notions of ancient ethics. Living a values-based life was essential to be virtuous. Happiness wasn't a feeling or experience as we understand it today but rather a way of life. This is true for Aristotle, Plato, Augustine, and many other philosophers that came after them.

The word "virtue," which sounds a little dated, comes from the Latin "virtus," which means strength or excellence. Aristotle spoke about many virtues, although among the moral ones, there are four virtues – the cardinal virtues – that make up the foundation of Aristotle's moral philosophy: prudence (wisdom), justice, temperance, and courage (fortitude). Possessing these virtues was necessary to be happy and live at one's full potential. Aristotle made a distinction between intellectual and moral virtues. The cardinal virtues are moral. The ideal to aspire to was to become a mix of wisdom, self-discipline, and courage and to be just.

Moral virtues are psychological traits and moral habits that one can rely on when facing ethical decisions – something we all have to do every day. Imagine having to consciously consider every moral decision you must make without having values to back you up or show you the way. You might get stuck.

Spending time with my close friends and those I love and enjoy is essential to me. Being a good friend is important to me and something I've worked at for a long time. But it's not the only value that I care about. I also believe in being honest, courageous, kind, acting with integrity, working hard, and always learning. These values are important to me because they've helped me grow, learn from my mistakes, and become a better person, partner, friend, sister, and coach. As long as I continue to work on these things, I'll be able to achieve many things but most importantly: I'll always feel satisfied, whatever the outcome.

You can control how you act, not how other people react to you

In an achievement-based world, we constantly strive for the next thing and often forget to enjoy the process and the journey. We get so wrapped up in what we're doing that we forget to live. Achievements are important, but they shouldn't be the only thing that matters to us. When trying to progress in our lives, we must keep our values in mind and use them to guide our actions. That way, we can ensure that we're not just achieving things for the sake of achievement, but that we're doing things that are truly meaningful to us. Valued living means knowing where you're going, but while working toward something, you pay more attention to the journey than the destination.

We often feel like our happiness depends on other people, what they think of us, how much they like us, and the praise or attention they give us. When we're children, we need that attention and love from our parents or caretakers. If we don't get it or are mistreated in any way or experience any other painful event, trauma can set in and influence how we view the world.

I touched on trauma, attachment styles, and their effect on being and staying stuck. I address it a bit more below. For now, know this, if other people and how much they like or praise you are the most important barometer for your measure of success or happiness, you're in for a wild ride.

I'm sure you've come across people and situations that made you very unhappy in the past. Perhaps you're currently struggling with a narcissistic parent, a bully at work or in your professional network, someone who called themselves your friend but, as soon as a disagreement arose, decided to make you look bad by gossiping behind your back, an ex-partner who makes you want to scream every time you're trying to agree on child support and visitation. There are so many examples of situations where people will not be their best selves. Why? Because people are people: flawed humans (just like us) dealing with their own (unconscious) trauma, pain, and issues that you can't (and shouldn't want to) control.

"Hell is other people" is one of Jean-Paul Sartre's, a well-known French philosopher, most famous quotes. The quote appears at the end of his play "Huis Clos"[76] from 1944 – *"No Exit"* in English, which isn't a great translation because the words in French mean something like "judicial proceedings without the presence of the public, behind closed doors." The play is about three characters – Garcin, Estelle, and Inez – finding themselves in a drawing room that appears to be hell. While the characters make sense of where they are and try to understand what they did – what sin brought them there and what their punishment might be – it starts to dawn on them that there's no one coming to save them. There's no fire to burn them, no torturer to hurt them. It's just the three of them. Forever. That's their punishment. Their gaze on one another, what they think of each other, what they say to each other.

Stay true to yourself and your values

Ever since I read the play when I was a teenager, I found a lot of truth and solace in it. At school, I was never one of the cool kids. Throughout my teenage years, I was bullied on and off, mainly by girls who would gossip about me and not allow me to be part of their group of friends. Because of this, I always felt like an outsider. When I was still at school, I tried to outsmart them to make them like me to be accepted. It never worked. There was no way to stop it, so I had to learn to live with it. At that age, other people were like hell to me sometimes.

I always thought that bullying would end when my childhood ended. I believed that adults didn't gossip or do bad things to one another. Following Maya Angelou's famous quote that "Once we know better, we do better" I thought adulthood would be bliss, with insightful people treating each other with respect and kindness. Unfortunately, not everyone grows up to *know better*.

When someone or something negative happens to me today, I remind myself that, as the Stoics say, we're only our capacity to make *choices*. Other people can't harm us; only bad decisions can. This means that good choices can benefit us. And luckily, people might treat you badly all they want; you're the only one who has power over your choices. That is what self-leadership is all about.

Knowing what you stand for is powerful. Your values can help you find your purpose or help you to react in a meaningful way when facing difficult situations. Using your values when making decisions can help you protect your boundaries by helping you decide what is right. Living your life in accordance with your core values can increase your self-confidence by giving you a greater sense of who you are and what's truly important to you. Finally, and most importantly, identifying your core values helps define the path to your dream life, career, or business by knowing what matters most to you. Let's look at that in a bit more detail.

Identifying your five core values

Getting unstuck, as you know by now, is a process of unraveling, imagination, and creation. It starts with discovering more about yourself and what you want. Finding out what your core values are is an essential part of that. We all operate with an internal set of values. Still, as we've seen in Step Two, our inherited dreams often bury them deep beneath social expectations, false beliefs about ourselves and the world, the pressure to conform, and the unwritten rules we believe we must live by, passed down to us in childhood. Through the following exercise, you'll identify what matters to you and your five core values, allowing you to make better choices about what you want to be, have, and do in life.

Prompt: Identifying the values that speak to you.

This exercise aims to identify the values you feel connected to intuitively, not those you've inherited or been conditioned to identify with. Below is a list of values. Read through the list, and circle or write down all the values that speak to you. If you possess some values that aren't on the list, feel free to add as many as you like. Try to do this as a free-flow exercise without overthinking why you choose certain values over others.

Abundance	Enjoyment	Performance
Acceptance	Entertainment	Perseverance
Accomplishment	Enthusiasm	Persistence
Accountability	Entrepreneurship	Philanthropy
Accuracy	Environment	Playfulness
Achievement	Equality	Popularity
Activity	Equitability	Positivity
Adaptability	Ethics	Potential
Advancement	Excellence	Power
Adventure	Excitement	Practicality
Advocacy	Experience	Pragmatism
Affection	Expertise	Presence
Agility	Exploration	Proactivity
Alertness	Expressiveness	Productivity
Altruism	Extrovert	Professionalism
Ambition	Exuberance	Progress
Amusement	Fairness	Prudence
Appreciation	Faithfulness	Punctuality
Approachability	Family	Purity
Assertiveness	Fearlessness	Purpose
Attentiveness	Feelings	Quality

Attractiveness
Autonomy
Availability
Awareness
Balance
Beauty
Belonging
Benevolence
Boldness
Bravery
Brilliance
Calmness
Candor
Capability
Carefulness
Caring
Certainty
Challenge
Change
Charity
Cheerfulness
Cleanliness
Cleverness
Collaboration
Comfort
Commitment
Common sense
Communication
Community
Compassion
Competency
Completion
Concentration

Fidelity
Fierce
Firm
Flexibility
Flow
Focus
Foresight
Forgiveness
Fortitude
Freedom
Friendships
Frugality
Fun
Generosity
Genius
Gentleness
Giving
Goodness
Grace
Gratitude
Greatness
Growth
Guidance
Happiness
Hard work
Harmony
Health
Heart
Helpfulness
Heroism
Honesty
Honor
Hope

Radiance
Rationality
Receptiveness
Recognition
Reflection
Relationships
Reliability
Resilience
Resourcefulness
Respect
Responsibility
Responsiveness
Restraint
Reverence
Rigor
Risk Taking
Sacrifice
Safety
Satisfaction
Security
Self Awareness
Self-Reliance
Selflessness
Sensitivity
Sensuality
Serenity
Seriousness
Sharing
Significance
Silence
Silliness
Simplicity
Sincerity

Concern for Others
Confidence
Conformity
Connection
Consciousness
Consistency
Contentment
Contribution
Control
Conviction
Cooperation
Courage
Courtesy
Craftiness
Creativity
Credibility
Curiosity
Daring
Decisiveness
Dedication
Delight
Dependability
Depth
Determination
Development
Devotion
Dignity
Diligence
Directness
Discipline
Discovery
Diversity
Down-to-Earth

Humility
Humor
Imagination
Impact
Impartiality
Inclusiveness
Independence
Individuality
Innovation
Insightfulness
Inspiration
Integrity
Intelligence
Intensity
Introspection
Intuition
Inviting
Joy
Justice
Kindness
Knowledge
Leadership
Learning
Listening
Liveliness
Logic
Longevity
Love
Loyalty
Making a difference
Meaning
Merit
Meticulousness

Skillfulness
Softness
Solitude
Spirituality
Spontaneity
Stability
Status
Strength
Structure
Success
Support
Sustainability
Sympathy
Synergy
Talent
Teamwork
Temperance
Tenderness
Thankfulness
Thoughtfulness
Tolerance
Traditionalism
Tranquility
Transparency
Trustworthiness
Truth
Understanding
Uniqueness
Usefulness
Value
Versatility
Virtue
Vision

Dreaming
Drive
Duty
Eagerness
Education
Effectiveness
Efficiency
Elegance
Emotionality
Empathy
Empowerment
Encouragement
Endurance
Energy
Engagement

Mindfulness
Moderation
Modesty
Motivation
Mystery
Nurturing
Obedience
Open-Mindedness
Openness
Optimism
Originality
Passion
Patience
Peace
Perfection

Vitality
Vulnerability
Warmth
Wealth
Welcoming
Well-Being
Willfulness
Wisdom
Wonder
Zeal

Use the outer circles of the diagram below to group your core values in a way that makes sense. This could be based on what they represent to you, a particular category of values, or anything else that makes them stand out as a group for you. Once you're done, pick the most important one from each group and write it in the center of the diagram. Those are your five core values. Congratulations!

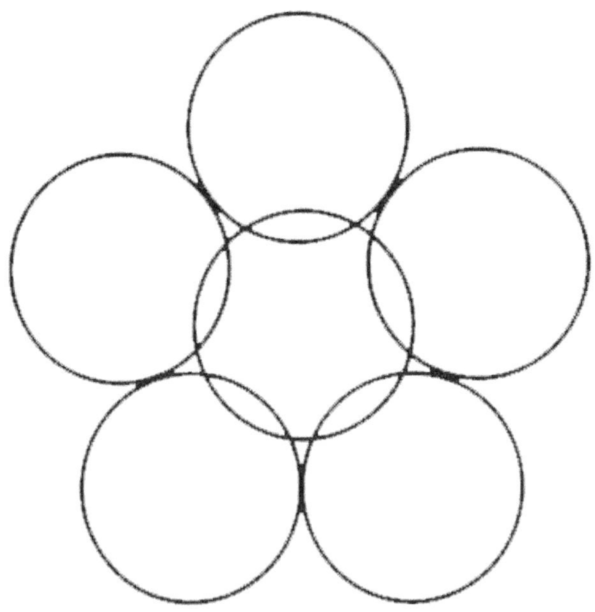

Write them down on a piece of paper in order of importance (the most important one at the top) and put your list somewhere visible so you can have your five core values close by when you need them as a reminder of what you stand for. I have mine hanging on my office wall, but you can also stick them in your planner, bag, or purse. Whatever works best for you.

Chapter Two: Using Every Excuse in The Book Not to Change.

"Not managing your time and making excuses are two bad habits. Don't put them both together by claiming you 'don't have the time."
– Bo Bennett

So far, I've mentioned the people who do nothing because they have too many choices and get overwhelmed, the ones who try everything but never stick to anything long enough to make it work, and the ones who think themselves out of everything because they find flaws in whatever it is they're thinking about doing. Before we start to put a plan together for your dreams, I want to address the fourth type of people who are stuck: the ones using every excuse they can find *not* to change. Instead of finding flaws in every idea they come up with, these types find reasons why *they* can't do what they want to do.

"There is absolutely nothing I can do about it."
"I don't know anything about business."
"I can stop drinking whenever I want. I just don't want to right now."
"I'm not creative."
"It's too late to start a new career."
"Nobody will ever take me seriously."
"I don't have time to learn a new language."
"It's been a long day; I'm going to watch Netflix; I deserve it."
"It's just the way things are. You can't change some things."

Remember Step One, where we talked about growth versus fixed mindset? Excuses are a way for the fixed mindset to show its ugly head, but not only that. Making excuses can be a way to avoid leaving your comfort zone, losing something, having to admit you're not perfect, changing yourself or your reality, or justifying why you haven't done what you said you were going to do. In many cases we don't actually believe we're too old or not creative, but we let fear convince us of those things, so we don't have to do the scary thing we secretly want to do. Fear has a way of sabotaging your plans this way.

If this sounds familiar, know that this is a natural way for fear to try and keep us safe. Doing this is fear's number one task. Finding excuses not to do something is not a sign of weakness or laziness, even though it's often called that. If you follow the excuses you come up with not to do something, fear is in the driver's seat, and you're a passenger on the bus that is your life.

When my client Chiffa first connected with me, she'd been making excuses for not switching careers for almost ten years. Yes, you've read that right, nearly ten years! She felt undervalued and miserable at work and couldn't stop thinking about everything she could do instead. She was at her wits' end. She'd also been making so many excuses for herself over the years that she was in an absolute deadlock about what to do next.

The problem with excuses is that they keep you stuck. They feed your fears, keep you from growing and learning, prevent you from doing what you want, and, most importantly, make you avoid making tough choices you know you should make. Nobody can guarantee that change will improve your life, but we all owe it to ourselves to try.

A vital step to stop making excuses is realizing that you control your destiny. Instead of making excuses, you can make choices. Now that you've identified your five core values, you have a firm anchor on which to base them. Whenever you're faced with a choice and feel an excuse coming up not to do it, rely on your values to help you move forward. This will enable you to live a more intentional life.

By choosing choices over excuses, you take back control. You also stop wasting precious time trying to defend why you're not doing something and instead focus your energy on finally doing what you want. That's how it should be. *You* belong in the driver's seat of your life, nobody else. Instead of spending every minute you have letting fear convince you that you shouldn't do something, thank fear for looking after you so well and tell it that you've got this, then use that time to come up with creative ways to change your life, find the career of your dreams or start your own business!

Prompt: Stop making excuses for yourself.

If you often find yourself coming up with excuses for not pushing an idea forward, or the next time you're tempted to give up because you came up with a *perfect* excuse not to do something, try addressing the reasons you're coming up with by asking yourself the following questions:

- Is this thought realistic? Is it really true?
- Is this excuse valid? Would I believe it if someone else was saying this to me?
- Why am I afraid of moving forward? What is fear trying to tell me?
- What's the worst that can happen?
- If I listen to this excuse and do nothing, what will happen?
- What will happen if I don't listen to this excuse and take action?
- What if everything turned out the best way possible?
- Do I really want to change? And, if so, what is my next step?

Yes, but-ing

A few years back, I enrolled in an improvisation class. I've been doing these types of classes and workshops for some years now to force myself out of my comfort zone and experience new things and emotions. And, wow, did I get what I signed up for! For someone like me, who is ambivalently introverted, on the spectrum, loves her alone time, and is highly sensitive, landing in a group of twenty-five happy souls ready to play pretend and laugh for an entire Sunday morning was challenging. It took me a while to get into things, but I was all in once I did!

The class was great, and our teacher was too. He taught us many things about the techniques of improvisation theater. The most important thing I learned, and applicable outside of shady open mic bars, is the concept of "yes, and" instead of "yes, but." In improv, you cannot use the word "but" when handed a story by another actor; you must accept it by saying "yes" and follow it with "and" to add your own story to it. Before improv, I'd never thought about how fatalistic the word "but" really is. It's like a stop sign. As soon as someone says "but" you know things aren't going anymore. That's why you're not allowed to use it in improv theater because the whole point is to keep the show moving forward and let whatever the actors create take shape.

When people make excuses for themselves, often there is some "yes, but-ing" going on. Have you ever listened to a friend tell you why she hates her job, only to find that as soon as you offer some alternatives (after being asked to do so, of course), you get a big, ugly "but" in reply?

"Yes, you're right, I could do that, but…"
"Yes, I know, but…"
"Well, normally I'd say yes, but…"

"But" is a terrible word when trying to get unstuck. A better strategy is to use the one from improv. When you're thinking about your options, instead of talking yourself out of them with a "but," try and see what happens if you start with "yes, and."

When you feel like excuses are running your life, there's only one thing you can do (well, three, actually):

- Recognize when you're making excuses for yourself.
- Question your excuses as you've done in the previous exercise.
- Say "yes, and" instead of "yes, but" and decide on a step forward instead of listening to your excuses and doing nothing.

The "good enough" trap

Another way excuses show up in disguise is by making us think things aren't that bad, what I call the "good enough" trap (or crap, depending on my mood).

I was stuck there for many years. It's where you know things could be better, but because the nail isn't hurting all the time or not that much, you convince yourself that things are okay. More importantly, you convince yourself that things could be worse.

"My job sucks, but I could be unemployed."
"I'm undervalued at work, but I could have a toxic boss."
"My apartment is falling apart, but I could still be in my parent's basement."
"I party too much on the weekend, but I could be out every day."
"My partner is cold and distant, but I could be a single parent."
"I never have time for myself, but I could be alone."
"My father drinks too much, but he could be violent."
"My wife often screams at me, but she could leave me."

When we focus on what could be worse, we lose track of our situation – of what is. Our mind plays this trick to help us cope with the stress of living an unsatisfying or difficult life. If this is you, I want you to know that you're doing nothing wrong; this is a normal reaction for many people. But accepting your situation as "good enough" reinforces the status quo; you accept a way of life, a habit, or a behavior that isn't serving you. You make excuses for yourself or those around you about why it's okay to stay where you are and do what you do.

The relationship I had with my ex-husband wasn't particularly loving or caring. We lacked communication and never really knew each other, not even after almost a decade spent together. Looking back, the signs were there from the beginning. The person I am today, with the growth and self-discovery I've gone through and all the self-love and self-esteem I've gained over the years, would not work with that relationship at all. Working on yourself makes you strong and powerful, that's for sure! But I wasn't always like that. I was an anxious people-pleaser, trying to do what I believed society wanted me to do.

Throughout that relationship, the only thing I did was get sucked deeper into the "good enough" trap. Every time something happened, I would find a reason why it wasn't so bad and compare my situation to what, in my mind, was a worse one. When we wouldn't be able to communicate and resolve conflicts in a healthy way, I would call myself lucky that we "didn't fight a lot." Even though we had few common interests and did most things on our own, I would call myself lucky that we came home to each other at night.

Because there was always a possible worse scenario, I convinced myself that my situation wasn't as bad as it was. When I finally got divorced, I realized how unhappy I had been, how much of myself I had lost in that relationship, and how trapped I felt by the "good enough" I'd accepted for so long.

In the end, it was a hard but crucial lesson. I don't participate in toxic relationships anymore. My confidence and self-esteem are stronger, I'm no longer a people-pleaser, and I don't take unhealthy behavior from people. To become the person I am today, I needed to see through the "good enough" trap and let go of the idea that because something might be worse, I should be happy with what I have. That's just not true. Things are either good, or they're not. If they're not good, you work on improving them, or you change your situation.

Don't stay with someone who doesn't love you or who mistreats you. Whatever the reason for staying, it's just an excuse to hide your fear of change. Don't hang on to a job that leaves you burned out every night because you're afraid to be unemployed.[77] There's plenty of work and great jobs that will make you feel valued and fill your cup instead of depleting you.

"It's not that bad" should signify it's time for a change. Remember that a "not that bad life" is not a good one. You deserve a life that makes you happy, that makes you jump out of bed in the morning. Instead of focusing on how things could be worse, remember that things could be better and aim for that. Trust your gut; it knows, even if you'd like to convince yourself otherwise, *especially* when trying to convince yourself otherwise.

Connected to the "good enough" trap are three psychological occurrences that I often encounter in my work: perfectionism, cognitive dissonance, and sunken cost fallacy. Before addressing fear itself – the most crucial reason people don't act on their dreams – I want to quickly explain how these three phenomena can affect how you see the world and keep you stuck, especially when you're in a situation you know isn't good for you.

Perfectionism

The opposite of the good enough trap, one might say, is the perfectionist one. While the good enough trap makes you settle for less than you deserve or desire, perfectionism makes you aim for the absolute best. When you're a perfectionist, you don't get stuck because your expectations are too low; you get stuck because they are too high.

Perfectionism is rooted in all-or-nothing thinking. When you're a perfectionist, you believe that if you can't do something right (aka perfectly), you shouldn't do it at all (remember the fixed mindset from Step One?). You can draw a perfect picture the first time you try, or you shouldn't draw at all; you either stick to early morning runs every day of the week, or you shouldn't even take out your running shoes. When you can't stick to the unrealistic plan you've created for yourself, you feel like a failure. So you do nothing.

One of the problems with perfectionism is the stiff thinking that goes along with it. Perfectionism is disguising itself as "having high standards," which in our achievement and success-driven society is often seen as a virtue. As a recovering perfectionist, I know how the lack of compromise with myself kept me stuck for years. I would enroll at the local gym and decide to go "every day." It went well for a few weeks until life, and its busyness or demands got in the way. Instead of reviewing the plan and being less demanding of myself, as soon as I missed a day, I would beat myself up. Not long after that, I would quit – every single time.

Perfectionism is an illusion. According to Plato (yes, him *again*, you can't take the philosopher out of the coach I'm afraid), "perfection only exists in the world of forms."[78] He believed that the objects and matter in the physical world were nothing more than imitations of the real and true, perfect, absolute, unchangeable version of those objects and matter (which he called ideas) that could only be found somewhere in the heavens. The perfect circle is found in that realm, not on earth, just like the perfect bird, house, or virtue. I love this example because I believe perfection only exists in our minds. When we think of something, we see the perfect version of it; we see it as we want it to be. But that's not how things are or how we can make them come true.

Perfectionism is often a trauma response, or a way of being created in response to a demanding environment, usually in childhood. As such, perfectionism is a way to keep us safe. If we do everything perfectly, the caretaker, schoolteacher or bully will have no reason to be mad at us, criticize what we're doing, or make fun of us. Children learn this strategy early on. Unfortunately, as we've seen before, what worked to protect you when you were a child can become a burden if you take it with you into adulthood. Without realizing it, many perfectionists (my former self included) continue to try and keep themselves safe using the same strategies – when there is no danger anymore.

I often come across this in my work. Clients who imagine an action they could take towards their dream job or life share it with me, and immediately after that, start to "yes-but" themselves out of it. In their mind, they're calculating what I call *perfectionist risk*. This type of risk assessment, even though it looks like it's about the success or failure of their idea, is, in fact, about the likelihood of someone criticizing them for not executing their idea perfectly.

One such client, a wonderful creative producer with years of experience putting together the most amazing shows for her artist clients, was ideating activities with me to help her transition from the role of producer to creative director. She came up with a list of big names in the industry she was in good standing with, and that she could easily reach out to for a push in the right direction. As soon as the action was set, I could see her perfectionistic muscle take over as she started to think herself out of every conversation she could have. "I'm worried they will criticize me," she said when I asked her what was going on. "I don't know what I'll do if they criticize me, because I only have one shot to speak with them." To someone who isn't a perfectionist, this way of thinking may sound odd, but to someone for whom making a mistake has been conditioned into them as being the worst thing in the world, protecting themselves from "harm" this way is not unusual. The only problem is, even if our parents or caregivers spent years trying to convince us that we couldn't do anything right, that is just not true. It certainly doesn't serve the grown-ass adults we've become.

A better way to approach how to be in the world is to aim for excellence. Instead of holding too high standards for yourself (and others!), cultivating sustainable effort will help you get unstuck. Yes, you can have it all, but you can't have it all right now – and it won't be perfect anyhow. And you can only have it all if "all" is realistic, doable, really what you want, and not just another reason or excuse not to do something.

To help you recognize when perfectionism is keeping you stuck, here are some examples:

- **Unrealistic expectations.** Achieving a goal can't be messy but must be linear; when you try something new, you immediately want to be good at it, you can *never* say or do the wrong thing.
- **Fear of failure.** If you try, you must succeed; if you fail, it means *you're* a failure, and you worry about what people will think.
- **It's all about the result.** It's hard for you to be present, to live in the now, and to appreciate the journey when you're trying to achieve something; you're *only satisfied* when you've reached your goal. Immediately after that though, you're already thinking about the next goal, and the satisfaction disappears.
- **All-or-nothing thinking.** Either you do it perfectly or *don't do it at all*; you're tough on yourself and hold yourself to unrealistic standards.

Whenever I feel perfectionism is holding me back, I think about Vladimir and Estragon waiting for Godot,[79] who never shows up. Waiting for Godot is the worst thing you can do; life will pass you by while you wait for the perfect time, conditions, or plan. Perfection is not coming, so you can stop waiting for it. I spent years waiting to lose those last 10 pounds before feeling good about my body, allowing myself to enjoy food, and wearing a bikini without feeling uncomfortable at the beach! I know this is true for so many people, and not just with a number on the scale.

Whatever you do, always go for good enough instead of perfect. It sounds contradictory to the good enough trap, but it's not. Don't settle for less, but don't aim for perfection either. Choose the middle ground, do what you want and go after your dreams but do it with a dash of realism, enthusiasm, flexibility, patience, and compassion for yourself. Always aim for progress, not perfection.

Procrastination

In a way, this entire book is about procrastination: not doing something or delaying or postponing it, staying where you are even though you know what you could do to help you get unstuck. At this point in the MOVE method, let's look at it directly, especially to understand that it has nothing to do with laziness or that it's not a flaw you might think you're born with.

When I talk about procrastination – and I do that a lot, believe me, because it plagues so many people (including myself) – the first thing clients tell me is how disappointed they are with themselves, how ashamed and guilty they feel, and don't understand why they can't simply do what they know they should be doing.

Some of the most common reasons why we procrastinate are very similar to why we get and stay stuck; that's why they're often used interchangeably. They include:

- Lack of self-confidence.
- Perfectionism and people-pleasing.
- Lack of focus or motivation.
- Fear of failure.
- Fear of criticism (big one!).
- Decision fatigue, too many choices.
- Difficulty defining your goals and tasks.

- A lack of vision for your future.
- Lack of energy or too much of it.

We all avoid doing things sometimes, but that doesn't make us procrastinators. The critical difference between occasional procrastination and chronic procrastination is that a person with the latter habitually delays or puts off tasks or projects, even when they know it's in their best interest to do them.

Fortunately, several strategies can help to overcome the habit of chronic procrastination. While different approaches will work for different people, some of the most effective strategies I know include the following:

- Getting organized and clearing out your work and living spaces.
- Breaking down complex tasks into smaller ones (don't put goals on your to-do list!).
- Setting realistic goals and deadlines.
- Not breaking promises to yourself (huge one!).
- Creating incentives and rewards for yourself (life should be fun, make play part of your days).
- Focusing on the present moment.
- Limiting distractions as much as possible.
- Celebrating small wins along the way.
- Taking breaks, movement, and deep breathing.
- Eating nutritious food.
- Getting enough sleep!

These strategies can help you become more productive, efficient, and focused in your daily life. However, the best way to break free from procrastination is to start taking action – today.

Apart from what I mentioned above, not working in your zone of genius might also be why you procrastinate. It can be hard to stay motivated if you're not doing something that brings out the best in you. Feeling like your skills are being underutilized can make you delay tasks or projects (unconsciously). You know that what you're asked to do won't satisfy you, so there's no motivation to do it. When working within our zone of genius, it's easier to get things done, so it's worth being honest about what you love to do most and focusing on doing more of that.

Cognitive dissonance

Leon Festinger,[80] the social psychologist who developed the theory of cognitive dissonance in 1957, based his theory on the belief that humans want all their actions and beliefs to be consistent. When contradictions enter our lives – which happens a lot, and certainly when you hold two contradictory beliefs or believe one thing and act differently – we feel uncomfortable. That's the "dissonance" Festinger identified, and it is all around us.

Some signs that you may be experiencing cognitive dissonance are:

- An uneasy feeling before making a decision.
- The need to justify your beliefs, decisions, and behavior (even when nobody's asking).
- Doing things because you think you must do them, not because you want to.
- Feeling guilt, shame, or embarrassment over decisions that you made in the past.
- Experiencing stress and anxiety when you've decided or done something.
- Feelings of regret over past behavior or decisions.
- Feeling like a failure for not living up to your standards and expectations.

Cognitive dissonance is one of the most common human experiences, and I'm sure you've experienced it many times before.

The guilt you feel when you've decided to start eating healthier and end up eating a bag of irresistible Kinder chocolate; that's cognitive dissonance. Or when you're looking for biased information online to confirm the conspiracy theory you just came up with, that's a way to cope with the uneasiness that cognitive dissonance creates between the knowledge you have and the new knowledge that contradicts it. Or when your manager at work has poor leadership skills and often makes mistakes. To overcome cognitive dissonance, you'll rationalize why you're not speaking up but instead listen to them and do what they say because that's what you're "supposed to do."

It's no surprise, then, that cognitive dissonance keeps us stuck, especially by producing excuses for our behavior. This psychological mechanism aims to restore balance and harmony between what we think, believe, and do. If you're stuck in a job that drains you, in a romantic relationship that isn't working for you, in a town you dream of leaving every day, at home living with your parents, in a dire financial situation, chances are you've found all sorts of reasons to explain why, and perhaps even concluded that this is your life, and this is what's meant for you.

The fact that I stayed with my ex for so long has to do with cognitive dissonance. "Being married" was a way for me to brush off a lot of what was going on in the relationship. Even when things where bad, I kept on rationalizing that I "just needed to work on it a little harder" and that marriage wasn't supposed to be fun all the time. I made excuses for our behavior, so I could rationalize the situation I was in, and thought things like "I probably should not have raised my voice" or "I just need to try a little harder to understand him" or "he's probably right, it must be me." None of this was helpful, but it took my marriage falling apart for me to see it.

That's how powerful cognitive dissonance can be, even in the little things. After a long day of work, I'll catch myself wanting some ice cream or a slice of pizza, and I always rationalize it by saying "I deserve it" after the stressful, busy day I just had. But is that true? Or is my mind trying to make sense of two opposing beliefs: that I deserve relaxation and self-care *and* that I want to make healthy decisions and be mindful of what I put in my body? Perhaps you can relate.

How can you spot cognitive dissonance and not let it guide our decisions? This is a significant and juicy question. It's not easy to do, especially since 95% of our thinking is unconscious.[81] One thing that's helped me is to spot and pause when I make excuses. I'll ask myself if what I'm saying is true or if perhaps there's something else going on. Besides that, being more mindful has helped me spot my dissonant thoughts. When you're more aware of what you're thinking, you start to see where that thinking might be flawed. Meditation is a mindfulness practice[82] I do every day. Still, if that's not your thing, a few minutes of breathing with your eyes closed can be helpful, or some grounding exercises where you allow yourself to be in the now by focusing on the sensations of your body rather than your thoughts.

Sunken cost fallacy

Did you ever finish a book you didn't like? Overeat yourself simply because you ordered too much food? Or stay to watch the ending of a movie that wasn't worth your time or money? If you did, your actions were most likely driven by the investment you'd already made. If you didn't finish the book, didn't eat all the food, or didn't stay to watch that terrible movie's ending; your time, effort, or money would have been wasted. Right?

Making us draw this type of conclusion is what sunk costs do. They make it hard for us to abandon a course of action, a strategy, or a decision because we've already invested in it substantially, even when we know that giving up on what we're doing, changing course, or making a new decision would be the most beneficial thing to do. If we stop mid-way, we're left with a sense of loss, of costs that we can't recoup – which, to be fair, is true.

The problem with the sunken cost fallacy is that we only look at the costs we've already incurred and don't give any attention to the costs we still have to make if we persist and stubbornly keep going in the same direction.

I did this with books for many years. As soon as I'd read the first paragraph, however uninteresting or bad, I felt a strong urge to keep going. I'd started, so I needed to finish. I had invested time and energy; no way that could go to waste! While I was doing that, the pile of books that were good and worth my time steadily increased, as were the book wish lists I made every year on online book-selling platforms. At the age I am now, if I do an outstanding job of reading, let's say, 52 books a year (my current average), I can read another 2,000-ish books in my lifetime. It sounds like a lot, but it isn't. There are more than 600,000 books published every year in the United States alone. In 2021 more than 2,465,000[83] new book titles were published worldwide!

The sunken cost fallacy is a psychological phenomenon we all experience. Some domains are more conducive to it than others, like the financial sector or gambling, where sunk costs always include economic losses, which makes it more difficult for the person incurring the expenses to stop and take those losses: the next bet or the next investment might make up for all that has been lost so far. When you feel stuck and have felt that way for a while, the sunken cost fallacy might be at play too. You went to college for four years to get a degree in engineering, and even though you'd like to start your own bakery business and sell vintage books, you're convinced you need to become the hotshot engineer your parents are so keen for you to be.

Carlos was lucky enough to escape the trap of the sunk cost, but it took him several years. He came to me complaining that he wasn't happy but wasn't able to put the finger on what bothered him. "I don't know," he said, "when

I get up in the morning, I should be happy. I don't have anything to complain about. I have a great partner, a sweet baby boy, a well-paying job where I'm appreciated. What's wrong with me?" I nodded and smiled in agreement as Carlos shared his story with me. He was a funny and witty storyteller. After sharing a little more about his family, friends, and his wide range of interests, Carlos circled back to his job.

"You know," he started hesitantly, "I've never told this to anyone, but I don't really like being a lawyer." I could see Carlos was shocked by what had just come out of his mouth, as if he had shared something with me that even the secret service wasn't allowed to know. I knew we were on to something. "It's all my parents ever wanted, I just can't imagine doing something else, but at the same time, I'm dreaming about all the things I could do if I wasn't stuck in that law firm writing affidavits, checking official letters and filling out court documents all the time." I still hadn't said a word. Carlos, who I could see felt relief for finally sharing his truth with someone, continued, "Sometimes I think about leaving the firm. Then I remember all the nights I stayed up studying, all the money my parents paid to get me an education, and all the debt I'm still paying off. I've invested so much; it would be crazy to shift gears now and do something else."

There's something to say about Carlos's arguments – he's a lawyer after all. It's true he invested a lot in his law career: time, energy, and money. But he still has his whole life ahead of him; should he spend that life feeling unhappy at work every day? Even if it already cost him? It's going to end up costing him much more if he doesn't change course. Every day he's losing more time, energy, and perhaps even money doing something that doesn't make him happy. Wouldn't you agree? If Carlos was your best friend and told you what he told me, what do you think he should do?

As I coach, I help clients dig deep into their inner well[84] to figure out what they truly want. I help them align with their true desires and values, see the world for what it could be, give themselves permission to choose happiness, and come up with solutions and a vision for their lives. It took Carlos a few sessions to start seeing that he didn't need to keep investing in something he didn't like and that he was allowed to pivot and change careers. It took him a couple more to find out what he wanted to do, or better, to remember.

Since he was a child, Carlos had always wanted to work with animals. During the summer, he would stay with his grandparents at their dairy farm and help them care for the animals. "It was the happiest time of my life," he recalled in one of his last sessions, "I've never felt more alive than when I was surrounded by nature and animals." After remembering this childhood dream, Carlos put a list together of all the careers he could have that involved caring for animals. He came up with this list:

- Become a legal consultant for businesses and people who work with animals.
- Start an animal shelter.
- Work at an animal shelter.
- Work at a law firm that deals with protecting animal rights.
- Become an animal rights activist.
- Become a legal consultant for animal rights activists.
- Start a farm or work at my grandparent's farm (now run by my uncle).

Once he had his list, Carlos had a direction. He decided to pay a visit to an animal shelter in town to understand their needs and if they could use someone to assist them with legal issues. Paul, the shelter owner, was a lovely 55-year-old man with an immense love for animals but no legal insights. When Carlos knocked on his door, he was about to give up on a dispute he'd had with the town officials, who'd been pressuring him for a year to move his shelter elsewhere. It was Carlos's first consulting job but certainly not his last. After he helped Paul save his shelter, he knew this was what he was meant to do. He left the law firm and launched his freelance legal business. Even though he was leaving security behind, and he would never be able to make his mother's dream come true of becoming a partner in a big law firm, Carlos had found his calling by combining his interests into a new career. He could have stayed in the job that didn't make him happy, claiming that he had invested too much in it to change, but that would only increase the sunk cost and make it even harder for him to leave. By cutting his losses instead of staying stuck and investing more, Carlos gave himself the most beautiful gift: a career that he loves.

Prompt: What do you really want?

Now that you've gained insights about all the tricks your unconscious mind can play on you to keep you stuck, go back to your answer to the question "What do you really want?" and review what came up.

Then, to list your dreams, goals, and desires, ask yourself these questions:

- Are there other options available that I didn't consider before?
- Is this really what I want? Am I keeping my desires small, or am I going all in?
- Am I making excuses for myself?
- Am I talking myself out of the things I want by finding flaws in everything?
- Is what I want realistic? (E.g., Can I become an astronaut at 37?) If not, what could I do instead? And what do I really like about the idea of being an astronaut?
- Is perfectionism making my dreams impossible?
- Am I staying where I am because I've already invested a lot in this relationship, career, etc.?
- Is this dream important enough to me that I do everything to achieve it?
- What is the first step to making this my new reality?
- How am I going to keep myself accountable and motivated?
- What am I missing to go after this dream?

Chapter Three: Fear Itself.

"We are more often frightened than hurt; and we suffer more from imagination than from reality."
– Seneca

As you're nearing the end of this book, you know now that we create and live out self-fulfilling prophecies. Every day we live up to our self-image, we act as the person we think we are, and so we become that person. The world is what you think it is. We are who we say we are. If you want to change, it's essential to tell yourself a different story. Your inner dialogue needs to change, including your relationship with fear. Recognizing its voice, knowing when it's fear talking to you and not yourself or your intuition, catching the actions you're taking based on that fear and voice and not on what you really want or set out to do… it's all part of getting – and staying – unstuck.

Defining your fears

As you might have noticed, the older I get, the more truth and wisdom I find in philosophy, especially the Stoics. Seneca, particularly with his way of approaching fear and suffering, has helped me to overcome some of my deepest worries. "We suffer more often in imagination than in reality." It's one of his most famous quotes that I remind myself of every time I go into overthinking or catastrophizing my future.

In a 2017 TEDtalk,[85] Tim Ferriss, an American entrepreneur, writer, investor, podcaster, and freedom lifestyle advocate, talks about how defining his fears helped him overcome some of his life's darkest moments. In the talk (that I recommend you watch if you're plagued by procrastination, overthinking or future-tripping), he offers a way to define and analyze your fears to disarm them or at least put them in perspective. By defining your fear, you're getting a better grasp on what might happen if you do what you're afraid to do, but also – and this is important – what it will cost you not to do it.

In a recent coaching session, Elizabetha, a Croatian creative who came to me with a dream of building her own business but no idea on how to get started, admitted that what she was most afraid of was feeling the negative emotions that go along with not achieving her goals. "It's not so much that I'm afraid to fail. I know that when I fall, I can get back up; I've done it many times before. What I'm afraid of is the feeling when I'm down. I hate to feel hurt, sad, and, well, afraid." I nodded as Elizabetha continued to share how she didn't want to experience certain feelings. "I've felt this way in the past, and it's horrible! I never want to feel that again," she said while she crossed her arms in front of her chest decisively.

Elizabetha was sharing one of the biggest truths about fear. What we're afraid of is often the feelings that we experience when something bad happens or when things don't go our way, more than what is happening. I'm not talking about life-threatening events or loss; those are scary and painful things I wouldn't wish upon anyone, but for many other events or changes, like losing a job, separating from a partner, moving to a different country or state, deciding to switch careers, letting go of alcohol or food as a coping mechanism, being let down by someone, and so on, it's the emotion that accompanies the event rather than the event itself that we fear.

That's why it's interesting to define our fears and map them out like Tim Ferriss shares in his talk. By doing so, you realize that your worst fears won't probably happen and that the cost of not doing something might outweigh the cost of taking a chance on it and jumping.

Ask yourself this: "If you're not afraid to feel, what are you really afraid of?" Probably, not much.

This question returns to accepting uncertainty and *becoming comfortable with being uncomfortable,* a superpower that changed everything about my life. By allowing any emotion to pass through you, not reacting to those emotions immediately but instead letting them exist knowing that they're fleeting and will soon be gone, you become unstoppable. It is the most powerful way to get unstuck.

To become comfortable with being uncomfortable, you need to know that everything will be ok, that there is a light at the end of the scary, dark, sometimes painful tunnel. Because there is, and it's called trusting yourself that you've got this. Let's explore.

Overcoming fears and insecurities

In her bestselling book, *Feel the Fear And Do It Anyway*®, Susan Jeffers[86] says that underlying all fears is the fear or belief that we're not good enough. She continues that fear is connected to an even more profound idea, that we don't trust ourselves, which we've seen in this book. This lack of self-trust finds its way insidiously into our thoughts and mind in the form of, guess what, beliefs.

Often what keeps us from achieving our goals are fears and insecurities that take form in our minds rather than exist in the real world. What you think and believe influences what you do – *everything* that you do.

Five truths about fear

In the above-mentioned book, Susan Jeffers shares five truths about fear. I find those fears so powerful that I include my version here. They're based on Susan Jeffers, but they're not entirely the same. I've added some twists and my take on them to help deepen your understanding of how fear can keep you stuck.

#1 Being fearless is a myth.

There's no such thing as not being afraid. Everything you do that matters, is done with a dash of fear. Every time you decide to do something that you've never done before or that feels bigger or bolder than what you think is possible, you experience fear. This means that fear will come back over and over again, as you grow and strive for bigger dreams and goals. That's perfectly ok! Everyone experiences this. As Susan Jeffers so powerfully put it, the trick is to *feel the fear and do it anyway.*

#2 Being confident comes after you've done something, not before.

As I mentioned, you'll wait forever if you wait for absolute confidence or fearlessness before doing something. Waiting to feel ready, courageous, or confident enough before doing anything will result in you probably never doing it. It's by doing something that you overcome the fear that goes along with it. It's also by doing something that you slowly built the courage needed to do it in the first place. I know, it's so backwards! Every time you do something that scares you, your comfort zone expands.

#3 Ignoring your fears will only make them grow stronger.

It's an illusion that ignoring your fears will make them go away. We know we should not suppress our emotions, but somehow, when our fears are concerned, we believe that we do. Only by taking them on will you be able to make them smaller. It's the same with working through any emotion. The longer you work around your fears instead of through them, the more your confidence shrinks and your fears grow bigger. Fear gets smaller the closer you get to it. The only way to stop fear from ruling your life is to get as close to it as you can.

#4 Everyone experiences fear.

You might think you're the only one scared of doing something, but this is another myth used by fear to keep you small. The truth is: everyone's scared. Pretty much all the time. As I've shared before, on any given day I'll try to crawl under a rock at least ten times. Everyone is running around thinking about all the terrible things that might happen if they do anything. How do I know? Besides the rock thing I just shared? I speak to people about their dreams every day and fear is one of the biggest things that keeps them stuck.

#5 Most of what we believe will happen, never does.

85% of what we fear and worry about never happens[87], but when we're anxious and stressed out, 85% of what we think about are all the horrible things that could happen. This is nothing new; French philosopher Michel de Montaigne said it five hundred years ago: "My life has been filled with terrible misfortune, most of which never happened." Still, we insist on believing the unrealistic thoughts that fear puts in our minds. To get unstuck, you need to switch the script and focus on all the good things that could happen – which are more realistic! – then what could go wrong.

Fears and beliefs can prevent us from doing what we truly want. To recognize these fears for what they are, I invite you to do the following fear examination exercise whenever fear is holding you back.

- **Review your fears.** A powerful question that has helped many clients and I is: "What's the worst that can happen?" Whenever you experience fear, ask yourself this question and write down everything you can think of. When your list is ready, review the items and try to identify the worst outcome. Now compare that worst outcome with the life you'll have if you don't pursue your passion, goals, or dreams.

- **Embrace your fears.** After you realize that your worst outcome is probably much better than the unhappiness and unfulfilled life ahead of you if you don't follow your dreams, accept that answering your calling is scary. That's okay and something we all experience. This is why befriending and accepting your fears is so powerful, especially when undertaking new and exciting things.

- **Transform your fears.** A great way to live with your fears and make them work for you is to channel them into something empowering. Transform your negative thoughts into positive mantras that you repeat to yourself daily, and your fears will change in your favor. It might be something as simple as starting to say "I can" instead of "I can't" or "yes, why not?" instead of "no, not me." A mantra that has helped me many times to move through fear is: "it's not dangerous, it's old programming." I use it whenever I feel fear or anxiety taking over, especially when I'm about to do something bold and new. Reminding myself that it's a reaction of my nervous system to the past helps to stay grounded and focused in the present (where there is no danger!).

- **Avoid letting fear shut you down.** When you experience fear, please do whatever it takes to avoid shutting down. The simplest way to accomplish this is to sit with your fears and "do it anyway." There's no easy way to do this except through practice. However, by using fear as a trigger, you'll diffuse it from the start, and it *will* get easier.

- **Don't let fear guide you.** I'll be the first to admit that fear is very powerful. If left alone and free to play games with your mind, fear will eventually lead you away from your dreams and desires, cloud your judgment, and drag you down. The first step to avoiding this happening is recognizing your fears and knowing when they try to lead you. Awareness of your thoughts, feelings, and emotions will help you stand against fear and not let it guide you.

- **Prevent fear from deciding for you.** Fear is not only powerful, but it's also *very deceiving*. If a fear stays with you long enough and you don't challenge it, it will become part of your belief system. When this happens, fear starts to dictate your decisions and give direction to your life. Prevent fears from becoming familiar by habitually questioning your belief system and turning inwards. Doing this is essential to know what makes you happy and give your life the direction you want.

As I was finishing writing for this book one morning, a former client connected with me on Instagram. Proudly, Serena sent me a message and told me that, for the first time, she would post a picture and caption on her Instagram account about her writing work. While I was getting ready for a coaching call, I saw her message come through. I congratulated and encouraged her to post and let me know when she did it. That was a Tuesday. By Friday, I still hadn't heard from her. First, I went to Selena's Instagram account to see if I could find the post. Nothing. I sent her a message to gently inquire if there was something wrong with my eyesight. Selena messaged me back almost immediately. She sent me a happy emoji and said: "Well, as I was thinking about writing the caption, I realized it was going to be a long one. So I had a better idea! I'm going to write a blog post instead. But to do that, I realized I had to redo my website first because I don't like how it looks anymore. When that's done, I'll post the caption. It'll be much better because I'll be able to link it to my new website and blog."

What do you think is happening here? And, more importantly, does it sound like you? If you've come this far, it might. I know I was like Selena, and I still am at times, especially when I set big goals.

Sometimes, what we need is a friendly kick in the butt

When Selena told me her plan to redo her entire website, I knew what was going on. Having worked with her in the past, I knew what a talented creative and writer she is, but also how hard it is for her to get into action when she sets out to do something that scares her. Through our work, she managed to get unstuck and do some fantastic things, but life is a journey, and as we progress, our goals get bigger. We must keep reminding ourselves that fear will always be lurking and tell us not to do something to keep us safe (thanks, fear, but we've got this!). I couldn't help myself; I had to say something.

The following conversation ensued:

Sounds great! Can I challenge that a little bit?

Yes please!

Many creative generalists start with one thing and end up with a much bigger one, I'm not saying that's happening here, but going from publishing one post on IG to writing articles and relaunching your website could be clever fear or resistance disguised as practicality :)

I'm not saying it's your case!

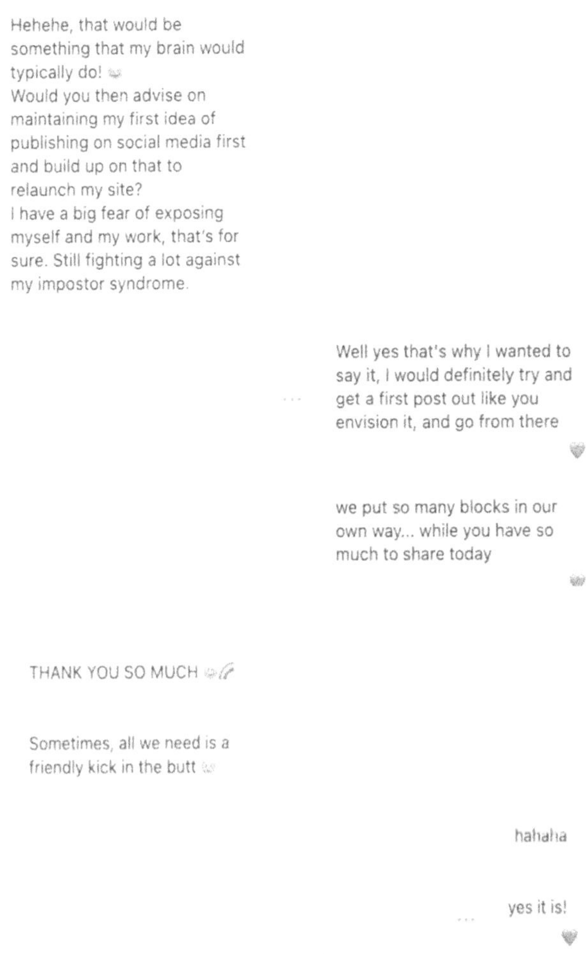

Selena posted her work and caption about 30 minutes later because that's all (!) the time she needed to get it written up and published. Had she waited for her website to be updated, she wouldn't have posted anything about her work for weeks, maybe months, even though she writes every day, publishes books, and knows her stuff so well!

I love what she said at the end: "sometimes, all we need is a friendly kick in the butt." It's true; we do. But not sometimes, most of the time. Many clients come to me stuck because of fear, and they're not doing anything because they're waiting to "feel different" or for the fear to go away. When they feel entirely ready, that's when they'll do it! By now you know it means they probably never will.

False evidence appearing real (FEAR)

When you're stuck, all the thinking, analyzing, and questioning you do isn't helpful. You've been over all your options a gazillion times; you're clearly not coming up with new solutions. Instead, you're going around in circles, another thing fear loves; for as long as you're going around, guess what you're not doing? You're not moving forward! Or, as Frank Herbert wrote in *Dune,* Fear is the mind killer.[88] The only thing that helps you out of a "fear loop" like that is to give yourself a kick in the butt (or have a well-intentioned and trained coach do that for you). Remind yourself of this powerful acronym for fear: false evidence appearing real. What you're feeling is real; the evidence, however, isn't. Snap yourself out of the overthinking cycle, especially when you're contemplating another, much more time-consuming idea than the one you were (finally!) ready to execute. Ask yourself: what can I do right now? Then, without hesitation, please do it!

A few days after our message exchanges and the friendly kick in the butt Selena needed, she came back to me with exciting news. Her Instagram post caught the eye of a content creator at a national television channel. She was offered a literary critic role and a column for one of their media! I mean, need I say more?

We can all use a little more grit

By finding the courage to give ourselves a kick in the butt sometimes, what we're doing is cultivating grit: a word that resonates with strength, determination, and unwavering resolve. Google speaks of courage, resolve, and strength of character. I believe it's what separates the dreamers from the doers, those who succeed from those who fail. In a world where instant gratification often takes center stage, the importance of grit cannot be overstated. Truly.

Recently, Adrian, a friend and client in his late thirties, who owns a chain of restaurants, shared a rather compelling story with me. One of his pizza places had just hired a new employee. It was her first week, and in the middle of a busy shift, she suddenly took off her apron and left on the spot, claiming that the hectic pace of the restaurant "was not good for her."

Now, this incident might seem like just a momentary blip, but it reflects a broader issue in today's world – a lack of grit and resilience in the face of challenges. In a society where everything should be frictionless, I see many people struggling to navigate demanding environments like a restaurant. As ambitious creatives, dreamers, careerists, entrepreneurs, or business owners, we must recognize the significance of grit in our personal and professional lives. Grit isn't merely about tolerating difficult situations; it's about embracing them as opportunities for growth and learning.

But what is grit, really? It's an invisible force. Because I've witnessed its power in my life and that of so many of my clients, I believe it's what keeps us pushing forward when everything seems to be against us. It's the unyielding fire that fuels our progress and pushes us towards our goals. Yet, in today's fast-paced society, it feels like grit is slowly fading away.

We live in a world where distractions are all around us and where the allure of immediate success can be tempting. We start something with enthusiasm, only to abandon it when the going gets tough. But here's the truth: true success rarely comes overnight. It's forged through tenacity, resilience, and, yes, grit.

When I was younger, I would start many things but never finish them. Of course, some of that resulted from my generalist brain, but there was more than that going on. I believe that at the time, I didn't have the resolve or the grit that is necessary to push through challenges and see things through to completion. I would often give up when faced with setbacks or when things became too difficult. It was easy for me to lose interest and move on to the next shiny object that caught my attention.

As I grew older, I realized the importance of finishing what I started and its impact on achieving success and personal growth. I began to understand that the habits that would allow me to succeed included perseverance, determination, and the willingness to do the necessary work, even when I didn't feel like it or faced obstacles. I consciously decided to develop my grit and cultivate a mindset that would help me overcome adversity. The book you're holding right now is a testament to that.

Ready is not a feeling, ready is a decision

One of the ways I started building grit was by using Mel Robbins' 5-second rule. When I saw her TEDx talk in 2013, *How to stop screwing yourself over*, I'd just embarked on my self-development journey. Mel Robbins is an American lawyer, television host, author, and motivational speaker. Her talk is one of the most popular TEDx talks of all time.[89] She was one of the first inspirations to change my life, stop slacking, and finally do the things I always wanted. By making her 5-second rule a habit, everything shifted. It made me realize that *being ready isn't a feeling; being ready is a decision*. Selena's story is a beautiful example of that. Throughout the years, I've shared the talk and the 5-second rule with many people who benefited from it. I'd love to share it with you.

Prompt: The 5 Second Rule (by Mel Robbins)

Whenever you feel like you're talking yourself out of an idea, try Mel Robbins' 5-Second Rule. This American Lawyer turned self-help author, and motivational speaker explained how the rule works in her book, *The 5 Second Rule*. It goes like this:

"The 5 Second Rule is simple. If you have an instinct to act on a goal, you must physically move within 5 seconds or your brain will kill it. The moment you feel an instinct or a desire to act on a goal or a commitment, use the Rule. (...) When you feel yourself hesitate before doing something that you know you should do, count 5-4-3-2-1-GO and move towards action."[90]

It wasn't so much that I didn't have a plan or an idea of what needed to happen to get unstuck. For the longest time, I'd look at the plan and tell myself that I would start with it tomorrow. I was in action, but only in my mind. In the real world, I was only "working on the plan," aka. I procrastinated, waiting for the moment I would "feel" like starting. The problem is that we hardly ever feel ready before we do something. Most of the time, the feeling of being able to do something comes after the fact, when we've done it and realized it wasn't that hard or that bad after all. Right?

When we're waiting to feel ready, we don't fear immediate danger; we fear possibilities: possible pain, loss, and worst-case scenarios. Then we conclude that we're *not ready* so we can avoid the negative feelings that come up because of fear. If we're not careful, this becomes a vicious cycle from which we have no escape. We focus so much on our feelings that we never take a step.

When we're playing out all the disaster scenarios in our heads, what we're overlooking is that most things we do work out. The probability of you achieving what you're trying to achieve is, in most cases, much higher than for things to not work out in your favor. That's why I love the 5-second rule, or any other trick to get yourself out of thinking mode for just long enough to do something. It short-circuits the overthinker in you, and pushes you into the action-taker mode so you realize that you are, in fact, as ready as you'll ever be.

I invite you to take this rule to heart and try it out the next time you feel you're talking yourself out of doing something or are waiting for a particular feeling to get started. It works, I promise you, and it's one of the keys to getting unstuck.

As a reminder, here's a (non-exhaustive) list of how fear can show up and keep us stuck:

- Disaster scenarios.
- Talking yourself out of things (instead of into them).[91]
- Coming up with excuses and yes-but-ing your way through life.
- Perfectionism and people-pleasing.
- Black and white, all-or-nothing thinking.
- Not knowing what you really want.
- Lack of self-confidence and self-esteem, impostor syndrome.
- Breaking promises to yourself.
- Procrastination.
- Not having clear boundaries.
- Settling for what you have, not what you want.
- Activities that keep you from working on your goals, such as binge-watching Netflix, busyness, compulsive shopping.
- Not pushing through, giving up before the finish line, impatience.
- Not wanting to take risks.
- Not wanting to change.

Getting unstuck means we stop avoiding what we fear. Instead, we can experiment so that, slowly but surely, our comfort zone becomes bigger! There's no other way than to feel *the fear and do it anyway*.

Chapter Four: Trauma and Childhood Wounds.

"Trauma is a psychic wound that hardens you psychologically that then interferes with your ability to grow and develop. It pains you and now you're acting out of pain. It induces fear and now you're acting out of fear."
– Gabor Maté

Whatever fear makes us do, it does so to protect us and keep us safe. The problem is that fear doesn't grow up the way we do. What worked for fear to keep us safe when we were children doesn't work anymore. The outdated programming from our younger years brought us to this point, but it will not take us where we want to go. To get there, we need to have a conversation with fear and help it understand we're not the same person anymore. We've grown, we can think for ourselves, and the world that might have been terrifying once is safe now.

I used to be anxious and stressed all the time. There was a good reason for that. For the longest time, up until my parents passed away, I was in an almost constant *crash state,* as my therapist calls it. A crash state is where your trauma controls you, often without knowing what's happening. I was a people-pleasing perfectionist with anxiety who lived for one thing and one thing only: to do what I thought was expected of me. I used unhealthy coping mechanisms to try to relieve the incessant stress and worry that I was feeling, and I had no connection to my emotions or my body.

In a recent conversation with a fellow coach about trauma and attachment wounds, he made a comment that stayed with me. As I was sharing how I'd been in a crash state for so long, without even realizing I was flooded with PTSD and being hyper-reactive to trauma triggers, he said: "at least you feel when you're being triggered." I had to stop and pause for a second when he said that because, yes, it's true that I feel when I'm triggered now. Before I reconnected with my body and started to heal, I didn't feel anything from the neck down. When something triggered me, I thought that what I felt was my truth and I needed to act upon my perception of reality.

One of my most significant wounds is abandonment, and it's been one of my biggest fears throughout my life. When you fear being abandoned due to an unhealed wound, anything that resembles it will set you off. Whenever a partner or someone close to me would create any distance between them and me, I would be triggered and need a lot of reassurance. I would also start to exhibit sabotaging behavior to have them prove that they loved me and weren't abandoning me. I know a lot of people do this and carry similar wounds.

The interesting thing is that we almost all – if we have unhealed trauma – think we're reacting to an actual situation happening in the present moment. But we aren't. Nobody's abandoning us, people are simply living their lives, and the feelings that come up in us are not a reaction to their behavior (going to the gym, showing some independence, traveling for work) but to something from the past. See how tricky this is?

Healing your trauma and (childhood) wounds

In a conversation with my friend Holly, a grief and trauma counselor, we talked about how everything comes down to trauma and attachment wounds. After working through my stuff for so long, I'm more convinced than ever that this is true.

In the past decades, I've healed a lot of what was stuck in my body, mind, and nervous system. Whenever I uncovered a new layer of pain and gave it my attention, I became stronger and more resilient. Don't get me wrong, this process was long and arduous. I didn't take a magic pill that would fix everything. But what I experienced was magical, nonetheless.

Almost all the anxiety and worry that plagued me then is gone, and so is my tendency to procrastinate and my inability to finish projects; my boundaries are more robust, my determination and tenacity have expanded, and an overall sense of happiness and well-being is a constant in my life.

A few years ago, something unexpected happened after I'd already healed so much of the pain that was holding me back from living the life I wanted. While a global pandemic struck the world, I was zooming with my therapist when I shared what felt like an insignificant detail. Glenn picked up on it. He stopped my ramblings about what was happening in my life and made me pause. "I'm wondering," he said, "what do you mean by what you just said?"

A challenging but eye-opening conversation followed. I'd just stumbled on my most profound trauma, what I call my *primal trauma*. This trauma had been with me since about the age of five, so almost my entire life. It dictated significant aspects of my life without me knowing it, forced me into choices I didn't want to make, and pretty much decided everything I did and thought I wanted. Behind it was a lot of fear that came out during the night and when I was alone.

When I realized I was carrying this trauma, all my choices gained new meaning. As I was healing my wounds, it got harder to keep acting on auto pilot. Eventually, I chose myself and my healing over fear. That meant I had to face my fears and do the things I was most afraid to do.

I love the life I have now. Healing that trauma – truly healing it – allowed the fear and anxiety to leave completely. In and of itself, this is a fantastic accomplishment. But that's not the end of it. When I healed my primal trauma, I got free. Absolutely free. Without realizing it, the crash state I was in was hiding behind layers of protective behaviors. The fears at night were just one of the symptoms. Suddenly, I wasn't afraid of many other things: speaking to large crowds of people, stepping into spaces I didn't know, meeting strangers and talking to them, asking for what I wanted or needed, standing up for myself, being more visible and claiming my truth, writing books, sharing my views on my podcast, and so much more.

The ripple effect of trauma

We all carry childhood wounds and trauma. Gabor Maté, who I mentioned before, says that very few people reach adulthood without some trauma. It doesn't have to be "big T" trauma; "little t" trauma is often as painful and challenging to overcome, especially if you're unaware of it.

Big T trauma refers to life-threatening situations or events. A car crash, natural disaster, an accident of any sort, like a house fire, a violent crime or a robbery, a school shooting, or the death of a parent or loved one. This type of trauma causes acute psychological distress. Ongoing, chronic distress that threatens the victim's physical safety, such as repeated abuse or when children are neglected or unsafe, also qualifies as big T trauma.

Little t trauma is more subtle but no less distressing. The difference is that little t trauma usually doesn't involve a threat to the victim's physical safety, only a psychological one. However, this can create the same distress and trauma responses as big T trauma. Being bullied, falling out with a friend, breaking up with a partner, losing a job, being ostracized by a group or not accepted into one, receiving physical but not emotional care from a caregiver, having to live up to the standards of a perfectionistic or narcissistic parent, or something as simple as a parent not allowing a child to have their own opinion, or punishing them for being spontaneous or speaking up. All of these create trauma responses like big T trauma. Some studies even suggest that repeated exposure to little t trauma can cause more harm than exposure to one big T trauma event.

Everyone who goes through traumatic events will have some trauma as a result. The way my marriage ended was so abrupt, and my worldview was so shattered that I developed PTSD. It took months of intensive therapy to get that shock out of my nervous system and for the emotional distress to subside. With time, support from friends, and professional help, I recovered.

I suffered a lot of little t trauma in my life, but my primal trauma is of the big T kind. Unlike my painful separation, what I experienced as a child was never adequately addressed, the recovery process – if there ever was one – was interrupted, and the coping mechanisms I developed back then became my way of being. On the outside, I was a confident go-getter who knew what she wanted; inside, I was a little, anxious mess. This trauma crash state had terrible consequences for what I believed was possible, how I saw the world, and rippled into all my relationships with other people – and mostly with myself. The problem was: I had no clue this was going on!

What I believe is most damaging about trauma, is that most people don't know they're carrying it. You can't recover from it if you don't know it's there. As long as I was unaware of the extent to which my behavior and life were dictated by it, I was stuck. I saw the beautiful dreams I had waiting for me on the other side of the procrastination and self-sabotaging bridge, but I couldn't cross it. Whatever I tried ultimately failed. Not entirely, thank goodness. But moving forward and building my dream life was so much harder than it needed to be. Unconsciously, I was carrying a weight that pressed me down and made everything challenging, and scary.

Once I realized trauma was stuck deep in my nervous system, I decided to do something about it. It took a few years of therapy, consistent self-awareness, a healthy dose of courage, and a diligent willingness to grow and change, but eventually, I overcame what had been keeping me small for so long. I got myself unstuck once more. I peeled another layer of the onion. Everything started to flow and became more manageable. Life didn't feel like a fight anymore (nor a flight, for that matter). I was free, and what I wanted started coming to me almost effortlessly.

Reconnecting with your inner child

When I focused on healing, my therapist first asked me to start a conversation with my inner child. It probably was one of the hardest things for me to do. Without being aware of it, I was utterly disconnected from the little girl I had once been. In time, I learned this happened to protect myself because I couldn't consciously face what had happened to me growing up. But ignoring, silencing, or forgetting about my inner child didn't mean she was gone or didn't influence my adult behavior. On the contrary.

We all have an inner child inside ourselves. That child was the first version of ourselves that consciously experienced the world, picked up beliefs about society and our place in it, and underwent the vast array of human emotions. These first tentative steps into life left marks and patterns that shaped us and our future. Those patterns and marks came from positive, nurturing experiences or neglect and trauma. That's important to know and recognize because our inner child isn't gone; for many of us, it's become our way of being. When you're traumatized, hurt, or neglected as a child, and you grow up and move on, you still carry that weight. Somewhere, somehow what is unresolved will show itself in your life, even if you don't see it. My *primal trauma* is a perfect example of that. I never questioned the fact that I was afraid and anxious; I just made sure (unconsciously) that I avoided situations that made me feel that way.

A part of the work I had to do was reconnecting with my inner child. Even though it was hard at first, it's also one of the most amazing experiences I've ever had. Glenn, my therapist, guided me and introduced me to experiments and strategies to connect and talk to her. It caused a lot of stress and negative emotions to surface. My inner child was holding a lot of pain, sorrow, and anger but below those burdens, there lived a vibrant, carefree, adventurous, and courageous little person that wanted nothing else but to live a happy life.

Reconnecting with your inner child to see what it wants to share with you is always helpful and inspiring. If you have childhood wounds or trauma, your inner child will help you figure out what's going on and what to work on. If you don't, reconnecting with the bubbly, young, innocent, and joyful part of yourself will still enrich your life.

Some ways to reconnect with your inner child:

- Remember what you liked doing as a child and try it now.
- Think about your best childhood memories (think about your best childhood dreams if you don't have many positive memories).
- Give your inner child a voice: listen and speak to what it says.
- Give yourself a hug and imagine you're giving it to your inner child.
- Connect with children and let their imagination and joy bring your younger side back.
- Bring a pen to paper and journal about your childhood years and what you loved most about them, dreamed of for yourself, and wanted to be when you grew up.

Uncovering your childhood wounds

Connecting with your inner child can help you understand your adult experience. Until I started doing this work, I thought that I'd left my childhood behind, that it was a closed box, a done deal. I believed I'd moved on from the pain of those years and healed my wounds. Now I know that's not how it works. If you want to get unstuck, you must work through the problem, not keep it buried (this is such a big realization that I'm using it as the foundation and plot for a thriller I'm currently working on).

I knew I had not been given the love and care I was supposed to get, but I thought it made no difference. I believed I'd *fixed* myself, that I understood what had happened, and that I was healed from it. The problem with childhood trauma is that, when it's left untreated, it's hard to be happy. A feeling of impending doom and lack of safety is constantly throbbing below the surface. We feel lonely and shameful. We still believe that, somehow, all of this is our fault. If we'd just tried harder. If we'd just been *good*, none of this would have happened. Of course, all of that is untrue.

Every child deserves love, and it's never the child's fault when an adult isn't offering the safety, care, and support the child needs. Unfortunately, children always think it's their fault. I was no exception. Growing up in a stressful environment, I experienced a severe lack of connection with myself, bouts of depression and sadness, and chronic anxiety throughout my early adult life. I was stuck – without even knowing it!

Childhood wounds left unresolved will continue to affect us as adults. Healing requires us to return to the child we were when the pain and trauma occurred. It is our starting point. The emotions our inner child experienced are still lingering inside of us. As long as we don't address those feelings and work through them, we will never be free.

If you were neglected as a child, it might be hard for you to trust others or the world. Luckily, it doesn't have to be this way. Through inner child work, you can heal these wounds and become a happy, successful, and joyful person. I did; that's why I know you can too. And it all starts with looking at your wounds and how they keep you stuck.

Prompts: The wounds that keep you stuck

Friendly reminder: I'm not a therapist, psychologist, or healthcare professional. I'm a coach. If you have severe trauma, attachment, or childhood wounds or need medical support, please get in touch with a healthcare professional. I've added a resource page with a list of organizations that can help on my website here: https://www.muriellemarie.com/healing-from-trauma-resources.

For this exercise, I want you to (re)connect with your inner child. You don't need to write anything down if you don't feel like it, but writing is the best way to connect on a deeper level with yourself. Find a quiet spot to sit or lay down. Once you've read through the questions, start writing or close your eyes and ponder:

- How was I as a child?
- What is my happiest childhood memory? My wildest dream?
- Were there any decisive events that shaped how I see the world today?
- How does my inner child see the world?
- What beliefs about the world started in my childhood for me?
- When I was a child, what did I want to be when I grew up?
- What's a funny yet embarrassing moment from my childhood?
- What is my inner child saying to me today?
- What does my inner child need from me today?
- How will I give my inner child the love and support I wanted as a child?
- What is one step I can take to get unstuck?

Attachment styles and how they keep you stuck

Our childhood wounds shape our attachment style. Our attachment style defines how secure we feel in the world and how we trust ourselves and others. We all know lack of trust is a huge hurdle in our relationships. But did you know it can have equally detrimental consequences for other aspects of your life, your career, or business? If you have trust issues, your attachment style is likely playing a role in your lack of trust toward others, which might be keeping you stuck. Are you readily able to trust the people you work with? Do you believe your friends when they tell you they'll show up for you? Do you believe a co-worker when they tell you they'll handle an issue at work? Do you trust them to do a good job, or are you micromanaging everything and everyone around you?

Your lack of trust and the micro-management or control following from it might be because you're anxious and don't want to be hurt (again). What has probably been a great, life-saving defense mechanism at some point could be keeping you stuck in toxic relationships, a career you don't like, or unable to move forward with your business or project idea. It might even stop others from entering into professional or personal relationships with you.

On the surface, it doesn't seem like trust issues have anything to do with keeping us stuck, but when we dig a little deeper, it's easy to see how this can affect success and why it deserves attention and might even require healing. Trust issues are often linked to anxious attachment, one of four attachment styles. People who have developed an anxious attachment lack trust in almost everyone and everything, often making them anxious, scared, or worried.

What is attachment theory?

Attachment theory examines how the caregiver-child bond develops and impacts child development. Psychologist and psychoanalyst John Bowlby was the first to talk about attachment and formalize its theory in the 1950s and 1960s. Bowlby theorized that attachment is an inbuilt survival instinct that ensures infants seek proximity to their mothers or primary caregivers. If they cannot do so, infants might feel "distress," a form of discomfort and dissatisfaction when confronted with anything other than what they need. In Bowlby's words: *"Attachment is a deep and enduring emotional bond that connects one person to another person across time and space."*[92]

According to Bowlby, there are four attachment styles: *secure, anxious-ambivalent, disorganized, and avoidant.* Let's review them quickly. Refer to the resources section at the end of this book for more extensive information.

#1 Secure attachment.

Securely attached children feel safe and comfortable with their primary caregivers. They explore the world around them but return to a secure and safe place when needed. Securely attached people tend to have healthier relationships in adulthood because they feel more confident in their interactions with others and don't experience fear of abandonment.

Securely attached individuals will have an easier time sticking to a job or business idea, trusting coworkers or business partners, and making decisions based on opportunity rather than fear. In their careers or as business owners, securely attached adults are more likely to rely on others for help and support because they have a more vital trust. They're also less anxious about their lack of control in work-related situations.

When we're securely attached, we tend to be warm and loving in our relationships. We're comfortable with intimacy and are not afraid to show affection for others. Being securely attached is magical; it gives you such an advantage in the world, yet we hardly talk about it.

Dana Dozzyy, a nervous system practitioner I follow on TikTok (yes, you read that right, and you can find her info in the resources section at the end of this book because she's awesome!), shared a thought about secure attachment that rings so true to me, especially after healing so much of my trauma and helping so many people get unstuck. She said: "When you understand how the nervous system works, you realize that the real rich are people that grew up in a household with two loving parents that were very emotionally regulated, that prioritized healthy relationships, quality sleep, quality nutrition, exercise, movement, sunlight, family time. I don't actually think that most people understand how much of a leg up growing up in a household like this actually gives you in real life. (...) It is better for somebody to grow up in a home like that, where there is less money, versus a home with dysregulated parents that don't prioritize those things and make more money."[93]

#2 Anxious-ambivalent attachment.

Anxious-ambivalent children are more clingy, needy, and lack self-confidence. They get anxious when away from their caregivers and distrust them, leading them to explore their environment with fear rather than excitement. Children with anxious-ambivalent attachment constantly seek approval from their caregivers and continuously observe their surroundings out of fear of being abandoned or in danger. This anxious behavior can translate into less ease and more perfectionistic tendencies in adulthood because they're constantly dwelling on what could go wrong. The decisions they make are often based on (unconscious) fear, which can result in complicated personal relationships or professional opportunities or promotions they want but don't take.

#3 Avoidant attachment.

Avoidant children lack the attachment bond with their caregivers and show very little interest in exploring or trying new things. They seem uninterested, detached, and lack empathy for others. When they explore the world, it's usually to get away from adults rather than get close to them; when faced with a challenge that requires help, they don't seek support. They often struggle with expressing their feelings and find it hard to understand emotions – especially their own. As a result, avoidant adults tend to lack trust in people, reflected in their relationships, careers, or businesses as difficulty to delegate, trying to do it all themselves, failing to ask for support when needed, and often struggling to work with others as a team.

#4 Disorganized attachment.

Disorganized attachment is a combination of avoidant and anxious attachment caused by various reasons, such as a lack of bonding with the caregivers or frequent changes in caregivers. Children with a disorganized attachment style often display intense anger and rage and difficulty controlling their emotions, affecting their relationships later in life. As adults, they avoid trusting others and have little to no self-confidence when facing challenges. This lack of self-confidence and low self-image often leads to accepting less than what they're worth both in their private life and at work, doing other people's jobs, and accepting without a fight not being recognized for their accomplishments. In business, it leaves them prey to their customers and service providers, often because of a lack of non-violent communication and aiming for smaller goals than they could achieve if they trusted themselves more.

The law of familiarity and how it can affect your life

About 50% of the population has a secure attachment style, so why are those people not often part of the social fabric of those with non-secure attachment? I believe the main reason is that like attracts like. Even with half the population having secure attachment, it doesn't mean you'll have a lot of those people in your life if you don't have a secure attachment style yourself (remember what we learned about our environments and how the people in our lives shape who we are). A reason for this is what's called the *law of familiarity*.

Suppose you grew up in a household where dysregulation was the norm. In that case, you're not used to peaceful, regulated parents who care for you with love, stability, and warmth and teach you how to develop a secure attachment to others. If you've grown up in a dysregulated household, what you'll be familiar with is the emotional chaos, the insecurity, the lack of trust, the trauma maybe, so that's what might – unfortunately – feel safe to you. Just like securely attached people will attract other securely attached people based on unconscious behaviors, those with an insecure attachment will be drawn the same way to others who share their insecure attachment.

The good news is that you can change your attachment style. It takes effort, but it's worth it to become more secure in your relationships, both personally and professionally. This has been my reality, and the same is true for many of my clients. Through our coaching work, they learn how to trust themselves more and become more confident, even if they're working on entirely different goals, like changing careers or starting their own business. In a way, what's happening is you're learning how to attach to yourself securely. By focusing on getting unstuck and achieving your dreams, you're gently nudged to believe in yourself and become your own safe haven.

Is your attachment style keeping you stuck?

If you have an anxious or ambivalent attachment style[94] (well, hello there, I see you!) there's a chance that you learned not to trust others at a young age. A lack of secure attachment with caretakers during our early years affects how our brain develops and responds to interpersonal relationships later in life.

Lack of trust can express itself in various ways, both in your personal and professional life, such as:

- You're exhausted because you feel you need to do everything, and the help you're getting is (according to your perfectionistic standards) never up to par.
- You're micromanaging everyone's tasks (including your partners, children, colleagues, business associates, and service providers) because you're not confident they can do the job.
- You never ask for help or accept it because you believe you must do everything alone, and it makes you suspicious whenever someone offers. You wonder what the ulterior motives are, so you say no, even when you need it most.
- You're always waiting for the other shoe to drop because you're anxious things won't work out. Everything might look good now, but you don't believe it will stay that way.
- You have a hard time making decisions, especially about a career change or a new business venture. One day you're ecstatic about the idea; the next, not so much.

Anxiously (and ambivalently) attached people are generally preoccupied with thoughts about relationships – whether personal or professional ones. They can be cautious to the point of being fearful and may withdraw from a relationship if they have an uneasy feeling that it's going downhill. This, of course, is bad for business. A successful career or business requires networking, reaching out, and connecting with others.

If you lack trust in your professional or personal relationships, try the following:

- Make sure you're not micromanaging everything and everyone around you. Be a supportive team player instead of always telling others what to do. You don't want them to feel like their work is never good enough because this might further complicate your relationship or collaboration.
- Trust others by giving them more responsibility (not less!) and let go of the reins. Your lack of trust will show if you don't delegate some tasks, so try trusting someone with something small first and see how they do before handing over more significant projects or responsibilities.
- Have a candid conversation with your partner, children, business associate, or service providers, and tell them that your attachment style has held you back from trusting them. You don't need to give them the reasons why, but it helps to develop solutions together.
- Keep working on developing a more secure attachment. You might never get where someone naturally trusts others, but you can get close. It starts with understanding your style and being willing to work at it.

Building a more secure attachment with yourself

To heal your lack of trust, you need to work on healing your attachment wounds. It's one of the most liberating things you can do for yourself, but it's not something that happens overnight. I've added an exercise below to get you on the path to secure attachment. Still, if you feel your attachment style is keeping you stuck, start with finding a therapist or coach who knows about attachment theory so they can help guide you through this process. You may also want to read or research this topic to understand it better.

When we're raised in a dysregulated environment, we not only lack secure attachment with others but also with ourselves. We've addressed this when talking about self-trust before. Trust and security are connected. Security requires trust that someone will do what they say they'll do, but also that we can rely on our understanding of how someone is and will treat us, even if they don't promise us anything.

In recent years, I've worked hard at becoming a safe person, friend, coach, and business partner for the people in my life. I've cultivated reciprocal safe attachment with my inner circle of friends, which has helped them and me grow into a more secure attachment. I've learned to recognize the triggers that made me pick partners that didn't have a secure attachment style, and I've learned how to make safer choices instead. A lot of what I've shared in this book so far has been instrumental in going from anxious to secure attachment:

- Being present with myself,
- self-love,
- self-trust,
- self-compassion,
- living a values-based life,
- changing my mindset and beliefs,
- living in integrity with myself,
- committing to myself daily,
- being fiercely disciplined in my growth journey.

What helped me the most is the realization that I always have my own back and that abandoning myself, as I've done so many times in the past, doesn't need to be my destiny. I can choose, moment to moment, to be there for me, to be safe for myself, to be my most trusted friend. Every day, I have the choice to be the best version of myself that I've ever been. By shifting my life this way, I've become more confident about what I can accomplish and gained a level of inner peace and calm that I didn't know existed. Not to mention the ease with which I make choices and decisions, which keeps me from getting stuck again.

Prompt: How can I build a more secure attachment with myself?

Imagine someone you'd feel secure being around. Someone that has your back no matter what and who supports you while giving you the freedom to explore the world. Maybe you have someone like that in your life; in that case, think of them.

Now think about how this person shows up for you. What do they do when you need help? When you're sad? When you feel lonely or misunderstood? How do they help you navigate difficult situations? What do they do when something great happens in your life? How do they celebrate with you? What happens when you don't speak to them for a while or when you're busy with your life?

For each aspect below, reflect on how the person you've imagined above would embody them. Then, modeling them, imagine how you can give more of these things to yourself.

- Being present with yourself.
- Loving yourself.
- Trusting yourself.
- Being compassionate towards yourself.
- Living a values-based life.
- Changing your mindset.
- Living in integrity with yourself.
- Committing to yourself daily.
- Being fiercely disciplined in your growth journey.

Finally, ask yourself what you need to feel more securely attached to yourself. What is the one thing you can start doing right now? Then commit to doing it.

Chapter Five: The Most Effective Way to do Something, is to do it.

"Sorry; I have no space left for advice. Just do it."
– Donald E. Westlake

Let's go back to Chiffa for a moment. She'd been through all the excuses in the book not to quit her job. Because she had thought herself out of so many things, she believed there were no options left. "I don't know what to do, I've thought about everything, but nothing feels better than the one I have now. It's boring, yes, but it also pays well, and the money is in my bank account on the first of every month. I can't risk not having that money come in." Chiffa had a well-paying job that felt safe, even if it bore her brains out, and her boss and colleagues undervalued her.

I see this often in my practice: people stuck in *golden cages* or handcuffs. The door to the cage isn't closed, the key to the handcuffs isn't lost, they could step out at any time or release themselves from the burden, but the cage is so cozy and the handcuffs so shiny. Even with open doors, it remains a cage; even with all the bling and luster, they're still handcuffs, and that's difficult to escape, even though everyone I coach wants to get out. So did Chiffa.

After she opened up about her job, it became clear that she wasn't taking any action to switch careers because of her need for financial security. It's a need many people share and that I have as well. The problem with that need is that it's a perception, not reality. Having a job offers more security than not having one, but no job is 100% secure, and almost no job is *for life*. After months of being in limbo, of self-doubt and frustrations, trying to move forward by thinking about things more had no point. There was only one thing left for Chiffa to do: take action.

Convergent thinking vs divergent thinking

We get stuck by looking at our challenges and problems from just one point of view. To get unstuck, you must be willing to look at your situation differently and investigate how it relates to you. This is called divergent thinking: you question the accuracy of what you think about yourself and reality, and change things that don't serve you.

As we've covered in Step Two, introducing new and unknown information into a system, and looking at it from various viewpoints is how we can gain new insights and get moving again, right? Well, yes, obviously! But only to a certain point, after which the questioning and inquiring become an excuse not to do something. This point, which many of us reach at least a few times in our life, is what I call *the graveyard of diffluent ideas.* It's where nothing happens anymore, not even thinking, and exhausted and overworked ideas break down and eventually dissolve until nothing is left of them (dramatic music playing in the background).

Knowing when to step away from divergent thinking and move into convergent thinking is essential. To get unstuck, you can't keep thinking about all your options without taking action; at the end of the day, you must do what? That's right! Get up and get going!

So far in this book, I've invited you to open your mind, step outside your comfort zone, and expand your divergent thinking. It's time to bring everything together and let what you've learned and discovered about yourself, and your dreams take root in meaningful, focused, productive action. It's time to bundle all your ideas into an actionable plan. Are you ready?

What's your glue?

One of the things that many people have a hard time with is finding the one thing that will keep them inspired and going forward. Creatives and entrepreneurs (not to mention creative generalists) can have difficulty knowing what to focus on – they simply have too many ideas.

In his book *Start With Why,*[95] Simon Sinek shares a fundamental idea about people and why they buy: "People don't buy what you do, they buy why you do it." Sinek's TEDx talk from 2009, which is now the world's 3rd most-watched TED talk of all time[96], emphasizes the importance of a company knowing why they do what they do. At its heart is the concept of purpose and the idea (that is now mainstream) that businesses with a strong purpose grow faster. I believe this is true. However, I've also seen in my coaching practice how looking for your "why" can keep some people stuck, especially when they're looking for the type of purpose Simon Sinek talks about: *"The compelling higher purpose that inspires us and acts as the source of all we do."*

When I met Ella many years ago, an American singer-songwriter living in Paris, I was immediately enchanted by her natural energy and beautiful voice. Ella was about thirty then and had just finished recording the first two songs of the new album she was producing independently. Ella paused as we discussed her goals and dreams and how she wanted to grow an audience and platform for her work. She looked at me, and while I could see some hesitation in her eyes, she said: "You know, I've been breaking my head over this and thinking about it for so long, but I just don't know what my *why* is. Actually, that's not true," she continued, "I know what my why is, it's just not this big purposeful thing everyone says you need to have to be successful. I love to make music. I love writing songs, being in a studio, collaborating with others when recording songs, and hearing the music come to life. If I'm honest, that's why I do what I do. It makes me happy to use all my creative skills this way."

Ella and I went on to have a wonderful and inspiring coaching relationship. Over time I witnessed how she got herself unstuck and took on some big and beautiful goals that she achieved one by one. But in that first conversation, Ella raised a point that stayed with me and that I've since heard many times. People who feel stuck, ashamed even, for not having a clear higher purpose, a reason outside themselves why they want to do what they do. The question is, do you have to? Isn't your happiness enough to guide you – as long as what you want isn't hurting anyone, or does it need to be bigger than yourself to be worthy of your time?

As I finish this book, my *"Get Unstuck with Murielle Marie"*[97] podcast is nearing 6000 downloads! And guess what? It's all about inspiring people to say "f*ck it" and helping them to get unstuck in their lives and careers. Finally, I'm also working on a new online course and group program. The course is a step-by-step guide to help you get unstuck using my proprietary 4-step MOVE method that you've read about in this book. If I've worked according to plan, that should be available by now.

That's a lot of "getting unstuck," isn't it? But hey, what can I say? It's my "glue," the common thread unique to me that makes everything else come together and make sense, combines creativity, curiosity, a need for freedom, and a deep belief in the power of connection. It turns out that my "why" – getting people unstuck – benefits greatly from my glue. To find it, I followed the breadcrumbs. I asked myself what career would allow me to combine everything that makes me happy daily in a meaningful way (the ideal day exercise really helped!).

We all have our unique glue. The clearer you get about *your glue*, the easier it becomes to choose what to focus on and eventually make progress on your goals. Not an easy thing to do for people with more ideas than hours in a day, but once you get a handle on it, it's gold.

Sometimes our glue looks like Simon Sinek's "why" or will lead to it, but not always. Our glue can be a thing or a specific career path or interest, but that too, only happens sometimes. In many cases, like Ella's, our glue is more of a feeling, a sense of flow, or a way of being that we experience when doing certain things, especially creating. And that's perfectly ok. Even if you're an entrepreneur or freelancer, doing something you love can be enough for other people to see the value in your offer. If you do it long enough, your why will probably emerge. You don't need to save the world – adding some positivity to it is good enough. Like Frank Tyger says: "Doing what you like is freedom. Liking what you do is happiness."

Prompt: What's your glue?

What unique theme or common thread makes everything come together and make sense for you?
The questions below will help you identify your main theme. Don't despair if you can't pinpoint one clear thing; a sense of what that theme might be for you is good enough to get you started. As you progress on your journey of self-discovery, and as you live more and more aligned with your values and authentic self, your glue will continue to manifest itself.

- When are you the happiest?
- What activities quickly get you into flow?
- What makes you come alive?
- What topics interest you the most?
- What type of work do you like to do?
- What motivates you to keep going?
- What's your most secret dream?
- When do you get to use your entire skillset?
- What do you enjoy doing?
- What keeps you interested and gives you energy?

Look at your answers to the questions above and try to distill a common theme or thread from them. What are the reasons why you do what you do? What's the number one thing that makes you feel alive?

When Muhammad, a bright and energetic Norwegian client with a master's in history and a Ph.D. in archaeology, did this exercise, he realized that his glue was *creating*. "I love people, knowledge, and history," he told me. When I'm connecting dots between all the knowledge I have when I put exhibits together that make people understand what I see when I look at an ancient artifact, that's when I'm the happiest."

Just choose something!

You're almost at the end of this book and, hopefully, by now, at the beginning of (finally) getting unstuck. If you haven't done the exercises in this book and are still feeling rather stuck, now is the time to do them. In what follows, we're going to make some decisions and start taking action.

Chances are you'll get started a bit unsure and without absolute clarity. That's perfectly fine. It's the only way to do anything anyway. Isn't waiting to feel ready or confident enough not what got you stuck in the first place? It's time for a new approach, the one that works. One where you trust that you will figure things out as you go, not that you need to have all the answers before you start.

Throughout this book, I've asked you a few times what you wanted. Each time you pondered that question, you did so with a little more understanding of how your mind works and how it might keep you stuck. After the last exercise, you should know your glue, the common thread that makes everything come together and make sense to you. Now is the time to be bold and take a step. Now is the time to choose something to get started with. Not forever, just for a start. The thing that you know you really want the most right now.

Prompt: The thing I'm going to get started with is...

Review the "What do you really want?" exercises if you need to, and when you're ready, focus on the one thing you want to get started with. I'm not asking you to dismiss anything if you have many things you want to do; just choose one that you'll get started with right now. Write it down as a positive mantra and put it where you can see it daily.

Here's the example of Martha, a client stuck in a demanding job that left no room for any creative pursuits, who realized she wanted to go back to theater after having enjoyed it so much as a child.

"Enroll in an acting class at my local community center so I can step on stage and feel alive again."

Or take Hamza's example, who felt stuck in his final year of college and was pressured by his parents to attend medical school. Hamza could only see the pile of debt he was amassing and the years spent studying for a career he knew wasn't his dream but his parents'. After a few sessions of digging deep into what Hamza wanted, here's what came up:

"Build the courage to follow my dream of becoming a documentary maker and get the funding I need for my first project about young entrepreneurs and their impact on creating sustainable communities."

Phew! How does it feel to finally have clarity about what you want to do? Getting to this point was pivotal for me. Knowing what we want gives us the wind to spread our wings and fly – so we can become wild and free again, even if we don't know exactly where we'll land. That's okay. By now, you know that you can never fully know or control where you're going anyway; you can only give yourself a direction and jump. The co-creation with the world that happens once you take a step is the journey; it's the magic, the life that unfolds for you. Your only job is to keep going, learn as you move forward, and make sure that what you say yes to is aligned with your values and dreams. That's all.

Being a victim versus being in control

You didn't magically wake up one day and decide to get stuck. You took steps and made decisions every day until you arrived where you are now. You might not get unstuck overnight, either. Does that mean you should give up? Get impatient? Blame others for your lack of progress? Probably not.

Katrin, a client who enrolled for a short brainstorming package with me recently, thought differently. Faced with two options, she came to me for help deciding the next steps to take in her career. In her initial coaching session, everything went well. We talked about her lack of clarity, set a goal to help her move forward, and followed up with clear action steps for her to do in the two weeks that followed.

Because I want to support my clients in-between sessions, I often call myself their "secret business partner" or "career counselor." They can connect with me via email or text messaging when we work together. And here's when things started to take a different turn. The day after her session, Katrin messaged me to tell me that she wasn't progressing with her actions. She hadn't done any of the things we had agreed and asked for tips on how to get out of procrastination. I messaged Katrin with several suggestions and told her not to beat herself up too much about it. There's no point in adding guilt and shame to the mix when you're procrastinating; it only makes things worse. The next day, I got a similar message from Katrin. And the next. And the next. By the end of week one (for a two-week package), Katrin had only worked on one of her action steps and was starting to feel anxious about her lack of progress. As a result, she began to blame me. She sent me a few text messages telling me the tips I gave her weren't helpful and that she wanted more – and better – ones. By then, I'd given her at least ten things to do, none of which she had given a try, but that wasn't enough for her. She was looking for the magic pill to get unstuck and blamed me for not handing it to her.

Now that you're at the end of this book, I hope you know such a pill doesn't exist. That's what I told Katrin, after which we parted ways.

To get unstuck, you must take responsibility for life. If you don't, you'll always feel stuck because you will leave it up to others to change your circumstances for you. To be clear, I'm not blaming Katrin; I'm simply saying not to blame anyone (that includes yourself) for being stuck or staying stuck. Don't be mad when someone doesn't hand you the easy solution you're looking for. That solution doesn't exist, and looking for it is probably why you're still stuck. Instead, go to work and do something about it.

Take responsibility for your choices

Nothing is more counterproductive than waiting for someone else to fix our problems. Luckily, in my practice, I come across many inspiring people ready and willing to do the work. Sometimes though, I'll meet someone who complains about their situation more than they take steps to change it. When I work with people at that stage of their journey, I first try to make them realize it's their experience and that they have a choice – and responsibility – over how they act and react to the world.

Getting to the point of having a choice is hard work; it's a journey. Accepting that you are responsible for your experience means that you must first be willing to recognize what's happening. You can be stuck in negative feelings like anger, judgment, fear, and worry. There are many signs that you're not taking responsibility, most of which are emotional responses.

We all know the jealous friend who lacks self-confidence and hides it by being spiteful and mean. Alcoholics are known to sooth complicated and painful feelings by drinking them away. We've all heard of the unhappy boss who takes it out on the people trying to do good work for them. It's easy to find someone to blame for everything that goes wrong in life. People who are not ready to take responsibility for their actions might tell you for months or years why they're unhappy or stuck without ever doing anything about it. If you ask them, they might lash out at you or blame you for making them feel miserable – on top of being stuck! In the coaching world, such a person is considered not coachable.

Just like the first step someone with an addiction needs to take is to realize they have a problem, the first step for someone who's been blaming their stuckness on everything and everyone except themselves is to recognize that they have a part to play in getting themselves unstuck. This is, again, where self-trust comes in – but also where making a firm decision to take responsibility for your life must occur. Luckily, there are ways to make taking control of your choices easier. To get you on your way, I want to share the three most important ones with you before you go.

#1 The myth of willpower

At some point, when all the excuses have been used up, when you've been going around in circles, when you've thought of everything you could think of, and still, you're not making any progress, you must have the courage and willingness to be honest with yourself and ask: ok, so, what will it be? Are you going to repeat the same patterns, or will you finally keep the promises you make to yourself?

Getting unstuck is a process; we're clear on that, but it's also a change in mindset and mental candor. Think of it as working your way through the jungle. You've just landed on an island with a bunch of strangers after a plane crash, and you need to find some food and water. You gather a few brave souls, and together you enter the jungle that makes up most of the island. The vegetation is so thick that you need to sable your way through it using a sharp part of the plane's wing you found on the beach. You're the one leading the way. After a few hours of this, you're tired and ready to give up. You have yet to find a single coconut or berry; by now, you could use a fresh and cold glass of water. What are you going to do? Are you going to give up and, without trying to sound dramatic, potentially die? Or are you going to push through? What if help doesn't come immediately, and you're stuck on that island for weeks, months, or even years? What if you and everyone else there are lost? How are you going to handle yourself? What are you going to do (apart from pushing the button)?

When we think of being stuck like being on an island, it clarifies many things. First, a burst of willpower won't get you very far. It might help to get you going the first few days, but if no help is coming, and if there's only a limited number of coconuts hanging from the trees, your enthusiasm and good mood will eventually run out. Why? Because willpower is a myth.

When we muster the willpower to do something, it means there's a tension between what we know we should do and what we're doing. We've discussed this internal conflict before when we talked about the main reasons why people stay stuck in Step One. We often hear that willpower is a "muscle you can train." It's not only true; much of what you've learned in this book will help you do that. However, if you rely on willpower alone, you must also remember that you can overuse a muscle, exhaust it and that it needs time to rest to recover and grow. According to psychological research, this is true of willpower as well. When the study's authors examined the human ability of self-regulation, they concluded that people have a limited capacity to resist temptation. When they did so successfully, it was harder for them to say no to temptations right after that. Their conclusion (suggestion) is that self-control, aka willpower, is like a muscle that can be temporarily fatigued.[98]

Diligence, determination and the willingness to change

Willpower can help you get started, but after that, you need something more profound, more permanent: you need the unshakable will and the mental power to move forward. You need discipline and a good reason. You need the ability to kick yourself in the butt by reminding yourself why you decided to get unstuck in the first place. Let me help you with that one: you were miserable where you were (or perhaps still are), remember?

Discipline, daily habits, and rituals allow you to exercise the muscle of resolve and diligence you need to get unstuck and achieve your goals. It's what will give you the willpower you think you lack. Because what you lack is knowledge about how humans achieve things, and because you've tried and failed at using your willpower so much (every time you broke a promise to yourself) you don't believe you have any anymore. Let us clear that up right now and get you going.

#2 The paradox of choice

Without trying to sound like a broken record, I've asked you several times throughout this book to think about what you really want. Every time you moved through another step of my MOVE method; I asked you to revisit the question. I've done that with a clear goal: to help you choose. Not forever, not absolutely, but for *right now*.

I asked you to make a clear choice only a few pages ago. This is something that I know a lot of people dread. Let me reassure you: we're not closing all the other doors and options, we're putting them in the fridge for now so you can return to them later once you're done with your *first* choice. I'm returning to it one last time to ensure you've made that choice. If not, please pause reading this book and do it now. Take a piece of paper or open the workbook companion to this book and write it down. I'm adamant about this because having many options available to you, rather than improving the odds of your success in getting what you want, can cause stress, anxiety, and overthinking, and make it hard to make a choice at all. It's called *the paradox of choice*.

The more options we have, the happier and more comfortable we think we'll be with our decisions. It's quite the opposite. We've seen before how we don't compare options based on all the facts available, that we only do that after we've made a choice. This is one of the reasons why having too many choices is hard to deal with. Another reason is that we don't want to make mistakes; we want to make the *right* choice and *feel* that it's the right one before we make it. We often only feel that something is right for us once we've eliminated other options, usually by, guess what, that's right, trying them out!

100% decisions versus 98% decisions

As long as you haven't made a clear choice – a 100% decision versus a 98% decision (as former Harvard Business School professor Clayton Christensen[99] called them), you'll still contemplate other options when they arise. This unconsciously undermines your self-trust because you cannot predict with 100% certainty what you will do in the future. If you've decided to give up alcohol, but you've only committed to it 98%, you can only be partially sure you won't drink a glass of champagne at the office's Christmas party. If you're 100% committed, you do. That glass will stay on the tray while you try out all the mocktails on the menu.

Benjamin Hardy, the author of *"Willpower doesn't work, "*[100] says that "if you have to use willpower, it's because you haven't made a choice yet." The reason you must use willpower to keep the (promises) decisions you (almost) made to yourself is that in your mind, while that well-meaning co-worker or friend is telling you that "one glass of champagne never hurt anyone," you're debating whether that's true, which in turn influences whether you're going to have that glass or not. The 2% window you left open by not committing fully to your decision or the promise you made to yourself will eventually cause decision fatigue and deplete your willpower and motivation.

Once you've made a 100% decision, however, you don't have to think about alternatives anymore. The decision has already been made; your job is to stay true to it! When a glass of champagne is offered, there's no second-guessing, no wondering because you're clear on what you want. Change requires simplicity. If you make things too complex for yourself, you'll have too many options to overthink or use as an excuse not to do what you said you would. By making clear-cut decisions, you're simplifying your life to the point where you can't find arguments not to do something except come back on the word you've given yourself. Once you've understood the importance of keeping promises to yourself, it will be something you won't easily do anymore.

#3 We become the decisions that we make

Making 100% decisions also shapes you as a person. The Buddha said, "We are the result of what we have thought." Our thoughts create actions that make our life. If you're committing to 100% decisions, you cannot but become the person that you want to be because your actions will reflect the decisions or promises that you've made to yourself.

Greta, a remarkable 28-year-old witty and fun activist, creative, and writer, came to me after going through weeks of coma and rehabilitation following a covid infection during the first months of the pandemic. Greta fought hard to survive and won but is now partially disabled for life. Her body endured so much shock and trauma that she will also be chronically ill for the remainder of her life. Through my work, I get in touch with many people who deal with illness, physical disabilities, or health issues, and although all of them are inspiring and teach me lessons about life, I've rarely encountered someone like Greta.

When we connected, she was about to move out of the house she'd shared with her partner of many years, she was waiting for the right equipment to start writing again, and she was picking up on her client and creative work. Greta gave a big and juicy middle finger to the predictions doctors, and the people around her were making about what she would and wouldn't be able to do.

How you evaluate yourself and what you're capable of is based on what you do, not what other people say or think about you. The problem is many of us believe those outside voices. If we're not careful, we give in to them and quit. But not Greta. One difficult morning, when everything that could go wrong for her did go wrong, she sent me a voice message to tell me what had happened in only a few hours: the handyman who was going to help her move furniture around and didn't show up, the shower curtain that broke loose and she couldn't hang back on while being butt-naked and all soaped up in her small bathroom, the friend who promised to help her with groceries but canceled. She continued her message with a sigh followed by the most powerful statement I've ever heard: "I'm deciding that this is not going to be my day, this is not going to be my story, this is not going to be my life. I will have a good day today because I said so!"

I remind myself of this whenever I'm having a difficult moment. Greta's story and resolve are a great reminder that we're not stuck in our lives; we only feel or think we are. We don't need to be the victims of our circumstances. We can decide our lives. We have choices. By changing what we do, we change as a person. Greta can't help what happened to her, but she can decide how she responds. And she's doing that every single day. She doesn't let anything define her except what she chooses to be determined by: her choices and beliefs about herself.

The same is true for you. Whatever your circumstances, if you start a business, you'll eventually see yourself as an entrepreneur. If you decide to go back to school and become a neuroscientist, eventually, that's who you'll become (wouldn't that be cool?).

Staying unstuck

That's it; you're almost done! You successfully went through the four steps of the MOVE method to help you get unstuck. By now, you should clearly understand what has kept you where you are for so long and what you can do to finally get moving again.

Before we say goodbye, I want to leave you with three ideas and strategies to help you *stay* unstuck. It's one thing to finally get the rust off and start moving again; it's another to keep up the momentum. Throughout my life, and in the many years I've now been a coach, I've come to believe that the following three things are the most important to help keep you in motion and working toward your dreams.

#1 Consistency is key – don't break the chain

Many years ago, someone shared *The Seinfeld Strategy* with me. I want to share it with you at the end of this book because it's been a game-changer for many of my clients and me.

The story goes like this: Once, someone at a comedy night asked Jerry Seinfeld about his secret to becoming a famous comedian. Seinfeld answered to buy a calendar and hang it on the wall. To become a renowned comedian, you need to have great jokes, and to have great jokes, you must write every day. When you're done writing for the day, mark the day off with an X on your calendar. After a few days, you'll have a chain. The only thing you have to do is: not break the chain.

In my life and work, I've become more and more consistent over the years, and Seinfeld's "don't break the chain" approach is one of the things that helped me the most. Consistency is key. Small steps repeated over time add to incredible results. This is also known as the compound effect. It's a simple strategy, but unfortunately, it's not always easy to follow. For consistency to work, you must focus on future gains instead of instant rewards. This is a hard thing to do for humans in general, but more so now that we live in a world of social media, same-day deliveries, and everything at our fingertips.

Resolve is a muscle that you must exercise for it to become stronger. Instant gratification, on the other hand, is something we are wired for. Ultimately, it comes down to this: what do you do when what you want is days, weeks, or months away? Do you do what you said you would? Or do you break a promise to yourself again? The promise of a brighter future, of a dream, of a healthy, happy, inspiring, successful life? Without realizing it, you're making those decisions every moment of your life with what you do or don't do in the moment. By breaking promises to yourself, you repeatedly tell yourself that you can't do something, that you're not good enough or capable enough. This shapes a different future than the one you want for yourself.

It's not that you can't do it; you haven't trained your resolve enough – yet. You have wisdom and power inside you; you just haven't learned how to tap into it. How do you learn? By reprogramming your mind to focus on getting yourself into action and by keeping the muscle moving and training it. Reading this book was a great way to exercise that muscle; staying close to yourself and aware of what's happening inside you will also help tremendously. In your day-to-day life, make it a thing to move forward slowly but diligently, and make it a habit to discover your defaults and triggers and how you operate. Reflecting on what you can learn from those things and showing up for yourself will help you grow. Understanding yourself better is part of shifting your focus from the goal to the process. Where in the process can you find happiness? That's where the magic is. You cultivate and grow your resolve muscle by learning to find joy in each moment, not by waiting for your moment of achievement.

Once you develop the habit, achieving mastery over yourself and your life will bring its rewards in the moment: pride for your progress, the good decisions you're making for yourself, and the insights and control you're gaining about who you are and how you operate. You'll see your life and work improve slowly at first, but once the compound effect starts showing, the changes will be palpable and exponential.

#2 Cultivate a state of flow

I believe that we're happiest and most creative when we cultivate a state of flow daily.

A few years back, I decided to become a writer. I'd wanted to write since I was 15; in fact, I wrote my first (crappy) novel when I was about that age. I still have it; it's a silly yet confronting medley of the thoughts and dreams of the teenager I was. After that, I wrote short stories on and off. Then life happened, and I started building businesses and a career. I was still writing, but most of it was technical documentation, sales offers, and reports. When I started my coaching business, as I've shared earlier, I agonized about writing again through blogging. Although I was excited to get back into writing, I experienced the biggest writing block I'd ever had. I felt like a fraud and thought I was the worst writer in the world. I didn't enjoy it at all. I got frustrated and anxious just thinking about having to write.

Since 2010, apart from the regular monthly, quarterly, and yearly goals I set for myself, I've been focusing on 5-year goals that I call "buckets." I started doing this the year my parents passed away when I realized how limited our time is. I'm convinced that in a period of five years, we can achieve pretty much anything: build and sell a business, change careers, and become an expert at something new. It's enough time to start, develop, and finish our bigger goals. It's also a way to filter out the noise and focus on what matters most. If you work in 5-year buckets, it's easy to know how many big goals you can accomplish in the time you have left. I'm in my forties now, so I have about seven buckets left if I live a healthy life until my eighties – still plenty to achieve some big goals, but not that much when you think about it.

It wasn't until a few years ago, when I decided to make the upcoming "five-year bucket," the bucket in which I was going to become a writer, that I started truly enjoying writing again. It took me a while to test out the best writing time for me and how I could make it easier to create a daily writing practice, but I've developed a formula that works well. I write every morning for 45 minutes using a Pomodoro timer; I take a 15-minute break and then study for 45 minutes. The studying is usually reading about the subject of the book I'm writing because, yes, since the beginning of my "writing bucket," I've kept the chain of daily writing going (except when I got sick or went away for the holidays). The result? I'm currently averaging one book a year (this is the second non-fiction book I've written). As I write this, I have two new book projects in the making. The secret? Flow.

When I wake up in the morning, I look forward to sitting at my desk and writing because I can almost immediately enter a state of creative immersion where time ceases to exist. I'm so engaged in writing that it focuses, energizes, and excites me and makes me feel successful at creating something. Feeling this way is what positive psychologist Mihály Csíkszentmihályi[101] describes as *flow*. Being able to experience this state of mind (almost) daily is what keeps me going. It's a beautiful place to be, and I believe it profoundly affects all other aspects of my life. It's almost like meditation, a state of being where I'm present with myself, in the now and nothing else matters.

What's interesting about cultivating a state of flow is that you need a lot of repetition and practice to get there: you need a chain that you don't break. I've found that having some rituals in place helps too. I have a writing playlist that I listen to every day, and that helps me get into flow quickly. I write at the same desk, in the same position, and at the same time every day. I always leave a sentence unfinished at the end of my writing time and give myself instructions to help me finish the thought and sentence the following morning. All of this helps to get and keep me writing, but the most critical part is the daily practice. The more you do it, the better you get at it, and the easier it is to enter a blissful creative flow state. Do I like books to be finished and published? Of course, I do. But do I like flow better? Yes, for sure.

Final prompt: Set a goal, the first one you'll take on when you're done reading this book.

Ask yourself for the last time what you want, but this time take all the knowledge of this book with you in your answer. Be as honest and truthful with yourself as possible. Then follow the steps below, one by one.

What do you really want?

- State a clear goal for yourself.
- List the reasons you want to achieve this goal (what will it bring to your life?).

- Are you setting this goal from your wounds, other people's dreams, or what you think you must do? Or are you wanting this from a place of freedom and joy (the right place)?
- Reflect on who you need to be(come) to achieve your goal. What shoes do you need to fill?
- List the steps you need to take to reach your goal in terms of doing and being.
- Make a list of the positive habits and rituals you will cultivate to achieve this goal.
- Reflect on what negative hurdles your environment might place in your way and devise ways to change your environment to help you accomplish your goals.
- Make a top three of the ways you're going to stay consistent in working toward this goal. How will you harness the power of the compound effect?
- By when do you want to achieve this goal?
- Buy a calendar (or download the one available on my website),[102] circle the day you've defined in the previous step and hang the calendar on a wall somewhere visible.
- Take one step today towards your goal, and mark this day on your calendar with an X.
- Do the same tomorrow, and mark that day with another X.
- Don't break the chain.

#3 Don't make one thing the focus of your life

We've talked so much about goals in this book that, before you go, I want to make one thing clear. The mono-focus you need when working on your goals cannot be the only priority in your life. You must focus on different things, not just one, for a full and rich existence. Having just one thing that matters in your life is dangerous. If that one thing disappears, you will get stuck again, and your life will feel empty. If you only have one thing in your life, and that thing isn't right for you, it will make it so much harder to get unstuck. Imagine if you're in a relationship or a job you want to leave but don't have anything else going on in your life. It will take a lot more from you to step away from it.

When I was holding on for dear life to my marriage, one of the reasons why I couldn't let it go, even if it was the best decision I could make, was because I was isolated from my friends and family. We had moved to another country where I didn't speak the language, and I had no immediate friends or social fabric to fall back on. I'm not saying that's the only reason I held on too tight, but the isolation didn't help. What was I going to do in that country by myself? Unconsciously that thought influenced me. Because of the move, we were more reliant on each other, another reason my life felt smaller and more complicated than it should have been.

My advice is to commit yourself to every part of your life. Be your own best friend. Build a strong and safe relationship with yourself. Then, practice being in the now as much as possible, doing what you're doing with all your heart. Make your life rich in friends, experiences, knowledge. Cultivate your interests and passions, be proud of who you are, don't be afraid to go after your dreams, speak your mind and your truth, and trust that you've got this – because you do.

That's it, you did it! You've now gone through all four steps of the MOVE method, and you're ready to get started! Before we say goodbye, here's a summary of what you learned in this final chapter.

Summary: Step Four – Execution

This fourth and final step of the MOVE method focuses on taking action and changing your environment, habits, and way of approaching your dreams so you can finally get unstuck. It's also the step in which you choose something to get started with.

In this fourth step, you learned:

- If you're looking for flaws, you'll find them.
- Trying everything is as bad as trying nothing.
- Don't get overwhelmed by the choices that you have.
- The power of valued living versus achievement-based living.
- The truth about fear and how to not let it stop you from doing what you want.
- The impact of trauma and childhood wounds on being and staying stuck.
- What your glue is and how you can use it to make sense of your life.
- The myth of willpower and the paradox of choice.
- Three strategies to stay unstuck.

I'm so proud of you for making it to this point. I know it wasn't easy. I asked you so many questions and wouldn't let you off the hook. But you did it, and now you're ready. I can't wait to see all the beautiful things you're going to create and the amazing life that awaits you.

Conclusion

How does it feel to finally *get unstuck*?

With this book, you've embarked on a journey of self-discovery, empowerment, and deep transformation. As you've journeyed through the MOVE method, you've peeled back the layers of overthinking, procrastination, and self-doubt that kept you from moving forward for so long. You've learned that being stuck is not a fact, but a feeling. And once you grasped the fullness of that truth, you finally got free.

The first step, Mindset, opened your eyes to the power of your thoughts. You dove deep into figuring out why you got stuck in the first place. By recognizing your thinking patterns and the limiting beliefs that kept you from taking action, you gained valuable tools to finally escape their grip.

Next, in the Options phase, you embraced the notion that true freedom lies in the choices you make. You learned that changing your mind can change your life and that the responsibility for your thoughts, emotions, and actions ultimately lies with you. By exploring the possibilities and opportunities available to you, you expanded your horizons and discovered the true power of making choices.

Vision, the third step, sketched your path forward. You crafted a clear, compelling vision for your life, one that is filled with passion and purpose. With this vision, you are no longer adrift in a sea of uncertainty. Instead, you have a clear direction and know what you want and why.

Finally, in the Execution phase, I asked you to muster the courage to take action. You know that this step might be uncomfortable, even daunting, after years of stagnation. But, armed with a plan and a calendar to stick to the wall, I know that you can see it through.

Now, as you stand on the cusp of a new beginning, you have the tools to stay unstuck, to navigate the twists and turns of life with resilience and grace. It is my wish that you use what you have learned in the pages of this book as a compass, guiding you toward a future filled with purpose, joy, and fulfillment.

As you close the pages of "Get Unstuck!" and step into your big and beautiful new life, remember that you are a well of wisdom, that you *had the power all along*, and trust in your newfound clarity and vision.

Your journey has just begun, and – as I hope you know by now – the possibilities are endless.

I believe in you. Now get up and get unstuck!

Acknowledgments

Writing a book is a journey of a thousand miles that begins with a single step. But it's also a step you cannot take alone. Traveling the long path of getting all one wants onto paper requires many individuals who provide support, encouragement, and inspiration, who pick you up when you can't remember why you're doing this work, or who bring you a chicken sandwich when you've finally found some flow and forgot to eat lunch.

I'm deeply grateful to everyone who has played a part in bringing this book together.

First and foremost, I want to express my heartfelt thanks and appreciation to Alexandra, Silvia, El, Carolien, Ewa, Barbara, Kirsten, Elizabeth, Lotte, Glenn, Kaatje, Samira, Marleen, Silvie, Sven and Mark. Your friendship, tips, unwavering support, valuable insights, and willingness to assist with proofreading, book formatting, and publishing were instrumental in helping me beat procrastination ☺ and finish this project. A special thank you to you, Olga, for designing such a cool cover for me!

To my clients, your trust in my coaching abilities has allowed me to explore the topics within these pages, and I'm genuinely thankful for the opportunities you've given me.

I want to acknowledge my brother Michel and sister Dominique, my cousins Valerie, Thomas, Andy, David, Sandrine, Marc, my aunts Rita and Sandy, my uncle Ron, and everyone else from my extended and international family for their love and belief in me. Your support has been a constant source of motivation and the strength I needed to keep going in some of the most challenging moments of my life. A tender thanks to my parents, who, even though they are no longer with us, I continue to learn from every day.

Lastly, I extend my gratitude to everyone who has contributed to this book through inspiration, their body of work, or provoking thought. Thank you for keeping me on my toes and interested in what it means to be human.

As you can see, like anything worthwhile in life, this book is the product of collective effort. I count myself lucky to have so many wonderful people in my life. I'm humbled and grateful for all you give me every day and for the gift of knowing you.

With the warmest gratitude and my deepest appreciation,
Murielle

About the Author

Known by her colleagues and clients as a mentor to the unconventional, Murielle Marie Ungricht is an internationally recognized and respected entrepreneur, philosopher, and a passionate advocate for social justice, equality, and inclusion.

She offers more than two decades of entrepreneurial experience and in-depth business acumen, having done everything from building, growing, and successfully selling a web agency to founding, and investing in early-stage start-ups, authoring two books on personal and professional development, and creating a successful coaching business.

Murielle has spent the last nine years specializing in integrative, mindset-focused business and career coaching and leadership development. Many of her clients – artists, creatives, start-up founders, creative entrepreneurs, and C-suite professionals – understand the need for growth but are unaware of how to achieve it. They feel "stuck." By integrating leading research in neuroscience, philosophy, trauma and attachment theory, business education, and her entrepreneurial experience, Murielle can help them move forward and create successful, and sustainable futures.

Murielle is a frequent public speaker, podcast guest and host, and TEDx speaker and idea generator who is committed to lifelong learning, including mindfulness training, feminist marketing principles, positive psychology, conscious business and leadership, neuroscience, and philosophy. Murielle is interested in investing in young and promising entrepreneurs who are trying to change the world in a sustainable way.

As an autistic woman, Murielle is acutely aware of the obstacles neurodivergent and other disadvantaged individuals encounter in their careers, which motivated her to launch a talent network that provides job opportunities as well as career coaching services exclusively tailored for marginalized groups.

With a passion for life and creative expression, Murielle keeps engaging in new experiences. Writing, drawing, improv theater, dancing, art history, tasting all flavors of Belgian chocolate, and making the most exquisite mayonnaise are only a few of her interests. Rarely does she say "no" to a challenge, especially one that serves a greater purpose.

Get in touch with her at www.muriellemarie.com
or on Instagram at www.instagram.com/muriellemarie

Endnotes

[1] Mail, T. (2021) *Most brain activity is "background noise" — and that's upending our understanding of consciousness: Salon.* [Online] Available from: https://www.salon.com/2021/02/20/most-brain-activity-is-background-noise-cognitive-flux-consciousness-brain-activity-research.

[2] Sones, B. & R. (2018). *Strange but true: 95 percent of brain activity is unconscious: The Okalhoman.* [Online] Available from: https://eu.oklahoman.com/story/lifestyle/2018/10/09/strange-but-true-95-percent-of-brain-activity-is-unconscious/60496296007.

[3] For more information about creative generalists, see Step Three of this book. Ungricht M.M. (2015) *What is a creative generalist?: Murielle Marie.* Available from: https://www.muriellemarie.com/quiz-creative-generalist-multipassionate.

[4] Palmer, A. (2014) The Art of Asking: How I learned to stop worrying and let people help. New York, Grand Central Publishing.

[5] I first read about the "ideal day" exercise in *Wishcraft*, an amazing book by Barbara Sher that helped me to make sense of all my dreams and passions when I felt completely lost. I recommend it to anyone who's looking for more clarity about what to do next or how to create a life they truly want. The book is available for download as PDF chapters at https://www.wishcraft.com. The original exercise can be found on page 55 of the book.

[6] Burkeman, O. (2021) *Four Thousand Weeks: Time Management for Mortals.* New York, Farrar, Straus and Giroux.

[7] Dobrijevic, D. (2021) *5,200 tons of space dust falls on Earth each year, study finds, Space.com.* [Online] Available from: https://www.space.com/extraterrestrial-dust-falls-on-earth.

[8] For a concise history of our solar system, visit https://www.futurity.org/earth-stardust-red-giants-2229632..

[9] *Rain Man* is a 1988 American road drama movie directed by Barry Levinson. The movie tells the story of an entitled, young and smooth, guy named Charlie Babbitt (played by Tom Cruise). When Charlie's estranged father dies, he discovers that he has left his multimillion-dollar estate to his other son, Raymond (played by Dustin Hoffman), an autistic savant, that Charlie didn't know existed. The autistic Raymond portrayed in the movie has extreme traits of intelligence. An example of this is when having lunch at a diner, while on the road, a box of toothpicks falls to the ground and Raymond can tell exactly how many toothpicks are on the floor just by looking at them. He is also extremely rigid and so set in his ways that any change in schedule sends him off into a panic. Although I don't want to claim that these aren't autistic traits, or difficulties people with autism experience, because of the lack of information about autism in the 80s and the success of this movie, for many people, and certainly for those of my generation, autism *was* Rain Man. The lack of representation that I could identify with caused me to never imagine this could be me. Without going into the representation debate, this is a problem

for so many minorities and underrepresented groups, and one of the reasons why I decided to come out about my diagnosis and put all my love, expertise, and passion behind the new app for diverse talent that I mentioned before.

[10] Maslow's hierachy of needs is an idea in psychology proposed by American Abraham Maslow in his 1943 paper "A Theory of Human Motivation" in the journal *Psychological Review*. Maslow subsequently extended the idea to include his observations of humans' innate curiosity. Maslow, A. H. (1943). A theory of human motivation. *Psychological Review* [Online] 50 (4), 370–396. https://doi.org/10.1037/h0054346. For more information, see https://en.wikipedia.org/wiki/Maslow's_hierarchy_of_needs.

[11] Kahneman, D. & Deaton A. (2010) *High income improves evaluation of life but not emotional well-being: PNAS.* [Online] Available from: https://www.pnas.org/doi/10.1073/pnas.1011492107.

[12] A great book to help you gain more control and leadership over your thoughts is Fox, A. E. (2013) *Winning from within: A breakthrough method for leading, living, and lasting change.* New York, Harper Business.

[13] To learn more about Tabby Biddle and her incredible work empowering women's voices, check out her website at https://www.tabbybiddle.com.

[14] For more information about leadership, see Wikipedia contributors. (2023) *Leadership. Wikipedia, The Free Encyclopedia.* Available from: https://en.wikipedia.org/w/index.php?title=Leadership&oldid=1173839147.

[15] Canfield, J. & Switzer, J. (2005) *The Success Principles.* Boston, Harper Business.

[16] If you're interested to learn more about Hegelian Philosophy, check out Habib, M. (2018) Hegel on Identity and Difference. In *Hegel and the Foundations of Literary Theory.* Cambridge: Cambridge University Press, pp. 72-86. doi:10.1017/9781108602952.006.

[17] If you want more information about Glenn or his work, you can reach out to him online via LinkedIn: https://www.linkedin.com/in/glenn-vervliet-21017a188.

[18] Clear, J. (2018) *Atomic Habits.* New York, Avery.

[19] For more about how our environment defines our habits, visit https://jamesclear.com/environment-design-organ-donation.

[20] Visit this link to sign up for your free session: https://www.muriellemarie.com/free-coaching-session..

[21] If you'd like to know more about how to combine your many interests and passions into a career, check out the blog on my website at https://www.muriellemarie.com/blog. Helping people to puzzle together portfolio careers is one of my superpowers.

[22] There is little evidence that the Greek philosopher Seneca said these famous words. We are sure, however, that Oprah did: https://www.oprah.com/spirit/thought-for-today-luck. I love this quote because to me it's a confirmation that to be lucky you must work at what you want and dream, because that is how you prepare for when the opportunities you've created manifest.

[23] The University of Edinburgh. (2009) *Michael Gazzaniga - The Interpreter.* [Online YouTube] https://www.youtube.com/watch?v=mJKloz2vwlc.

[24] An interesting observation is that, with the boom of AI services like ChatGPT, the same is said about those systems. The output they produce is only as good as the questions they're asked—not surprising considering we've modeled artificial intelligence to resemble our own thinking patterns.

[25] Anderson, J. (2022). *The Metaverse in 2040: Pew Research Center.* [Online] Available from: https://www.pewresearch.org/internet/2022/06/30/the-metaverse-in-2040.

[26] Leedy, M. G., LaLonde, D., & Runk, K. (2010) "Gender equity in mathematics: Beliefs of students, parents, and teachers. *School Science and Mathematics.* [Online] 203 (6). Available from: https://onlinelibrary.wiley.com/doi/10.1111/j.1949-8594.2003.tb18151.x..

[27] Saxe, R. & Baron-Cohen, S. *Theory of mind: A special issue of social neuroscience.* London, Psychology Press. Available from: https://www.routledge.com/Theory-of-Mind-A-Special-Issue-of-Social-Neuroscience/Saxe-Baron-Cohen/p/book/9781138877689.

[28] Baron-Cohen, S., Leslie, A.M. & Frith, U. (1985) Does the autistic child have a "theory of mind"? *Cognition*, 21 (1), 37-46. Available from: https://www.researchgate.net/publication/20222469_Does_the_Autistic_Child_Have_a_Theory_of_Mind.

[29] A Copernican Revolution (sometimes called a reversal or twist) is a radical change in how something in science or philosophy has been declared or believed to be true. The term derives from the name of Nicolas Copernicus, a Polish astronomer who was the first to propose that the planets might orbit the sun and not the earth. It was a dangerous proposition in 1515 that went radically against the anthropocentrism (the belief that the earth - humans - were at the center of the universe) of the time (the sixteenth century) and the Church. Copernicus escaped death, but others who proclaimed the same were less fortunate and were burned at the stake. Spencer, J. B., Brush, S. G., & Osler, M. J. (2022) *Copernican Revolution: Encyclopedia Britannica.* [Online] Available from: https://www.britannica.com/topic/Copernican-Revolution.

[30] A great way to start is to listen to my "Get Unstuck with Murielle Marie" podcast. I share an experiment to try at the end of every episode. Check out the podcast page on my website for more information: https://www.muriellemarie.com/podcast-get-unstuck-with-murielle-marie.

[31] The word "multipotentialite" was coined by Emilie Wapnick. Wapnick, E. (2010) *Welcome home: Puttylike Media LTD.* [Online] Available from: https://puttylike.com; the term "polymath" is much older in usage and dates back to the time of Leonardo Da Vinci, often considered one of the earliest creative generalists, and "multi-passionate creative" is a more recent term that found its way to a wider public thanks to Marie Forleo and other online creative entrepreneurs.

[32] For more information about my book about creative generalists, please visit my website at https://www.muriellemarie.com/.

[33] A more extensive quiz and additional information and resources for creative generalists are available on my website at https://www.muriellemarie.com/quiz-creative-generalist-multipassionate.

[34] Things are improving, luckily. More and more, companies are hiring for skills and talents, and actively looking for generalists who can juggle many hats and create bridges between ideas, projects, and people. We're also coming together to network and support each other. Check out my website at https://www.muriellemarie.com/creative-generalist-network-membership-page for more information about virtual meet-ups and to discover the Creative Generalist Network that I have created. We meet every month to brainstorm creative ideas and support each other's work.

[35] This is one of my favorite Gabor Maté interviews: https://www.youtube.com/watch?v=uPup-1pDepY. I cannot recommend his documentary enough: Maté, G. (2022) *The Wisdom of Trauma*. [Online]. https://thewisdomoftrauma.com. It was a game-changer for me, as are his books Maté, G. (2010) *In the realm of hungry ghosts: Close encounters with addiction*. Berkeley, North Atlantic Books, and his latest book, Maté, G. (2010) *The myth of Normal: Trauma, illness, and healing in a toxic culture*. New York, Avery. They are a must-read for everyone feeling like they don't belong.

[36] Get in touch at murielle@muriellemarie.com if you want to know more about the services this unique boutique agency is going to offer or have a great start-up idea you'd like to bring out into the world or get funded!

[37] Send me an email at murielle@muriellemarie.com if you want to know more or sign up for our revolutionary career advancement app and platform.

[38] Check out https://www.muriellemarie.com/blog/shift-shock-and-how-to-avoid-it for a more in-depth article about "shift shock."

[39] A longer version of this quote that I was able to find online reads: "Each time I write a book, every time I face that yellow pad, the challenge is so great. I have written eleven books, but each time I think, 'Uh oh, they're going to find out now. I've run a game on everybody and they're going to find me out." Unfortunately, my efforts to locate when and where Maja Angelou said these words were unsuccessful. If you do, please send me an email at murielle@muriellemarie.com and let me know!

[40] One of my favorite podcasts! Check it out on YouTube. Bartlett, S. (2020 to 2023) *Diary of a CEO*. [Online: YouTube]. Available from: https://www.youtube.com/c/thediaryofaceo.

[41] Watch this inspiring TEDx talk online here: TEDx Talks. (2014) *The prison of your mind | Sean Stephenson | TEDxIronwoodStatePrison*. [Online: YouTube] Available from: https://www.youtube.com/watch?v=VaRO5-V1uK0.

42 To learn more about the Socratic Method, visit the Wikipedia page dedicated to it: Wikipedia contributors. (2023) *Socratic method: Wikipedia, The Free Encyclopedia*. Available from: https://en.wikipedia.org/w/index.php?title=Socratic_method&oldid=1172340572.

43 The full translated dialogue is available in English at Plato. (380 B.C.E.) *Laches, or Courage: Classics MIT Edu*. [Online] http://classics.mit.edu/Plato/laches.html.

44 For more about Karl Popper, visit the Wikipedia page: Wikipedia contributors. *Karl Popper: Wikipedia, The Free Encyclopedia*. [Online] Available at: https://en.wikipedia.org/w/index.php?title=Karl_Popper&oldid=1173193197.

45 Grossmann, I. (2017) *Wisdom and how to cultivate it: Review of emerging evidence for a constructivist model of wise thinking: University of Waterloo.*" [Online] Available at: https://psyarxiv.com/qkm6v.

46 Ibid., p.3.

47 Ibid.; Grossmann et al., 2010.

48 Ibid., p.8.

49 Kounios J. & Beeman, M. (2015) The eureka factor: Aha moments, creative insight, and the brain. New York, Random House.

50 Zanjani, S., Yunlu, D.G. & Beigh, J.N.S. (2020) Creative procrastinators: Mapping a complex terrain. *Personality and Individual Differences*, 154. Available from: https://doi.org/10.1016/j.paid.2019.109640.

51 Eugene, A.R. & Masiak, J. (2015) The neuroprotective aspects of sleep. *MEDtube Science*, 3 (1), 35. Available from: https://www.ncbi.nlm.nih.gov/pmc/articles/PMC4651462/#:~:text=When%20one%20sleeps%2C%20the%20brain,help%20maintain%20its%20normal%20functioning.

52 Samples, B. (1976) The metaphoric mind: A celebration of creative consciousness. Fawnskin, Jalpur Press.

53 The Beautiful You Coaching Academy, founded by the amazing and incredibly inspiring Julie Parker. Visit https://www.beautifulyoucoachingacademy.com for more information. Enrolling in the course was my first step to transition into a coaching career. When I finished that course, I was ready to start! And what a journey it has been. I'm forever grateful to Julie and her team for giving me the tools I needed to believe in myself and to go for it!

54 I learned this "open or closed" exercise from Colleen-Page Joy, the founder and MCC coach that mentored and taught me when I was studying to become a Master Professional Coach at her coaching school *InnerLifeSkills*. I cannot recommend the school and Colleen's work enough. Follow this link for more information about her mentoring work and coaching courses: https://www.innerlifeskills.com.

55 The meaning of egocentric in this context is being centered in or arising from a person's own individual existence, context, or perspective, not being self-centered and thinking only of oneself, without regard for the needs, feelings, or desires of others.

⁵⁶ Visit this link to learn more about Kind Solomon: Wikipedia contributors. (2023) *Solomon: Wikipedia, The Free Encyclopedia*. [Online] Available at: https://en.wikipedia.org/w/index.php?title=Solomon&oldid=1173595171..

⁵⁷ More on Solomon's wives and concubines can be found here: https://en.wikipedia.org/wiki/Solomon#Wives_and_concubines.

⁵⁸ Grossmann, I., (2017) *Wisdom and how to cultivate it: University of Waterloo*. [Online], 13. Available from: https://psyarxiv.com/qkm6v.

⁵⁹ Cherry, V. (2022) *What is cognitive bias?: VeryWellMind*. [Online] Available from: https://www.verywellmind.com/what-is-a-cognitive-bias-2794963.

⁶⁰ Wikipedia contributors. (2023) *Motivated reasoning: Wikipedia, The Free Encyclopedia*. Available from: https://en.wikipedia.org/w/index.php?title=Motivated_reasoning&oldid=1170021201.

⁶¹ Wikipedia contributors. (2022) *My Wife and My Mother-in-Law: Wikipedia, The Free Encyclopedia*. Available from: https://en.wikipedia.org/w/index.php?title=My_Wife_and_My_Mother-in-Law&oldid=1109478354.

⁶² Flinders University. (2018) Age bias is subconscious, study indicates. [Online] Available from: https://news.flinders.edu.au/blog/2018/09/14/age-bias-subconscious-study-indicates.

⁶³ Doyle, S. (2015) *Before Lena Dunham, there was Anaïs Nin – now patron saint of social media: The Guardian*. [Online] Available from: https://www.theguardian.com/culture/2015/apr/07/anais-nin-author-social-media.

⁶⁴ Wonkmonk. (2015) *Cypher: I know this steak doesn't exist... Ignorance is bliss | The Matrix*. [Online: YouTube] Available from: https://www.youtube.com/watch?v=JODWCwycNmg.

⁶⁵ As a side note, according to Scientific American, there's a 50–50 percent chance we're all living in simulation. Exciting ideas, but that's for another book. Ananthaswamy, A. (2020) *Do we live in a simulation?: Chances are about 50–50: Scientific American*. [Online] Available from: https://www.scientificamerican.com/article/do-we-live-in-a-simulation-chances-are-about-50-50.

⁶⁶ Recode. (2016) *Is life a video game? | Elon Musk | Code Conference 2016*. [Online: YouTube] Available from: https://www.youtube.com/watch?t=142&v=2KK_kzrJPS8&feature=youtu.be.

⁶⁷ Big Think. (2021) *Is reality real? These neuroscientists don't think so*. [Online] Available from: https://bigthink.com/videos/objective-reality.

⁶⁸ I hope that trauma triggers aren't your daily experience. If they are, I feel you, and I'm so sorry you must go through that. If you need support with healing from trauma, I've compiled a list of resources on my website. You can find them here: https://www.muriellemarie.com/healing-from-trauma-resources.

[69] As I mentioned, I gave a TEDx talk about this idea: not to believe anything you think. TEDx Talk. (2017) *Is reality real? These neuroscientists don't think so.* [Online] Available from: https://www.youtube.com/watch?v=BxligD1idto.

[70] Wikipedia contributors. (2023) *Measurement problem: Wikipedia, The Free Encyclopedia.* Available from: https://en.wikipedia.org/w/index.php?title=Measurement_problem&oldid=1170098912 .

[71] "Insanity is doing the same thing over and over and expecting different results." Even though there is little evidence that this was said by Albert Einstein, it's such a great quote that can stand on its own, so I decided to add it anyway!

[72] Mesa, N. (2021) *Can the criminal justice system's artificial intelligence ever be truly fair?: Massive Science.* [Online] Available from: https://massivesci.com/articles/machine-learning-compas-racism-policing-fairness.

[73] For more information on disruption, and an immeasurable amount of insight and knowledge about meaning and purpose, listen to or watch professor John Vervaeke's lectures. (2019–2023) *Awakening from the Meaning Crisis.* [Online] Available from: https://www.youtube.com/playlist?list=PLND1JCRq8Vuh3f0P5qjrSdb5eC1ZfZwWJ.

[74] Learn more about professor John Vervaeke on his website at https://johnvervaeke.com.

[75] Gestalt means "shape" or "form" in German. In English, the definition reads: "An organized whole that is perceived as more than the sum of its parts." Guberman, S. (2017) Gestalt theory rearranged: Back to Wertheimer. *Frontiers in Psychology*, 8, 1782. Available from: https://doi.org/10.3389%2Ffpsyg.2017.01782.

[76] "Huit clos," by Jean-Paul Sartre (1944). Wikipedia Contributors. (2023) *No Exit: Wikipedia, The Free Encyclopedia.* Available from: https://en.wikipedia.org/w/index.php?title=No_Exit&oldid=1169549857.

[77] I'm not saying to jump without a plan, especially if you have bills to pay, but to actively work at being able to leave and transition into a job or career that will finally fulfill you and make you happy. Check my blog for more resources on how to do that here: https://www.muriellemarie.com/blog.

[78] Wikipedia Contributors. (2023) *Theory of forms. Wikipedia, The Free Encyclopedia.* [Online] Available from: https://en.wikipedia.org/w/index.php?title=Theory_of_forms&oldid=1173807976..

[79] Beckett, S. (1953) *Waiting for Godot.* New York, Grove Press.

[80] Britannica. (2018) *Cognitive dissonance of Leon Festinger.* [Online] Available from: https://www.britannica.com/biography/Leon-Festinger/Cognitive-dissonance.

[81] Kluger, J. (2015) *Why You're Pretty Much Unconscious All the Time: Time.* [Online] Available from: https://time.com/3937351/consciousness-unconsciousness-brain.

[82] If you want to learn more about mindfulness and experience its power, this 5-minute mindfulness meditation by Jon Kabat-Zinn (the grandfather of mindfulness in the West) is

a great place to start: Masterclass. (2022) *5-minute Guided Mediation with Jon Kabat-Zinn | MasterClass*.[Online] Available from: https://www.youtube.com/watch?v=7WnZisfYMsE.

[83] Wordsrated. (2023) *Number of books published per year*. [Online] Available from: https://wordsrated.com/number-of-books-published-per-year-2021.

[84] Another beautiful metaphor I learned from Colleen-Page Joy from *InnerLifeSkills*. Thank you for being such an amazing teacher Colleen! InnerLifeSkills. (2023) *Where Natural Coaches become Go-To Master Coaches*. [Online] Available from: (https://www.innerlifeskills.com).

[85] Visit this site to watch Tim Ferris's TEDtalk online: CMASES. (2017) *Why you should define your fears instead of your goals*. [Online] Available from: https://www.cmasas.org/why-you-should-define-your-fears-instead-your-goals.

[86] Jerrers, S. (2007). *Feel the fear and do it anyway* ®. *How to turn your fear and indecision into confidence and action*. Amazon: ASIN: B011T7KWO6. More information about Susan Jeffers and her important work can be found on her website at: https://susanjeffers.com.

[87] Sweeny, K., & Dooley, M.D. (2017). The surprising upsides of worry. *Social and Personality Psychology Compass*, 11 (4), p.e12311. https://compass.onlinelibrary.wiley.com/doi/10.1111/spc3.12311.

[88] "I must not fear. Fear is the mind-killer. Fear is the little-death that brings total obliteration. I will face my fear. I will permit it to pass over me and through me. And when it has gone past I will turn the inner eye to see its path. Where the fear has gone there will be nothing. Only I will remain." Herbert, F. (1965) *Dune* Sudbury, Chilton Books.

[89] Robbins, M. (2011) *How to keep from screwing yourself over: TEDxSF* [Online: YouTube] Available from: https://www.ted.com/talks/mel_robbins_how_to_stop_screwing_yourself_over?language=en.

[90] Robbins, M. (2017). The 5 Second Rule: Transform your life, work, and confidence with everyday courage. Amazon: ASIN: B01MUSNFOO.

[91] I have a popular podcast episode about this topic. Check out the podcast page on my website for more information: Ungricht, M. M. (2023) *#23 Grit: why it matters, and what you can do to get more of it: Murielle Marie*. [Online] Available from: https://www.muriellemarie.com/podcast-get-unstuck-with-murielle-marie.

[92] Bowlby, J. (1969). *Attachment. Attachment and Loss: Vol. 1. Loss*. New York, Basic Books.

[93] Dozzyy, D. (2022). *Nervous System*. [Online: TikTok] Available from: https://www.tiktok.com/@danadozzyy/video/7161027980561632517.

[94] If you're not sure of your attachment style, Diane Poole Heller, one of the attachment style experts I've learned so much from, offers a self-assessment test on her website. You can find it here: https://dianepooleheller.com/attachment-test.

[95] Sinek, S. (2011). Start with why: How great leaders inspire everyone to take action. Alberta, Portfolio.

[96] Watch, "The most popular TED Talks of all time.":[Online: YouTube] Available from: https://www.ted.com/playlists/171/the_most_popular_talks_of_all.

[97] Check out the podcast page on my website to listen: https://www.muriellemarie.com/podcast-get-unstuck-with-murielle-marie.

[98] Baumeister, R. F., & Vohs, K. D. (2003). Willpower, choice, and self-control. In G. Loewenstein, D. Read, & R. Baumeister (Eds.), *Time and decision: Economic and psychological perspectives on intertemporal choice* (pp. 201–216). Russell Sage Foundation.

[99] Clayton Magleby Christensen, an American scholar and corporate advisor, was renowned for developing the concept of "disruptive innovation," widely regarded as the most influential business concept in the early 21st century. Christensen Institute. (2023) *Disruptive innovation.* [Online] Available from: https://www.christenseninstitute.org/disruptive-innovations.

[100] Hardy, B. (2018) Willpower doesn't work: Discover the hidden keys to success." New York, Hatchette Books.

[101] Csíkszentmihályi, M. (2018). *Flow: The Psychology of Optimal Experience.* New York, Harper Perennial Modern Classics.

[102] Download your free copy of my Seinfeld Strategy Calendar here: https://www.muriellemarie.com/seinfeld-strategy-calendar-free-download.